MCAT
PSYCHOLOGY and SOCIOLOGY:
Strategy and Practice

D1364773

ABOUT THE AUTHORS

Bryan Schnedeker is Next Step Test Prep's National Academic Director. He manages all of our MCAT instructors nationally and counsels hundreds of MCAT students when they begin our tutoring process. He has over a decade of MCAT teaching and tutoring experience (starting at one of the big prep course companies before joining our team). He has attended medical school and law school himself and has scored a 44 on the MCAT and 180 on the LSAT. Bryan has worked with thousands of MCAT students over the years and specializes in helping students looking to achieve elite scores.

Dr. Anthony Lafond is Next Step's MCAT Content Director. He has been teaching and tutoring MCAT students for nearly 12 years. He earned his MD and PhD degrees from UMDNJ - New Jersey Medical School with a focus on rehabilitative medicine. Dr. Lafond believes that both rehabilitative medicine and MCAT education hinge on the same core principle: crafting an approach that puts the unique needs of the individual foremost.

Brian Syzdek earned his doctorate in psychology in 2014 from the Chicago School of Professional Psychology. He has been in test prep since 2009.

To inquire about doing tutoring work with Bryan, Anthony, or Brian directly, go to http://nextsteptestprep.com/ or contact Next Step at 888-530-NEXT.

Updates and other notes may be found here:

http://nextsteptestprep.com/mcat-materials-change-log/

Rev. 2015-05-01

TABLE OF CONTENTS

INTRODUCTION

Hello and welcome to Next Step's workbook for the new Psychological, Social, and Biological Foundations of Behavior Section of the MCAT. Since that name is quite the mouthful, we're just going to keep it simple for this book and call it "the psych section", understanding, of course, that the section includes sociology as well.

The book you're holding contains all of the information and practice that you need to start mastering this challenging new part of the MCAT. We'd like to start by giving you a brief overview of the Psych Section here in the Introduction.

The new Psych Section will consist of 59 questions which you'll have 95 minutes to answer. Those 59 questions will be presented in a mix of independent discrete questions and questions associated with a reading passage (much like the old MCAT). The 59 questions will include 10 passages with 44 associated questions and 15 independent discrete questions. We've followed the AAMC's precise guidelines for the practice sections in this book.

Each section of 59 questions will have roughly 30% of its questions drawn from introductory sociology, 60% from introductory psychology, and 10% biology. Within those broad categories, the AAMC estimates that the 59 questions will break down further as:

33%: Behavior, Learning, Personality
27%: Cognition, Emotion
20%: Identity, Social Interaction
15%: Social Structures, Demographics
5%: Social Inequality

As with the hard sciences, the key to mastering this new section involves taking a step-by-step approach, starting with reinforcing foundational content, then putting that content into an overall context, and finally practice, practice, practice!

Everyone here at Next Step would like to wish you the best of luck with your studies!

Thank you,

Bryan Schnedeker
Co-founder
Next Step Pre-Med, LLC

Free Online MCAT Diagnostic

Want to see how you would do on the MCAT and understand where you need to focus your prep?

TAKE OUR FREE MCAT DIAGNOSTIC EXAM.

Timed simulations of all 4 sections of the MCAT, including behavioral sciences

Comprehensive reporting on your performance

This exam is provided free of charge to students who purchased our book.

To access your free exam, visit:
http://nextsteptestprep.com/mcat-2015-diagnostic-practice-test/

HOW TO USE THIS BOOK

This workbook consists of five sections:

Chapter I is an outline of all of the content areas that will be covered in the new Psych Section, arranged by content area and topic. This outline is provided primarily as a reference tool. If you want to double-check if a particular topic will be on the Psych Section, come back to check this outline.

Appendix B is the self-study outline. Here, we have taken the outline from Section I and expanded it. This is where you begin the real work of learning new content. Next Step's workbook is **not** a textbook. For your content review, you will need to purchase Next Step's Content Review books or use other resources.

Instead, Appendix B is where we ask you to develop your **own** notes on these topics. By building up your own self-study outline, you will learn the material far better than simply skimming through some pre-written outline.

To use the Self Study version of the outline, fill in the space labeled "CL" with your confidence level (1, 2, 3, 4) on that topic. We suggest a simple self-assessment such as:

4 = total confidence. I could take the MCAT today and questions on this topic would be fine.

3 = strong confidence. I'd like to just refresh quickly, but I'd feel good seeing this topic on my MCAT.

2 = weak confidence. I've heard of it but can't explain it and I'd be nervous on this topic on my MCAT.

1 = no confidence. Is this English? I've never even heard of this before!

Once you've gone through and done a self-assessment, then use the large blank spaces under each topic to fill in your own definition or description of that topic for each topic you labeled 3 and 4. Once you've finished that, briefly investigate those topics using outside resources. For topics you already feel comfortable with, a quick skim of Next Step's content review book and the relevant Wikipedia articles should be more than enough. Remember, most of the concepts covered by this section are 101-level. The challenge of the section is not having an encyclopedic knowledge of advanced theories in psychology or sociology. Rather, it's interpreting data sets and studies to draw proper conclusions.If your descriptions were accurate, great. If you left things out or got things wrong, then highlight that topic in pink (or some color other than yellow). It's easy to learn new information, but harder to un-learn wrong information. So stuff you thought you knew (but you were wrong) have to be a priority in your studies.

After you're done with your strengths, move to the topics you're not sure on. For those, simply go through your outside content (Next Step's Review Books, old text books, Khan Academy, Wikipedia, etc.) and fill in a short description of each topic and sub-topic. If it looks like there's too much info to sum up in a few sentences, create a separate study sheet for your notes.

Once that's all done, give yourself a big pat on the back – that's the first major step in the process. As we said, the act of building up your own notes will have lead to much more learning than simply whizzing through a pre-written review book.

Appendix C is a glossary of every key term you will be expected to know for the Psych Section. With the same goal of turning this workbook into an active tool for learning (rather than something passive), we've arranged the glossary as a series of study sheets.

To use them, simply fold over the right-hand side of the page to cover the definitions. Then quiz yourself on the words on the right and check yourself.

It's important when learning these terms to avoid simply plowing through the terms in the same order over and over. You'll end up learning the terms in the context of the study sheet, rather than really learning each idea. We recommend that you use the following pattern:

1) Go through the words in order, twice.
2) Go through the odd-numbered pages, then the even numbered pages, then repeat.
3) Quiz yourself on the first word on each page, then the second word on each page, and so on.
4) Finally, go through the whole glossary backwards, twice.

By breaking up the order in which you review the words, you help your brain focus on learning each individual term rather than subconsciously memorizing the pattern in which the words are printed on the page.

Chapter 2 presents several practice passages and independent discrete questions and discusses some simple strategies for organizing the information they present. Work through this section **after completing the self-study outline** in Appendix B and **after learning the terms** in the glossary in Appendix C.

Chapter 3 consists of four full, 95 minute, timed sections. Complete each of these sections in order, under timed conditions. You do yourself no favors by "cheating" and not holding yourself to time. It takes a lot of practice to get used to the tight time constraints on the test, and these sections are your first chance to practice.

When going through the passages, we discuss the use of a highlighter pen. For these timed sections, a valuable way to review is to go back into the passages with a different color of highlight after you've reviewed your work. If there are any questions you got wrong because you didn't highlight something important in the passage, then highlight after the fact with the new color.

This lets you come back and review your work a couple of days later with a clear visual representation of how you should have been highlighting the first time through.

If you ever find yourself stuck and would like to ask questions or offer feedback, visit our forums on Student Doctor Network or contact us at www.NextStepTestPrep.com if you'd like to arrange for tutoring. (Hint – there's a discount on our tutoring programs at the back of the book!)

CHAPTER I
Outline: MCAT 2015 Psychology and Sociology

The following outline includes the concepts and topics to be covered on the psych section according to official AAMC documents. You'll want to have a good working knowledge of each of these concepts. Later in the book, you'll find a thorough glossary of terms and study sheets to master these topics.

PSYCHOLOGY

I. Sensation

1. Thresholds
2. Weber's Law
3. Signal Detection theory
4. Sensory adaptation

Particular Senses
1. Vision
   a) Parallel Processing
   b) Feature detection
2. Hearing and Auditory Processing
3. Auditory processing
4. Somatosensation and Pain
5. Kinesthetic sense

Perception
1. Bottom-up / Top-down processing
2. Perceptual organization – depth, form, motion, constancy
3. Gestalt principles

II. Consciousness and Thinking

Consciousness
1. States of consciousness
   a) Alertness
   b) Sleep
      i.   Stages and cycles of sleep
      ii. Dreaming
      iii. Sleep disorders
   c) Hypnosis
   d) Meditation

2. Drugs that change conscious perception
   a) Types of drugs
   b) Drug addiction

Memory and Attention
1. Selective Attention
2. Divided Attention
3. Memory encoding – process and how to increase it
4. Memory storage
   a) Types
   b) Semantic networks
   c) Spreading activation
5. Memory retrieval, effect of emotion
   a) Recall
   b) Recognition
   c) Relearning
   d) Retrieval cues
6. Memory loss
   a) Aging
   b) Alzheimer's disease
   c) Korsakoff's syndrome
   d) Decay
   e) Interference
   f) Memory construction and source monitoring

Cognition and Language
1. Cognitive development
   a) Piaget
   b) Later adulthood
   c) Effect of language
   d) Role of culture, heredity, environmental
2. Problem solving
   a) Approaches

b) Barriers
c) Heuristics
  i. Biases
  ii. Intuition
  iii. Emotion
  iv. Overconfidence
  v. Belief perseverance
3. Intelligence
  a) Various definitions and levels of ability
  b) Effect of heredity, environment
4. Theories of language development
  a) Learning
  b) Nativist
  c) Interactionist

III. Emotion and Stress

Emotion
1. Cognitive component
2. Physiological component
3. Behavioral component
4. Universal emotions
5. James-Lange theory
6. Cannon-Bard theory
7. Schachter-Singer theory

Stress
1. Stress appraisal
2. Stressors
3. Responses to stress: physiological, emotional, behavioral
4. Stress management

IV. Behavior and Personality

Biology Influences Behavior
1. Neurotransmitters
2. Endocrine effects
3. Genetic factors
  a) Temperament
  b) Interaction between heredity and environment
4. Environment and experience effect behavior

Attitudes and Motivation
1. Influences on motivation
  a) Instinct
  b) Arousal

c) Drive
d) Needs
2. Link between motivation and behavior
  a) Drive Reduction Theory
  b) Incentive Theory
  c) Cognitive Theories
  d) Need-based Theories
3. Specific behaviors explained by theories
  a) Eating, Sex
  b) Drug use
  c) Others
4. Regulation of motivation: biological factors, cultural factors
5. Components of attitudes
  a) Cognitive
  b) Affective
  c) Behavioral
6. Cognitive dissonance
7. Behavior and attitude affect each other

Personality
1. Perspectives on Personality
  a) Psychoanalytic
  b) Humanistic
  c) Trait
  d) Social cognitive
  e) Biological
  f) Behaviorist
2. Explaining behavior situationally

The Presence of Other People
1. Social facilitation
2. Deindividuation
3. Bystander effect
4. Social loafing
5. Peer pressure

Behavior Change and Learning
1. Habituation
2. Classical Conditioning
  a) Stimuli
    i. Neutral
    ii. Conditioned
    iii. Unconditioned
  b) Responses
    i. Conditioned
    ii. Unconditioned
  c) Acquisition

d) Extinction
e) Spontaneous recovery
f) Generalization
g) Discrimination
3. Operant Conditioning
a) Shaping
b) Extinction
c) Reinforcement
i. Positive
ii. Negative
iii. Primary
iv. Conditional
d) Reinforcement Schedules
i. Fixed ratio
ii. Variable ratio
iii. Fixed interval
iv. Variable interval
e) Punishment
f) Escape
g) Avoidance
4. Observational learning
a) Modeling
b) Mirror Neurons
c) Vicarious Emotions
5. Attitude change
a) Elaboration Likelihood Model
i. Central and Peripheral route processing
b) Social Cognitive theory
c) Factors that affect attitude change
i. Changing behavior
ii. Characteristics of the message and target
iii. Social factors

V. Identity and Interaction

Identity
1. Self-concept
2. Identity
3. Social Identity
4. Self-esteem
5. Self-efficacy
6. Locus of control in self-identity
7. Stages of identity development
a) Erikson
b) Vygotsky
c) Kohlberg
d) Freud
8. Social factors on identity development

a) Imitation
b) Role-taking
c) Reference group

Interaction
1. Attribution theory
a) Fundamental attribution error
b) Cultural impact on attribution
2. Self-perception shapes perception of others
3. Perception of environment affects perception of others
4. Prejudice
a) Power
b) Prestige
c) Class
d) Emotion
e) Cognition
f) Discrimination
i. How power, prestige, class affect discrimination
5. Stereotypes
a) Self-fulfilling prophecy
b) Stereotype threat
6. Interaction between animals
a) Signals used by animals
7. Social behaviors
a) Attraction
b) Aggression
c) Attachment
d) Social support

VI. Psychological Disorders
1. Psychological disorders
a) Biomedical approach
b) Biopsychosocial approach
c) Classification schemes and types
i. Anxiety
ii. Somatoform
iii. Mood
iv. Schizophrenia
v. Dissociative
vi. Personality
d) Incidence and prevalence
2. Psychological disorders as nervous system disorders
a) Schizophrenia
b) Depression

c) Alzheimer's

d) Parkinson's

SOCIOLOGY

I. Social Influences on Behavior

1. Peer pressure
2. Group polarization
3. Groupthink
4. Culture
   a) Assimilation
   b) Multiculturalism
   c) Subculture
5. Socialization
   a) Norms
   b) Socializing Agents
      i.   Family
      ii. Peers
      iii. Media
      iv. Workplace
6. Deviance
   a) Stigma
7. Obedience
   a) Conformity

II. Social Interactions

1. Types of Group
   a) Status
   b) Roles
   c) Groups
   d) Networks
   e) Organizations
2. Influences on interaction
   a) Responses to emotional displays
      i. Gender
      ii. Culture
3. Manipulating perception by others
   a) Front stage vs. Back stage
   b) Dramaturgy
4. Discrimination
   a) Individual discrimination
   b) Institutional discrimination
5. Ethnocentrism

a) In-group vs. Out-group

b) Cultural relativism

III. Structure of Society

Analyzing Social Structures

1. Functionalism
2. Conflict theory
3. Symbolic interaction
4. Social constructionism
5. Institutions that shape society
   a) Education
   b) Family
   c) Religion
   d) Government
   e) Economy
   f) Health care
6. Culture
   a) Material culture
   b) Symbolic culture
   c) Language
   d) Values
   e) Beliefs
      i. Norms
   f) Rituals
7. Social groups placement within the culture
8. Evolution

Demographics

1. Age
2. Gender
3. Race
4. Ethnicity
5. Immigration
6. Sexual orientation
7. Demographic shifts
   a) Fertility
   b) Migration
   c) Mortality
8. Social movements
9. Globalization
10. Urbanization

IV. Social Inequality

1. Spatial Inequality
   a) Segregation
   b) Environmental inequality

c) Globalization
2. Social Class
   a) Stratification into classes
      i. Status
      ii. Power
   b) Cultural capital
   c) Social capital
   d) Social reproduction
   e) Privilege
   f) Prestige
3. Class and race, gender, age
4. Social mobility
   a) Intergenerational
   b) Intragenerational
   c) Downward
   d) Upward
   e) Meritocracy
5. Poverty
   a) Relative
   b) Absolute
   c) Segregation
   d) Isolation
6. Healthcare Disparities
   a) Inequality in health status
      i. Race
      ii. Gender
      iii. Class
   b) Unequal access to healthcare
      i. Race
      ii. Gender
      iii. Class

BIOLOGY

I. The Nervous and Endocrine Systems

Nervous System
1. Neurons
   a) Reflex Arc
   b) Neurotransmitters
2. Peripheral nervous system
3. Central nervous system
   a) Brainstem
   b) Cerebellum
   c) Diencephalon
   d) Cerebrum

e) Cerebral cortex
   i. Voluntary movement
   ii. Information processing
   iii. Lateralization
4. Lab techniques for studying the brain

Endocrine System
1. Components
2. Effects on behavior
3. Negative feedback

II. Sense Perception

1. Sensation
   a) Thresholds
   b) Sensory adaptation
   c) Sensory receptors
      i. Pathways
      ii. Types
2. Vision
   a) Structure of the eye
   b) Function of the eye
   c) Visual processing
      i. Brain pathways
3. Hearing
   a) Structure and function of the ear
   b) Hair cells
   c) Auditory processing
      i. Brain pathways
4. Taste
   a) Chemoreceptors
5. Smell
   a) Olfactory cells
   b) Pheromones
   c) Olfactory processing
      i. Brain pathways
6. Pain perception
7. Kinesthetic sense
8. Vestibular sense

6

CHAPTER II
Passage and Question Strategies

Independent Discrete Questions

As we mentioned in the Introduction, each psych section will consist of approximately 15 independent discrete questions and 44 questions that come with a reading passage. Time is tight on the MCAT and you'll want to make sure you make the most of each minute.

To that end, the first thing you should do when you start the timer is go through the section and complete all of the independent questions. They're typically arranged in clumps of three to five questions and will say something like "These questions are **NOT** based on a passage." at the top of the screen.

To start, we'll look at a few examples of these sorts of independent questions.

1. A person with a genetic abnormality is unable to distinguish different colors from each other. Other components of vision and visual processing are unaffected. What part of his visual processing system is his genetic abnormality most likely affecting?
    A) Visual cortex
    B) Visual memory
    C) Optic nerve
    D) Retinal cones

This is an example of a relatively straightforward biology question. When reading through these independent questions, start by asking yourself, *"Exactly what is the question asking me for?"*. A classic sort of trap answer will be something that's the "right answer to the wrong question" – that is, it will be related to the topic of the question but not *exactly* answer the question.

Here, the question is asking us which system is abnormal. Once you've read the question and answer choices, and you know *exactly* what the question is asking for, re-read the question and ask yourself, *"What information is provided?"*. You've got to be careful not to make any unwarranted assumptions. The MCAT is a picky test and will expect you to pay attention to the exact information provided. We're told the only problem this person has is distinguishing color.

Next, ask yourself, *"What outside information do I need?"* The independent questions especially will draw heavily on outside knowledge. Here, you need to be familiar with the four terms in the answer choices.

Finally, *evaluate the choices, either by prediction or process of elimination*. In "prediction" you simply skim quickly through the choices looking for what you already know the answer will say. That's often the case when you have a good content background in an area. If you're not exactly sure what they're looking for, don't delay – start eliminating choices.

Remember, *answer every question, even if you're not sure!*

In this question, the answer is (D). Retinal cones are structures humans use to perceive information about color in visual images. An abnormality in retinal cones is likely to affect color detection, and for this reason the correct answer is (D).

> A: The visual cortex receives image-related information from the eyes and processes it; however, if visual information from retinal cones contains no color or less-well-defined colors to begin with, it would not make a difference whether the visual cortex is processing the information correctly or not.
> B: Visual memory has to do with the limited-term presence of visual images in the brain after having been seen. By contrast, a defect in retinal cones would cause inability to distinguish colors whether the image was previously seen or whether it is currently being looked at.
> C: The optic nerve transmits visual information to the brain from the retina. Abnormal retinal cones would have a more specific effect on color perception than would an abnormal optic nerve.

Now try another similar question:

2. A young child, after observing older siblings make breakfast for themselves by combining a bowl, a spoon, cereal and milk, unsuccessfully attempts to do the same thing. She tries again, this time with a parent helping her step-by-step, and is only then able to complete the process successfully. Two years later, she has learned to reliably add cereal, milk, and a spoon to a bowl without making a mess. What theory relates to the difference between her earlier behavior and her later behavior?
    A) Kohlberg's Pre-Conventional and Conventional stages
    B) Erikson's Stages of Psychosocial Development
    C) Vygotsky's Zone of Proximal Development theory
    D) Maslow's Hierarchy of Needs

Exactly what is the question asking me for?

The theory that compares the child's situation before and after two years pass.

What information is provided?

A description of a child being able to carry out a task with parental help and then later being able to do it on her own, and the names of various theories in the answer choices.

What outside knowledge do I need?

The MCAT will expect you to be familiar with the various theories presented in the answer choices and be able to match one to the description in the question.

Vygotsky's theory of a Zone of Proximal Development describes the difference between what an individual can do with assistance and what she can do without assistance. It also states that a child first attempts to learn by following the examples of others, and gradually develops the ability to complete tasks without help that previously required outside assistance. This describes the dynamic in the prompt, and hence the answer is choice (C).

> A: Kohlberg's stages have to do with morality development.
> B: Erikson's stages relate to the development of self, identity, trust and social independence, not the capability to perform procedural tasks with and without help.
> D: Maslow's hierarchy of needs relates to things that people need on physical, emotional and self-actualization levels; this hierarchy is not connected to the learning experiences described in the prompt.

Now that we've carefully examined a couple of questions, complete the questions on the next page to practice this process. The explanations follow.

3. A music fan often listens to his favorite band's songs on his music player. At some point, he decides to start attending concerts. He meets other fans at the concerts who wear the band's logo on their shirts. Many also have tattoos of the band's logo. Eventually, the fan gets a tattoo with the band's logo and purchases shirts with the logo. All of the following could characterize this situation EXCEPT:

    A) Influence of individuals on social identity formation

    B) Influence of a group on social identity formation

    C) Socializing to the norms of a subculture

    D) Locus of control in self-concept

4. A jogger in the park sees a bird swoop down from a tree and fly past in front of her. After jogging for another 25 seconds, she remembers the event but cannot recreate a specific visual image. Two days later, she passes by the same tree and is reminded of the event. What characteristics are involved with this chain of events?

I. Information recalled from short-term memory after disappearing from sensory memory.

II. Information recalled from visual memory after disappearing from short-term memory.

III. The semantic network model of memory organization.

    A) I and II only

    B) I and III only

    C) II and III only

    D) I, II and III

5. A paralegal is attempting to write a legal brief while also carrying on a conversation with a co-worker. She finds it very difficult to both write the brief and speak with the co-worker at the same time. What would the specific modality model of attention say about this?

    A) The fact that persons possess one undifferentiated pool of mental resources means that draining this pool through the use of one task leaves scant resources for other tasks.

    B) Neither the writing task nor the speaking task has been practiced enough to become automatic, meaning significant attentional resources must be devoted to each task.

    C) The fact that the verbal modality is being used for both the writing task and the speaking task means that the two tasks, since they must necessarily use the same modality due to the nature of each of them, will interfere with each other.

    D) The specific modality model of attention would not explain this.

6. All of the following characterize Cannon-Bard theory EXCEPT:

    A) A central role for the thalamic region in human emotion.

    B) A central role of hypothalamic structures in emotional expression.

    C) A stimulus causes physical arousal, which then causes a specific emotion.

    D) A stimulus causes physical arousal and specific emotions, but not necessarily in that order.

7. An English-speaking country imposes strict quotas on immigration from countries with non-English-speaking populations. The quotas are not lifted for 15 years. During this time, the percentage of English-only speakers in the country increases, and the percentage of people in the country who speak languages other than English decreases. What best accounts for this?

    A) A decrease in first-generation immigrants and an increase in second-generation immigrants.

    B) A decrease in first-generation immigrants and an increase in third-generation immigrants.

    C) A decrease in second-generation immigrants and an increase in third-generation immigrants.

    D) A decrease in third-generation immigrants.

Independent Question Explanations

3. A music fan often listens to his favorite band's songs on his music player. At some point, he decides to start attending concerts. He meets other fans at the concerts who wear the band's logo on their shirts. Many also have tattoos of the band's logo. Eventually, the fan gets a tattoo with the band's logo and purchases shirts with the logo. All of the following could characterize this situation EXCEPT:

    A) Influence of individuals on social identity formation
    B) Influence of a group on social identity formation
    C) Socializing to the norms of a subculture
    D) **Locus of control in self-concept**

Here, (A), (B) and (C) describe what is taking place. (D), however, relates to the extent to which a subject believes he can control the events affecting his life, and also relates to the ways in which this belief affects what a subject thinks of himself. The prompt does not connect to either of these. (D) is therefore the answer.
A: Individuals can often have an effect on a person's social identity.
B: Groups can often, and here seem to be having, an effect on a person's social identity.
C: Here, one norm of the subculture of concert-going fans described in the prompt seems to be wearing the band's logo. Socialization is a learned behavior that here causes the music fan in question to adopt this particular norm of this subculture.

4. A jogger in the park sees a bird swoop down from a tree and fly past in front of her. After jogging for another 25 seconds, she remembers the event but cannot recreate a specific visual image. Two days later, she passes by the same tree and is reminded of the event. What characteristics are involved with this chain of events?

  I. **Information recalled from short-term memory after disappearing from sensory memory.**
  II. Information recalled from visual memory after disappearing from short-term memory.
III. **The semantic network model of memory organization.**

    A) I and II only
    B) **I and III only**
    C) II and III only
    D) I, II and III

Here, choice (I) is correct – visual memory, a type of sensory memory, allows one to create a mental image of a visual scene, but typically lasts only for a half-second or so. Choice (III) is also correct – the semantic network model explains that certain triggers will activate associated memories – here, memories of the event are triggered by the jogger passing by the same place two days later. Choice (II), however, is the reverse of what has taken place and is not correct. Answer choice (B) is therefore the correct response.

5. A paralegal is attempting to write a legal brief while also carrying on a conversation with a co-worker. She finds it very difficult to both write the brief and speak with the co-worker at the same time. What would the specific modality model of attention say about this?

    A) The fact that persons possess one undifferentiated pool of mental resources means that draining this pool through the use of one task leaves scant resources for other tasks.
    B) Neither the writing task nor the speaking task has been practiced enough to become automatic, meaning significant attentional resources must be devoted to each task.
    C) **The fact that the verbal modality is being used for both the writing task and the speaking task means that the two tasks, since they must necessarily use the same modality due to the nature of each of them, will interfere with each other.**
    D) The specific modality model of attention would not explain this.

According to the specific modality model of attention, tasks that use the same modality are more likely to interfere with one another. Here, writing and speaking both require a person to use his or her verbal modality; therefore the writing and speaking tasks will interfere with each other according to the specific modality attention theory. (C) is hence the correct answer.

A: This describes Kahneman's theory of attention.

B: This describes the resource theory of attention.

D: This is, in fact, a situation for which the specific modality model has an explanation.

6. All of the following characterize Cannon-Bard theory EXCEPT:

   A) A central role for the thalamic region in human emotion.

   B) A central role of hypothalamic structures in emotional expression.

   C) **A stimulus causes physical arousal, which then causes a specific emotion.**

   D) A stimulus causes physical arousal and specific emotions, but not necessarily in that order.

Here, (C) characterizes the James-Lange theory, which postulates that physical arousal always precedes, and causes, emotional responses. Because it doesn't characterize the Cannon-Bard theory, (C) is the correct answer choice.

A: Cannon-Bard theory postulates that a stimulus causes excitation in the cortex, which in turn is directed by conditioned processes into a specific response, and this response then stimulates thalamic processes to activate in a particular combination in a way that sends signals to provoke a specific emotional response.

B: Neural projections from hypothalamic structures are postulated to play an important role in the emotional expression pathway of Cannon-Bard theory.

D: Cannon-Bard theory states that physical arousal and specific emotions arise independently, and often present at the same time rather than one after another.

7. An English-speaking country imposes strict quotas on immigration from countries with non-English-speaking populations. The quotas are not lifted for 15 years. During this time, the percentage of English-only speakers in the country increases, and the percentage of people in the country who speak languages other than English decreases. What best accounts for this?

   A) A decrease in first-generation immigrants and an increase in second-generation immigrants.

   B) **A decrease in first-generation immigrants and an increase in third-generation immigrants.**

   C) A decrease in second-generation immigrants and an increase in third-generation immigrants.

   D) A decrease in third-generation immigrants.

According to the three-generation model of assimilation, first-generation immigrants may speak some of their new country's language but they are mostly comfortable speaking their original language. Also according to this model, second-generation immigrants are bilingual, and third-generation immigrants only speak English. If this is the case, a country that dramatically reduces immigration of foreign language speakers will likely experience loss of first-generation immigrant population (through old age, emigration and other attrition). This can cause the immigrant population to become more heavily weighted toward second- and third-generation immigrants. As third-generation immigrants are the only group which speaks English only, an increase in their percentage and a decrease in the percentage of first-generation immigrants would best explain the percentage loss of foreign language speakers in the English-speaking country from the prompt. (B), which includes both of these elements, is the correct answer.

A: An increase in second-generation, bilingual immigrants would not have a clear effect on the percentage of English speakers or foreign language speakers.

C: A decrease in second-generation, bilingual immigrants would not have a clear effect on the percentage of English speakers or foreign language speakers.

D: A decrease in third-generation immigrants would not lower the percentage of foreign-language speakers, as third-generation people tend to speak only English according to the three-generation assimilation theory.

Social Science Passages

The social science passages on the MCAT will be anywhere from 250 – 550 words, and will often come with one or more diagrams. The types of information they present can be broadly categorized as informational or experimental. There are a number of different possible approaches here, but in this book we will opt for a relatively simple one: use the on-screen highlighter.

Some folks may like to go slowly and use the scratch paper to take notes, and others prefer to skim very quickly through the passage to get to the questions as quickly as possible. For some students those might work. But at least at first, we suggest you start with our "middle of the road" approach: don't skip right to the questions, don't bother taking notes on the scratch paper. Instead, read briskly – a little faster than you're normally comfortable with – and highlight important ideas as they come up.

When you come to experimental information, slow down and focus on one question: what does it measure? The MCAT loves to test your understanding of a passage by focusing on exactly what the experiment measured.

So what should you highlight?

There are four general categories of things worth highlighting: **Key terms, opinions, contrasts, cause and effect relationships.**

Keep in mind, we're using these category names very loosely. What matters is that you've spotted a key idea, not what name you give it. Having said that, here's what to watch for:

Key terms:	These are things like proper nouns, technical terms, numbers, dates, etc. They're the words that you're going to want to be able to find again quickly if a question asks about them.
Opinions:	Most importantly, the author's. Opinions can be a view expressed by a particular scientist, or a view espoused by a school of thought. The main thing to watch for here is the emphasis words like should, ought, must, better, worse, etc.
Contrast:	Just what it says. Watch for conflicting views, old vs. new, traditional vs. radical and so on.
Cause and effect:	We're going to use the phrase "cause and effect" to refer to any logical connection, association, correlation, or literal cause-and-effect relationship presented in the passages. Any time the passages offers us a "because this, therefore that" relationship, we'll call it "cause and effect". To be clear, we don't mean these are always literal, scientific causes. Rather, we're using this phrase in a loose, rhetorical way.

While using this book, have a yellow highlighter marker handy. Highlight in the book just like you would want to on the real exam. When you review the explanations afterwards, you'll see that we break down the material a couple of ways.

First, we use **bold and underlined** text to show you the words and phrases you should have highlighted. Then, underneath each paragraph, we use **bold text** to describe *why* you should highlight those terms. The material is analyzed using the four categories above.

If you're the type of test-taker who likes to take notes on the scratch paper, then our **bold text** notes under the paragraph can serve as an example of the sorts of things you should have jotted down.

Question Format

Once you have completed the passage reading, it is on to the **questions**, which is **where all the points are!** Just like the passages, each question the exam presents is looking to test your ability to complete a task. The four question types are:

Task 1, Recall: 35% or about 20-21 questions.
Task 2, Problem Solving: 45% or about 26-27 questions.
Task 3, Research Design: 10% or about 5-6 questions.
Task 4, Data-Based and Statistical Reasoning: 10% or about 5-6 questions.

Task 1: Recall of Scientific Concepts

A big part of your success both in medical school and on the MCAT is demonstrating a solid understanding of scientific concepts and principles. The exam will test your ability to recall key concepts and your ability to identify the relationship between closely-related concepts.

Task 1 Example Question

A person sees motion out of the corner of her eye and turns her head towards the motion in response. Which of the following lists the tissues involved, in the correct order, from the moment the light enters the eye until the visual stimulus is processed by the woman's brain?
A) Retina → Optic Nerve → Lateral Geniculate Body → Optic Chiasma → Visual Cortex
B) Retina → Optic Chiasma → Optic Nerve → Lateral Geniculate Body → Visual Cortex
C) Lateral Geniculate Body → Retina → Optic Nerve → Optic Chiasma → Visual Cortex
D) Retina → Optic Nerve → Optic Chiasma → Lateral Geniculate Body → Visual Cortex

This is a task 1 question because it simply requires you to recall the components of the visual system in the correct order. Here, only choice D places the elements in the correct order and so it is the right answer.

Task 2: Problem Solving within Scientific Concepts

The MCAT is not just about recall. The exam tests a student's critical reasoning about scientific concepts, theories, and applications. Solving these questions will involve analyzing and assessing scientific explanations and predictions across psychology, sociology, and biology. You will see plenty of these questions in this book but take a look at the sample question below.

Task 2 Example Question

A man holds a very strong allegiance to a particular political party. After a decade of that party being in power, its policies have proven to be disastrous for his country, and the party is rocked by scandals that catch most of the major leading figures of the party. The cognitive dissonance theory predicts that the man may do any of the following EXCEPT:
A) choose to de-emphasize the importance of the party's failed policies and dismiss the scandals as trumped up by the media.
B) tell himself that his party allegiance was never that important to him, and that what he was really attached to was a set of ideas, not the political party.

C) increase his allegiance to the party, accept the truth of the party's failed efforts, and feel upset at the downturn in the party's fortunes.

D) leave the party for another party with similar ideological foundations.

This is a task 2 question, because it asks you to recall a specific concept (cognitive dissonance) and then apply it to the situation described. The cognitive dissonance theory asserts that when a person has two cognitions, or a cognition and behavior, that are not consonant with each other, the person will feel discomfort. They can resolve this discomfort either by adding a new cognition (choice B), by changing behavior (choice D), or by changing a cognition to de-emphasize the importance of the dissonant cognition (choice A). So the man may use the strategies described by choices A, B, or D to help resolve his dissonance. What he likely won't do is described by choice C – increase his dissonance by both increasing his party loyalty and accepting his party's failures.

Task 3: Research Design

The new MCAT is looking to identify well-rounded future physicians. It will ask you to display a clear understanding of crucial components of scientific research. These questions will test your scientific inquiry skills by showing that you can actually carry out the "business" of science. You will be tested on your mastery of important components of scientific methodology.

To answer these questions correctly you will need to understand the methods that social, natural, and behavioral scientists use to test and expand the boundaries of science. These questions may seek to test your ability to recognize the ethical guidelines scientists must follow to ensure the rights of research subjects, the integrity of their work, and the interests of research sponsors.

Task 3 Example Question

In an experiment designed to test social facilitation, a group of highly skilled tennis players were asked to serve the tennis ball 10 times and to attempt to hit a small target with their shot. Group 1 did the serving exercise while being observed by other people, whereas group 2 did the serving exercise alone on the tennis court. What are the dependent and independent variables?

A) The dependent variable was whether the observers were present and the independent variable was how many times the subject hit the target.

B) The independent variable was whether the observers were present and the dependent variable was how many times the subject hit the target.

C) The independent variable was whether the observers were present and the dependent variable was how aware of the observers the subjects were.

D) The dependent variable was the sport being played and the independent variable was how many times the subject hit the target.

This is a task 3 question and requires knowledge of the concept of social facilitation and an understanding of which variables are dependent and independent in an experimental setup. The independent variable is the one controlled by the researchers (here the presence of observers) and the dependent variable is the one measured by the researchers (here how many times the person hit the target). Thus choice B is correct.

Task 4 Data-Based and Statistical Reasoning

The last task for the new MCAT is really not that new. Interpreting figures, tables, graphs and equations has long been a necessary skill in reading passages efficiently. With these questions, the test will make this task more formal. To succeed you must train yourself to be able to deduce patterns in data presented in graphs, tables, and figures. It will also ask you to draw conclusions based on the scientific data given in a passage or question.

Task 4 Example Question

The personality trait of novelty seeking is associated with impulsive decisions and extravagant behavior. When comparing personality models, research has found that novelty seeking is positively correlated with extraversion and negatively correlated with conscientiousness. Which of the following personality profiles is most consistent with this research?

A) Man A states that he "feels energized by being around other people" and has a tendency to overlook details in tasks at work. He likes to travel to exotic new lands and will often change his travel plans at a moment's notice while abroad.

B) Woman B scored very high on an inventory of novelty-seeking tendencies administered by her psychologist. She prefers to stay home and engage in hobbies like model ship building that require patience and precision.

C) Man C was experiencing anxiety while being around other people so he started seeing a psychiatrist. The man told his psychiatrist that he's been fired from his last two jobs due to sloppy work and that has added to his anxiety.

D) Woman D has serious financial issues due to her tendency to impulsively spend more money than she can afford on lavish presents for her cats. Her co-workers describe her as having a "larger than life" personality, but the woman doesn't socialize outside of work, preferring the company of her novels.

This is a task 4 question because to answer it, you must use reasoning about positive and negative correlations. We're told that novelty-seeking is positively associated with being extroverted but negatively associated with conscientiousness. Choice A best fits this profile, as the man described is high in novelty-seeking and extraversion but low in conscientiousness.

Use the five passages on the following pages as a way to practice your highlighting technique and your problem solving ability. You want to get comfortable with the different question types on the exam. For now, don't worry about time. Speed will come with practice.

Passage 1

In an experiment designed to test cognitive dissonance, researchers asked adult participants to rate their beliefs about eating meat on a 1-5 scale: "I believe the consumption of meat is 5: healthy and ethical; 4: somewhat healthy and ethical; 3: neither healthy nor unhealthy and neither ethical nor unethical; 2: somewhat unhealthy and unethical; 1: very unhealthy and unethical." Participants were then randomly assigned one of two essays to write – either a one-page essay defending a vegan lifestyle or a one-page essay defending meat-eating. Each participant was randomly assigned to one of five groups: Group 1 wrote the essay defending veganism and was paid $10; group 2 wrote the essay defending veganism and was paid $300; group 3 wrote the essay defending meat consumption and was paid $10; group 4 wrote the essay defending meat consumption and was paid $300; and group 5 was not asked to write any essay and was not paid.

Two days later, participants were asked to fill out the survey again about their attitudes about eating meat. The results are summarized below.

Initial Attitude	Group 1	Group 2	Group 3	Group 4	Group 5
5 (meat okay)	4.4	4.8	4.95	4.96	4.9
4	3.3	3.75	4.1	4.08	4.01
3	2.6	2.9	3.32	3.2	3.05
2	1.6	1.95	2.38	2.15	2.11
1 (meat not okay)	1.1	1.05	1.19	1.1	1.1

Table 1 Results of the essay-writing exercise on participants' beliefs. Data reported as the mean score on the 1-5 scale for all participants based on initial response and group assignment.

In a separate experiment, researchers placed five year old children in a room with a number of toys, including one especially tempting toy (the most popular children's toy of that Christmas season). One group of children were given no instructions about what to play with, and when left alone a strong majority of children selected the popular toy. The second group was told they could play with any toy but the popular one, and told they would be mildly punished if they disobeyed. The third group was told they would be severely punished if they played with the popular toy. After leaving each group alone for ten minutes, the researchers returned and told the children they could play with any toy they liked.

In group 3 (severe punishment), most children elected to play with the popular toy after they were told they were allowed to. In group 2 (mild punishment), however, the majority of children still avoided playing with the popular toy, even after they were permitted to.

8. Which of the following identifies a weakness in the experimental design of the first experiment?
    A) The amounts of money chosen do not reflect a constant marginal gain in value, given the differences in socioeconomic status among participants.
    B) Participants were asked to self-report their attitudes about meat consumption rather than an objective assessment.
    C) A five-point scale is too crude to make determinations about an issue as nuanced as food ethics.
    D) Both the initial and follow-up survey conflate two factors that may be different and have different effects on cognitive dissonance.

9. The participants in the second experiment differ from those in the first in that:
    A) they did not experience cognitive dissonance.
    B) their moral reasoning likely operated on a preconventional level.
    C) they did experience cognitive dissonance.
    D) their cognitive development was limited to the sensorimotor stage.

10. The results from experiment 1 suggest that those in group 3 who initially responded with a 1, 2, or 3 on the survey:
    A) experienced increased cognitive dissonance after the second survey.
    B) resolved their cognitive dissonance by increasing certain behaviors.
    C) resolved their cognitive dissonance by changing their cognitions.
    D) decreased their ethical behavior after the essay writing task.

11. Which of the following is NOT a method for resolving cognitive dissonance?
    A) Changing one's behaviors
    B) Adding new cognitions
    C) Projection of dissonant attitudes
    D) Denial of the truth of the conflicting information

12. The results from experiment 1 suggest that those in group 2 who responded with a 3, 4, or 5 on the initial survey experienced which of the following?
    A) Less cognitive dissonance than those in group 1 due to external justification of behavior
    B) No cognitive dissonance because they were writing an essay that was consonant or irrelevant to their attitude
    C) More cognitive dissonance than those in group 1 due to their willingness to write an essay opposing their views in exchange for a large sum of money
    D) An increased willingness to not be truthful with the researchers

Passage 1 Explanation

In an experiment designed to test **cognitive dissonance**, researchers asked adult participants to rate their **beliefs about eating meat** on a 1-5 scale: "I believe the consumption of meat is 5: healthy and ethical; 4: somewhat healthy and ethical; 3: neither healthy nor unhealthy and neither ethical nor unethical; 2: somewhat unhealthy and unethical; 1: very unhealthy and unethical." Participants were then randomly assigned one of two essays to write – either a one-**page essay defending a vegan** lifestyle or a one-page essay defending meat-eating. Each participant was randomly assigned to one of five groups: Group 1 wrote the essay defending veganism and was **paid $10**; group 2 wrote the essay defending veganism and was **paid $300**; group 3 wrote the essay defending meat consumption and was paid $10; group 4 wrote the essay defending meat consumption and was paid $300; and group 5 was **not asked to write any essay and was not paid.**

Key term: cognitive dissonance

Opinion: participants gave their opinion on meat-eating

Cause-and-effect: participants wrote an essay for or against meat eating and were paid a little or a lot

Two days later, participants were asked to fill out the survey again about their attitudes about eating meat. The results are summarized below.

Initial Attitude	Group 1	Group 2	Group 3	Group 4	Group 5
5 (meat okay)	4.4	4.8	4.95	4.96	4.9
4	3.3	3.75	4.1	4.08	4.01
3	2.6	2.9	3.32	3.2	3.05
2	1.6	1.95	2.38	2.15	2.11
1 (meat not okay)	1.1	1.05	1.19	1.1	1.1

Table 1 Results of the essay-writing exercise on participants' beliefs. Data reported as the mean score on the 1-5 scale for all participants based on initial response and group assignment.

Table 1 Attitudes remained relatively constant but that groups 1 and 3 (the $10 groups) had a bigger shift in response to writing their essays. We see that the biggest impact was on the group that felt meat-eating was okay and who were then paid $10 to write an essay defending veganism.

In a separate experiment, researchers placed **five year old children** in a room with a number of toys, including **one especially tempting toy** (the most popular children's toy of that Christmas season). One group of children were given no instructions about what to play with and when left alone a strong majority of children selected the popular toy. The second group was told they could play with any toy but the popular one, and told they would be **mildly punished** if they disobeyed. The third group was told they would be **severely punished** if they played with the popular toy. After leaving each group alone for ten minutes, the researchers returned and told the children they **could play with any toy they liked**.

Key terms: five year old children, tempting toy

Contrast: one group could play with any toy, one group was told mild punishment if they played with the popular toy, one group was told severe punishment

Cause-and-effect: after the initial threat of punishment, they were then let play with any toy at all

In group 3 (severe punishment), most children elected to play with the popular toy after they were told they were allowed to. In group 2 (**mild punishment**), however, the majority of children **still avoided playing with the popular toy**, even after they were permitted to.

Contrast: children who were only given a mild threat of punishment still chose not to play with the toy even when allowed to; other children played with the popular toy once permitted

8. Which of the following identifies a weakness in the experimental design of the first experiment?
   A) The amounts of money chosen do not reflect a constant marginal gain in value, given the differences in socioeconomic status among participants.
   B) Participants were asked to self-report their attitudes about meat consumption rather than an objective assessment.
   C) A five-point scale is too crude to make determinations about an issue as nuanced as food ethics.
   D) **Both the initial and follow-up survey conflate two factors that may be different and have different effects on cognitive dissonance.**

The self-reporting survey used conflates whether eating meat is "healthy" and whether it is "ethical". These are two very different considerations and people may have different attitudes about those two factors. In addition, differences in those attitudes may change how they react to the essay-writing exercise.

A: The difference between $10 and $300 was intended to be very different values, so asserting that they do not represent a constant gain in value is not a weakness in the experiment.
B: Many social science protocols require self-reporting. This is a standard practice, not a weakness.
C: An inventory that assesses basic agreement or disagreement can effectively use a five-point scale.

9. The participants in the second experiment differ from those in the first in that:
   A) they did not experience cognitive dissonance.
   B) **their moral reasoning likely operated on a preconventional level.**
   C) they did experience cognitive dissonance.
   D) their cognitive development was limited to the sensorimotor stage.

The second experiment involved small children. In Kohlberg's stages of moral reasoning, small children tend to operate at a preconventional level of moral reasoning. Adults typically employ conventional or post-conventional moral reasoning.

A: The fact that children who were not threatened with a harsh punishment chose later to not play with the popular toy suggests that the children experienced cognitive dissonance and so had to adjust their internal attitude ("well I didn't want to play with that toy anyway") so that the toy was not appealing even after the threat of punishment was removed.
C: While they did experience cognitive dissonance, this was not a way in which they differed from the adults, who also experienced cognitive dissonance.
D: Piaget's stages of cognitive development suggest that the sensorimotor stage is limited to 0-2 year olds.

10. The results from experiment 1 suggest that those in group 3 who initially responded with a 1, 2, or 3 on the survey:

    A) experienced increased cognitive dissonance after the second survey.
    B) resolved their cognitive dissonance by increasing certain behaviors.
    C) resolved their cognitive dissonance by changing their cognitions.
    D) decreased their ethical behavior after the essay writing task.

Group 3 was tasked with defending meat consumption, and those who initially answered 1, 2, or 3 did not initially express an opinion that meat eating was healthy and ethical. On the repeat survey, those numbers drifted upwards considerably, suggesting that some people resolved their cognitive dissonance ("I wrote an essay defending meat-eating for only ten bucks, but I didn't think eating meat was okay.") by changing their thoughts about whether eating meat was okay.

A: The assessment of cognitive dissonance comes through changes in the survey results between the first and second survey. We're given no data about what happens after the second survey.
B, D: The passage doesn't address behaviors exhibited by participants, only survey responses about attitudes.

11. Which of the following is NOT a method for resolving cognitive dissonance?

    A) Changing one's behaviors
    B) Adding new cognitions
    C) Projection of dissonant attitudes
    D) Denial of the truth of the conflicting information

Resolving cognitive dissonance requires changing thoughts or actions to reduce the dissonance. One can change one's behaviors to align with ideas (choice A), or add new ideas to reduce the dissonance (e.g. "I want to be on a diet but I ate that muffin. But that's okay because it must've been a low-fat muffin.") (choice B), or simply ignore the new, dissonant information (e.g. "I like this presidential candidate so this news story saying he did something I disapprove of must be wrong.") (choice D). By process of elimination, that leaves choice C as the right answer to this "NOT" question.

Projection is an ego defense mechanism, rather than a method to reduce cognitive dissonance.

12. The results from experiment 1 suggest that those in group 2 who responded with a 3, 4, or 5 on the initial survey experienced which of the following?

    A) Less cognitive dissonance than those in group 1 due to external justification of behavior
    B) No cognitive dissonance because they were writing an essay that was consonant or irrelevant to their attitude
    C) More cognitive dissonance than those in group 1 due to their willingness to write an essay opposing their views in exchange for a large sum of money
    D) An increased willingness to not be truthful with the researchers

Group 2 had to write an essay defending veganism, but those who answered 3, 4, or 5 did not express a particular attitude that eating meat was wrong. Thus they likely experienced some cognitive dissonance, and we can see that they resolved this dissonance by changing their ideas – in general the data on a re-test gave lower scores than the first test. However, the change in scores was not as great as for group 1. Thus group 2 likely experiences less cognitive dissonance. The difference is that they were paid a much larger sum of money and so could justify their essay-writing behavior to themselves rather than experience unpleasant dissonance.

B, C: Group 2 did not experience more dissonance or a lack of dissonance, as can be seen from the data in table 1. D: Nothing in the passage suggests that participants had a reason to lie or did so.

Passage 2

Joint attention refers to an individual's ability to coordinate attention with another person to reference a third object, such as when two people view a scene together or a class of students waits for a teacher to begin the lesson, for example. Infants develop this ability around age 3 to 6 months. Joint attention is involved in many social processes, such as learning, social cognition, and relationships. An infant's ability to develop joint attention skills can have a lasting impact on his ability to develop other skills, especially those acquired through interactions with others, which can last a lifetime. Three ways that an infant uses joint attention are 1) by following the direction of another person, such as if that person is pointing out an object, 2) by the infant, himself, indicating something, or 3) by the infant meeting another person's gaze to ensure that this person and the infant are both focused on a particular object.

Among the primary purposes of these behaviors are, first, to share the experience of the object to which the infant is paying attention. This desire is likely reinforced by the facial or emotional response the infant receives from the person with whom he is jointly attending. Types of joint attending behaviors which serve this purpose are known as declarative behaviors.

Another reason for an infant to jointly attend is to indicate something to another person, typically because the infant wants something. This type of jointly attending behavior is known as an imperative behavior. Both of these behaviors represent the capacity to learn through social cognition, a theory of learning that emphasizes learning socially. As much of early learning occurs in an observational and unstructured context, the capacity for social learning is an important skill.

Many early social interactions are related to developing social competence, or an ability to interact developmentally appropriately with others. A deficiency of social competency is highly related to long-term psychopathology. Researchers have found that ability to jointly attend and social competence are correlated. One way that they may be related is via language development, as researchers have found relationships between the ability to jointly attend and language development and language development and social competence.

Another way that joint attention ability is seen to relate to social competence is through caregiver scaffolding. Caregiver scaffolding refers to a process through which a caregiver incites infant learning by providing the infant with challenging, yet developmentally appropriate, stimuli through which the infant learns. Joint attention may encourage this process by helping the infant to be able to signal to his caregiver objects that he desires, and allows the caregiver to indicate objects to the infant. Both of these skills are necessary in an infant's learning through objects.

Researchers conducted a study in which the relationship between joint attention ability of infants between 6 and 9 months of age and language ability of these same infants at age 2 years was assessed. Researchers counted the number of joint attention behaviors they observed in one sitting with the infant and his caretaker. They then counted the number of unique words the infant was able to use at age 2.

Table 1 Correlation matrix for joint attention

Pearson correlation coefficient	Number of joint attention behaviors	Number of scaffolding behaviors	Number of unique words used
Number of joint attention behaviors	1.00	.78 (p=.039)	.89 (p<.0001)
Number of scaffolding behavior	.78 (p=.039)	1.00	.74 (p=.023)
Number of unique words used	.89 (p<.0001)	.74 (p=.023)	1.00

13. The age of onset of joint attention seems to refute what Piagetian concept of infant perception?
    A) Egocentrism
    B) Formal operations
    C) Animism
    D) Conservation

14. In what disorder is an infant's impairment to jointly attend a primary symptom of the disorder?
    A) Anxiety
    B) Conduct disorder
    C) Autism
    D) ADHD

15. In what way might a caretaker employ scaffolding to help a child learn to read?
    A) By giving him many books
    B) By naturally letting a child learn
    C) By helping a child sound out words he is struggling with
    D) By reading words with which he thinks the child will have difficulty so as not to discourage the child

16. Which of the following is NOT a possible explanation for the results of the study?
    A) Infants who can jointly attend can learn by watching other people speak
    B) Infants who can jointly attend can indicate what they want to learn
    C) Infants who can jointly attend are able to focus on the letters of the alphabet
    D) Infants who can jointly attend feel reinforced while learning by observing their caretakers' faces

17. Which of the following is NOT a mediating variable in the relationship between joint attention ability and long-term psychopathology?
    A) Social competence
    B) Language development
    C) Autism
    D) Social learning ability

18. If in the study, it was found that infants demonstrated a high number of imperative behaviors, what might this suggest in terms of language development?
    A) Infants who can attend to language the caregiver indicates can better learn language
    B) Infants who can indicate language they want the caregiver to help them learn can better learn language
    C) Infants who can follow caregiver scaffolding can better learn language
    D) Infants who can feel caregiver empathy can better learn language

19. Given the findings of the study and other associations described in the passage, in what other domain might an infant who is high in language development also be high?
    A) Scaffolding ability
    B) Empathic response
    C) Social competence
    D) Nativist language abilities

Passage 2 Explanation

Joint attention refers to an individual's ability to coordinate attention with another person to reference a third object, such as when two people view a scene together or a class of students waits for a teacher to begin the lesson, for example. Infants **develop this ability around age 3 to 6 months**. Joint attention is involved in **many social processes**, such as learning, social cognition, and relationships. An infant's ability to develop joint attention skills can have a lasting impact on his ability to develop other skills, especially those acquired through interactions with others, which can last a lifetime. Three ways that an infant uses joint attention are 1) by **following the direction** of another person, such as if that person is pointing out an object, 2) by the infant, himself, **indicating something**, or 3) by the infant **meeting another person's gaze** to ensure that this person and the infant are **both focused** on a particular object.

Key terms: joint attention
Cause and effect: By developing joint attention around 3-6 months, infants can carry out a number of tasks, especially tasks related to learning.

Among the primary purposes of these behaviors are, first, to **share the experience** of the object to which the infant is paying attention. This desire is likely reinforced by the facial or emotional response the infant receives from the person with whom he is jointly attending. Types of joint attending behaviors which serve this purpose are known as **declarative behaviors**.

Key terms: declarative behaviors, when an infant wants to share an experience of an object with another

Another reason for an infant to jointly attend is to **indicate something to another person**, typically because the infant wants something. This type of jointly attending behavior is known as an **imperative behavior**. Both of these behaviors represent the capacity to learn through **social cognition**, a theory of learning that emphasizes learning socially. As much of early learning occurs in an **observational and unstructured context**, the capacity to learn through social learning is an important skill.

Key terms: imperative behavior (indicate a desire to another person), social cognition
Cause and effect: Because infant learning is observational, they rely on social learning

Many early social interactions are related to developing **social competence**, or an ability to interact developmentally appropriately with others. A **deficiency of social competency** is highly related to long-term **psychopathology**. Researchers have found that ability to jointly attend and social competence are correlated. One way that they may be **related is via language development**, as researchers have found relationships between the ability to jointly attend and language development and language development and social competence.

Key terms: social competence, psychopathology
Cause and effect: joint attention is connected to language development, which is connected to social competence

Another way that joint attention ability is seen to relate to social competence is through **caregiver scaffolding**. Caregiver scaffolding refers to a process through which a caregiver incites infant learning by providing the infant with **challenging, yet developmentally appropriate, stimuli** through which the infant learns. Joint attention may encourage this process by helping the infant to be able to signal to his caregiver objects that he desires, and allows the caregiver to indicate objects to the infant. Both of these skills are necessary in an infant's learning through objects.

Key terms: caregiver scaffolding
Cause and effect: infants learn using joint attention by interacting with their caregivers

Researchers conducted a study in which the relationship between **joint attention ability** of infants between 6 and 9 months of age and **language ability** of these same infants at age 2 years was assessed. Researchers counted the number of joint attention behaviors they observed in one sitting with the infant and his caretaker. They then counted the number of unique words the infant was able to use at age 2.

Table 1 Correlation matrix for joint attention

Pearson correlation coefficient	Number of joint attention behaviors	Number of scaffolding behaviors	Number of unique words used
Number of joint attention behaviors	1.00	.78 (p=.039)	.89 (p<.0001)
Number of scaffolding behavior	.78 (p=.039)	1.00	.74 (p=.023)
Number of unique words used	.89 (p<.0001)	.74 (p=.023)	1.00

Table 1 shows us the relationships between scaffolding behaviors, joint attention behaviors, and unique words used in a symmetrical correlation matrix. We see an especially strong correlation (0.89) between number of words used and number of joint attention behaviors.

13. The age of onset of joint attention seems to refute what Piagetian concept of infant perception?
    A) **Egocentrism**
    B) Formal operations
    C) Animism
    D) Conservation

    Answer: A – According to Piaget, infants at age 3 to 6 months are unable to understand the perspective of others, a concept he termed egocentrism.

14. In what disorder is an infant's impairment to jointly attend a primary symptom of the disorder?
    A) Anxiety
    B) Conduct disorder
    C) **Autism**
    D) ADHD

    Answer: C – Autism is a disorder in which social contact and language is severely disrupted.

15. In what way might a caretaker employ scaffolding to help a child learn to read?
    A) By giving him many books
    B) By naturally letting a child learn
    C) **By helping a child sound out words he is struggling with**
    D) By reading words with which he thinks the child will have difficulty so as not to discourage the child

    Answer: C – Scaffolding is challenging the child in developmentally appropriate ways, which helping him sound out words is an example of.

16. Which of the following is NOT a possible explanation for the results of the study?
    A) Infants who can jointly attend can learn by watching other people speak
    B) Infants who can jointly attend can indicate what they want to learn
    C) **Infants who can jointly attend are able to focus on the letters of the alphabet**
    D) Infants who can jointly attend feel reinforced while learning by observing their caretakers' faces

    Answer: C – Joint attention is not strictly the same as attention. It refers to working in tandem with another, which answer C does not indicate.

17. Which of the following is NOT a mediating variable in the relationship between joint attention ability and long-term psychopathology?
    A) Social competence
    B) Language development
    C) **Autism**
    D) Social learning ability

    Answer: C – Joint attention ability deficits may be a symptom of autism, but autism does not mediate the relationship between joint attention ability and psychopathology.

18. If in the study, it was found that infants demonstrated a high number of imperative behaviors, what might this suggest in terms of language development?
    A) Infants who can attend to language the caregiver indicates can better learn language
    B) **Infants who can indicate language they want the caregiver to help them learn can better learn language**
    C) Infants who can follow caregiver scaffolding can better learn language
    D) Infants who can feel caregiver empathy can better learn language

    Answer: B – In the passage it was explained that imperative behavior was a way that infants could indicate something to the caregiver. Knowing that this type of behavior was displayed predominantly in the study then suggests that infants who can do that can learn language, as the high correlation coefficient indicates.

19. Given the findings of the study and other associations described in the passage, in what other domain might an infant who is high in language development also be high?
    A) Scaffolding ability
    B) Empathic response
    C) **Social competence**
    D) Nativist language abilities

    Answer: C – According to the data, infants high in language development are also high in joint attention. According to the passage, infants high in joint attention are high in social competence.

This page intentionally left blank.

Passage 3

The role traumatic experiences have in attention problems in children has become more recognized recently. During times of excessive stress, such as when experiencing traumatic events, the neurohormone cortisol is released in the child's body. Cortisol serves an important function to prepare the body to respond to physically demanding situations. However, due to the toxicity of cortisol, repeated exposure to it may lead to abnormal brain development. In particular, excessive cortisol has been associated with decreased hippocampus size. Decreased hippocampal area has been found to be associated with deficits in vocabulary and verbal performance, which can lead to difficulty understanding and attending to verbal communication.

In addition, the hippocampus, along with the prefrontal cortex, serves to regulate the limbic system, a process which helps regulate impulsive behavior. However, damage to the hippocampus through excessive exposure to cortisol makes the hippocampus less able to regulate the limbic system, resulting in more impulsive behavior.

The decreased hippocampal area of children exposed to chronic stress has been documented in studies comparing average hippocampal size of children exposed to repeated stressful situations versus children who have not had these experiences. The results of a recent study are presented in the following table. Researchers compared the average intracranial and hippocampal volume of children who had been exposed to at least 5 lifetime stressful situations and a control group of children, who had not been exposed to stressful situations. The table lists the volume of those measures and the p-value associated with the two-sample t-test comparing the average volume of each of those measures across groups.

Table 1 Effects of Stress on the Brain

Brain Area	Children exposed to stressful situations	Control (n=40)	p-value
Intracranial Volume	1245	1253	0.38
Hippocampus	5.08	7.1	0.0002

20. Which of the following facts about the children exposed to stressful situations and control group, if true, *weakens* the argument that children exposed to trauma have difficulties inhibiting impulsive behavior due solely to decreased hippocampal size?

    A) The average prefrontal cortex size between the two groups was not different.

    B) The average prefrontal cortex size between the two groups was smaller in the children exposed to stressful situations.

    C) The number of stressful situations the children exposed to stressful situations had been exposed to was at most 6 stressful situations.

    D) All children are exposed to a low level of background stress as a part of daily life.

21. Which of the following could potentially help children exposed to trauma improve attention?

    A) Preventative interventions

    B) Increased verbal instruction in classrooms

    C) Hippocampal neurogenesis

    D) Cranial dendritic pruning

22. Why was it important that the researchers measured intracranial volume as well as hippocampal volume to ascertain the relationship between experiencing stress and hippocampal volume?

    A) Through neuroplasticity, the hippocampus can come to process several other brain functions at once

    B) To explore the effect of trauma on the prefrontal cortex

    C) To know the ratio of hippocampal area to brain area

    D) To be able to assess the difference in brain size per stressful experience experienced

23. How does verbal performance mediate the relationship between hippocampal volume and attention in relation to this passage?

    A) Decreased verbal ability can make focusing on verbal information more difficult

    B) Decreased verbal ability leads to lower hippocampal volume

    C) Inattention is a byproduct of hippocampal volume, thereby impacting verbal ability

    D) Decreased verbal ability helps explain lower hippocampal volume and inattention

24. What is a limitation of the study cited above?

    A) Insufficient sample size

    B) Unable to generalize findings to individuals outside of the study

    C) The t-test comparison doesn't account for variability within groups

    D) Conclusions about trauma as a cause of decreased hippocampal size are unable to be drawn

Passage 3 Explanation

The role **traumatic experiences** have in attention problems in children has become more recognized recently. During times of excessive stress, such as when experiencing traumatic events, the neurohormone **cortisol** is released in the child's body. Cortisol serves an important function to **prepare the body** to respond to physically demanding situations. However, due to the **toxicity** of cortisol, **repeated exposure** to it may lead to **abnormal** brain development. In particular, excessive cortisol has been associated with **decreased hippocampus** size. Decreased hippocampal area has been found to be associated with **deficits in vocabulary** and verbal performance, which can lead to difficulty understanding and attending to verbal communication.

Key terms: traumatic experiences, cortisol, hippocampus
Cause and effect: trauma can cause and excess of cortisol which is correlated with decreased hippocampus size and verbal deficits.

In addition, the **hippocampus**, along with the **prefrontal cortex**, serves to **regulate the limbic system**, a process which helps **regulate impulsive** behavior. However, damage to the hippocampus through excessive exposure to cortisol makes the hippocampus less able to regulate the limbic system, resulting in **more impulsive** behavior.

Key terms: hippocampus, prefrontal cortex, limbic system
Cause and effect: damage to the hippocampus can result in dysregulation of the limbic system and more impulsive behavior.

The **decreased hippocampal area of children exposed to chronic stress** has been documented in studies comparing average hippocampal size of children exposed to repeated stressful situations versus children who have not had these experiences. The results of a recent study are presented in the following table. Researchers **compared the average intracranial and hippocampal volume** of children who had been exposed to at least 5 lifetime stressful situations and a control group of children, who had not been exposed to stressful situations. The table lists the volume of those measures and the p-value associated with the two-sample t-test comparing the average volume of each of those measures across groups.

Cause and effect: Chronic stress is also associated with decreased hippocampus volume.

Table 1 Effects of Stress on the Brain

Brain Area	Children exposed to stressful situations	Control (n=40)	p-value
Intracranial Volume	1245	1253	0.38
Hippocampus	5.08	7.1	0.0002

Table 1 shows us that despite similar total cranial volume, children exposed to stressful situations have a smaller hippocampus than the control.

20. Which of the following facts about the children exposed to stressful situations and control group, if true, *weakens* the argument that children exposed to trauma have difficulties inhibiting impulsive behavior due solely to decreased hippocampal size?

    A) The average prefrontal cortex size between the two groups was not different.

    B) **The average prefrontal cortex size between the two groups was smaller in the children exposed to stressful situations.**

    C) The number of stressful situations the children exposed to stressful situations had been exposed to was at most 6 stressful situations.

    D) All children are exposed to a low level of background stress as a part of daily life.

Answer: B – Answer B suggests that a smaller prefrontal cortex size could be a reason for the impulsive behavior, thus weakening the argument that impulsive behavior is due to a smaller hippocampus solely.

21. Which of the following could potentially help children exposed to trauma improve attention?

    A) Preventative interventions

    B) Increased verbal instruction in classrooms

    C) **Hippocampal neurogenesis**

    D) Cranial dendritic pruning

Answer: C – Hippocampal neurogenesis refers to the hippocampus regenerating cells, a process fairly unique to this brain area. If the hippocampus regenerates, that can potentially ameliorate attention problems caused by hippocampal damage from cortisol. A is not correct because preventative interventions would be helpful before a child was exposed to trauma. B is not correct because verbal attention is an area of difficulty for this group, leading to difficulties focusing on that type of stimuli.

22. Why was it important that the researchers measured intracranial volume as well as hippocampal volume to ascertain the relationship between experiencing stress and hippocampal volume?

    A) Through neuroplasticity, the hippocampus can come to process several other brain functions at once

    B) To explore the effect of trauma on the prefrontal cortex

    C) **To know the ratio of hippocampal area to brain area**

    D) To be able to assess the difference in brain size per stressful experience experienced

Answer C: This question has to do with neuroplasticity. If there is damage to the hippocampus, other areas of the brain may compensate for hippocampal duties, possibly resulting in increased size in these areas. Knowing that there is no increase in other brain areas limits the plausibility of that possibility. A describes neuroplasticity, but this would not be a reason to measure brain volume. B may be important to know, but researchers could not ascertain effects on the prefrontal cortex from a measure of the entire brain. D is not correct because there is no indication of the relationship between volume and number of experiences.

23. How does verbal performance mediate the relationship between hippocampal volume and attention in relation to this passage?

    A) **Decreased verbal ability can make focusing on verbal information more difficult**

    B) Decreased verbal ability leads to lower hippocampal volume

    C) Inattention is a byproduct of hippocampal volume, thereby impacting verbal ability

    D) Decreased verbal ability helps explain lower hippocampal volume and inattention

Answer: A – Decreased hippocampal volume has been shown to be associated with language problems, as stated in the passage. Therefore, focusing on verbal information is likely more difficult. B states an incorrect direction of effect. C and D don't describe the correct mediation process.

24. What is a limitation of the study cited above?
    A) Insufficient sample size
    B) Unable to generalize findings to individuals outside of the study
    C) The t-test comparison doesn't account for variability within groups
    D) **Conclusions about trauma as a cause of decreased hippocampal size are unable to be drawn**

Answer D: While there is a correlation between decreased hippocampal volume and trauma, causal effects are unable to be drawn.

This page intentionally left blank.

Passage 4

Perceptual organization refers to the way information that is visually perceived is organized by the organism perceiving it. The main way in which the organism organizes the information is by structure, or how parts of the image are grouped. Perhaps the most important way the structure is organized is in terms of part-whole structure, an increasingly more specific grouping of the structures by categories. For example, a child viewing a picture of his family might organize the structure of the picture in any of several ways. First, the child might organize the picture in terms of the whole picture. Then the child might form a whole called "family," of which the members of the family are parts. The child then might form a whole for each family member, with the individual body parts of the members forming parts. Another whole might be the background, which contains the parts that are observed, such as a tree or the sun.

The means by which the structure of the visual image is organized is called grouping. There may be several ways that the image can be grouped. For example, objects could be grouped by proximity, so for the picture of the family, family members who are standing together could be grouped together. Other examples of ways to group might be by size or color.

Related to grouping multiple objects, humans also have a tendency to perceive objects in a certain way. Amodal perception refers to humans tending to view objects that are partly occluded as whole objects. An example of this is given as follows:

Figure 1 Amodal perception example

In the above figure the figure in the background is partially covered by the oval. As humans view these figures they tend to complete the background figure. There could be many ways that the figure could be completed. The figure could be seen to have a jagged upper left corner or could end at the boundary of the oval figure. However, the way people tend to perceive the background shape is as a rectangle. There are likely at least two reasons why people tend to view the background figure this way.

First, people may tend to complete a figure in a way that is most similar to their prior experience. While people may have viewed a figure with a jagged corner or a piece missing, it is likely that people have far more often viewed an intact rectangle. Thus, because they have viewed that shape much more frequently they tend to perceive it this way again.

Next, people tend to complete shapes in the simplest way possible. Because the shape of the rectangle is the simplest shape, the background figure is pictured this way. This tendency to perceive figures in their simplest way is known as the minimum principle. However, it is not completely clear as to what constitutes the simplest shape. Is a rectangle the simplest shape or is a diagonal line that connects the intersections of the oval and rectangle the most simple?

Insight into how the brain perceives and organizes information is given from observing individuals with hemispheric lesions attempt to copy a given figure. Individuals with right parietal lesions tend to have difficulty replicating the whole figure, while those with left parietal lesions tend to have difficulty replicating details within the figure. This suggests that the right parietal lobe is responsible for processing the whole figure, while the left parietal lobe is responsible for processing details. It is not clear if these processes work in concert at the same time or if the brain perceives figures in a certain order, such as from details to the whole or from the whole to details.

25. If it was found that the brain processes figures first in the left parietal lobe and then in the right parietal lobe, this would be considered what type of processing?
    A) Top-down processing
    B) Bottom-up processing
    C) Inner-outer processing
    D) Outer-inner processing

26. What is the broad category for the principles of perception that are discussed in this passage?
    A) Vestibular sense
    B) Nativist theory
    C) Gestalt principles
    D) Weber principles

27. What is an evolutionary explanation for viewing objects as whole figures?
    A) The left parietal lobe has come to dominate human brains
    B) The details of an object do not contain information
    C) Viewing objects as whole figures is more similar as to how language is perceived
    D) Viewing an object as a whole figure allows humans to quickly judge the level of threat of the whole object

28. What is an example of how the visual data might be structured?
    A) A red and blue shape-whole; intersection-part
    B) A figure-whole; A rectangle and oval-part
    C) An overlapping figure-whole; a figure overlapping the background-part
    D) An oval within a rectangle-whole; a rectangle within a circle-part

29. How might a person with left parietal lobe damage recreate the figure above?
    A) By drawing the detailed parts within each figure
    B) By drawing the whole outline of the figure
    C) He would have difficulty seeing the figure
    D) He would have difficulty moving his left arm

30. Which of the following ways of grouping are NOT ways of perceiving the figure as two separate objects?
    A) Grouping by color
    B) Part-whole grouping
    C) Grouping by proximity
    D) Grouping by simplicity

Passage 4 Explanation

Perceptual organization refers to the way information that is visually perceived is organized by the organism perceiving it. The **main way** in which the organism organizes the information is by **structure**, or how **parts** of the image are **grouped**. Perhaps the most important way the structure is organized is in terms of part-whole structure, an increasingly more specific grouping of the structures by categories. **For example, a child viewing a picture of his family** might organize the structure of the picture in any of several ways. First, the child might organize the picture in terms of the whole picture. Then the child might form a whole called "family," of which the members of the family are parts. The child then might form a whole for each family member, with the individual body parts of the members forming parts. Another whole might be the background, which contains the parts that are observed, such as a tree or the sun.

Key terms: perceptual organization, structure, example of child viewing picture of family

The means by which the structure of the visual image is organized is called **grouping**. There may be several ways that the image can be grouped. For example, **objects could be grouped by proximity**, so for the picture of the family, family members who are standing together could be grouped together. Other examples of ways to group might be **by size or color**.

Cause and effect: grouping by size, color, proximity, etc. is how a visual image is organized

Related to grouping multiple objects, humans also have a tendency to perceive objects in a certain way. **Amodal perception** refers to humans tending to view objects that are **partly occluded** as whole objects. An example of this is given as follows:

Key terms: amodal perception means hidden objects are viewed as a whole

Figure 1 Amodal perception example

In the above figure the figure in the background is partially covered by the oval. As humans view these figures they **tend to complete the background figure**. There could be many ways that the figure could be completed. The background figure could be seen to have a jagged upper left corner or could end at the boundary of the red figure. However, the way people tend to perceive the **background shape is as a rectangle**. There are likely at least two reasons why people tend to view the blue figure this way.

Key terms: in the example, people see the background shape as a rectangle

First, people may tend to complete a figure in a way that is **most similar to their prior experience**. While people may have viewed a figure with a jagged corner or a piece missing, it is likely that people have far **more often viewed an intact rectangle**. Thus, because they have viewed that shape much more frequently they tend to perceive it this way again.

Cause and effect: the familiarity of rectangles makes people view the blue shape as a rectangle

Next, people tend to complete shapes in the **simplest way possible**. Because the shape of the rectangle is the simplest shape, the rear figure is pictured this way. This tendency to perceive figures in their simplest way is known as the **minimum principle**. However, it is **not completely clear as to what constitutes the simplest shape**. Is a rectangle the simplest shape or is a diagonal line that connects the intersections of the oval and rectangle the most simple?

Opinion: although people will tend to complete hidden shapes as simply as possible, it's unclear what qualifies as "simplest".

Insight into how the brain perceives and organizes information is given from observing individuals with **hemispheric lesions** attempt to copy a given figure. Individuals with **right parietal lesions** tend to have **difficulty replicating the whole** figure, while those with **left parietal** lesions tend to have **difficulty replicating details** within the figure. This suggests that the right parietal lobe is responsible for processing the whole figure, while the left parietal lobe is responsible for processing details. It is not clear if these processes work in concert at the same time or if the brain perceives figures in a certain order, such as from details to the whole or from the whole to details.

Contrast: right vs. left parietal lesions

25. If it was found that the brain processes figures first in the left parietal lobe and then in the right parietal lobe, this would be considered what type of processing?
    A) Top-down processing
    B) **Bottom-up processing**
    C) Inner-outer processing
    D) Outer-inner processing

    Answer: B – Bottom-up processing refers to processing details first and then processing the whole. Because it is assumed here that the brain processes from the left parietal lobe, which processes details, to the right parietal lobe, which processes whole, it can be assumed that this is bottom-up processing.

26. What is the broad category for the principles of perception that are discussed in this passage?
    A) Vestibular sense
    B) Nativist theory
    C) **Gestalt principles**
    D) Weber principles

    Answer: C – The way that people perceive objects as parts and wholes which they structure and the way people amodally perceive are Gestalt principles.

27. What is an evolutionary explanation for viewing objects as whole figures?
    A) The left parietal lobe has come to dominate human brains
    B) The details of an object do not contain information
    C) Viewing objects as whole figures is more similar as to how language is perceived
    D) **Viewing an object as a whole figure allows humans to quickly judge the level of threat of the whole object**

    Answer: D – This answer gives a reason which explains how humans are able to quickly perceive threat which would allow for increased chance of survival, an important motivation in evolutionary psychology.

28. What is an example of how the visual data might be structured?
    A) A red and blue shape-whole; intersection-part
    B) **A figure-whole; A rectangle and oval-part**
    C) An overlapping figure-whole; a figure overlapping the background-part
    D) An oval within a rectangle-whole; a rectangle within a circle-part

    Answer: B – This answer represents one whole object and two separate part objects.

29. How might a person with left parietal lobe damage recreate the figure above?
    A) By drawing the detailed parts within each figure
    B) **By drawing the whole outline of the figure**
    C) He would have difficulty seeing the figure
    D) He would have difficulty moving his left arm

    Answer: B – Someone with left parietal lobe damage has difficulty recreating details, so would likely draw the outline of the figure.

30. Which of the following ways of grouping are NOT ways of perceiving the figure as two separate objects?
    A) Grouping by color
    B) Part-whole grouping
    C) Grouping by proximity
    D) **Grouping by simplicity**

    Answer: D – If the figure was grouped by simplicity, the simplest figure would be one object, whereas the other answers separate the figure into two parts.

This page intentionally left blank.

Passage 5

Youth that chronically perpetrate violence may have neurobiological issues. It is first important to consider what type of aggression the individual primarily perpetrates. There are three main types of aggression. The first is premeditated aggression, in which the aggression is consciously planned and executed for some expected gain, such as a planned robbery. A second type of aggression is medically related aggression. This aggression is symptomatic of some medical condition. An example is that children with Down Syndrome may have trouble controlling their body and avoiding hitting others. A final type of aggression is impulsive aggression, which results from children having difficulty controlling their actions and reacting impulsively with aggression.

An area of the brain that is implicated in aggression is the prefrontal cortex, an area of the brain that controls many executive functions and other areas of the brain. An especially important function it controls is affect. Within the prefrontal cortex, the left prefrontal cortex primarily connects words to emotional experiences and encodes memories. The right prefrontal cortex controls the retrieval of memory and visuospatial information, both important in non-verbal problem solving. In normal human development, at about age 4 the left prefrontal cortex comes to dominate other areas of the brain, resulting in good interpretation of events and decision making. However, dysfunction in the prefrontal cortex can result in a number of dysfunctional behaviors, including inattention, impulsivity, and disorganization, among other conditions. The impact of this dysfunction can result in aggression, first, by making it difficult for the individual to choose non-aggressive responses. Second, having deficits in prefrontal cortex controlled processes, such as executive decision making, can lead a child to have a number of social problems. Children who demonstrate a number of these inappropriate behaviors, as listed above, can find themselves ostracized and unable to connect with peers. The result of this separation is a lack of social skill building and peer support. This predisposes this type of child to aggression because he has not learned alternative ways to handle conflicts or frustration and does not have social support to do so.

Another area of the brain associated with aggressive behavior is the anterior cingulate gyrus. The anterior cingulate gyrus is a part of the limbic system, primarily involved with processing emotional experiences. The anterior cingulate gyrus connects the limbic system with the prefrontal cortex, and thus serves to modulate the processing of emotional information. The anterior cingulate gyrus helps the brain to shift attention to relevant stimuli. The anterior cingulate gyrus serves to modulate attention between affect and cognition. Thus when the anterior cingulate gyrus is functioning properly the individual is able to encounter provocative situations that may lead to feelings of frustration. However, this individual can then reflect back on internal controls and modulate this arousal. When the anterior cingulate gyrus is dysfunctional an individual may only be able to focus on his own feelings of frustration and be unable to focus on the social expectations of a peer group, for example. This can result in the individual being uninhibited by social constraints and perhaps reacting with aggression.

A final area of the brain implicated in aggressive behaviors is the temporal lobe. The temporal lobe is involved with a host of bodily functions, including memory, mood, and perception, among others. Thus temporal lobe dysfunction can have far-reaching implications in terms of functioning. An area of the temporal lobe that is especially involved in aggression is the amygdala. The amygdala is primarily responsible for aversion emotions, such as fear or disgust. Low amygdala activity has been found in people with antisocial personality disorder. It is hypothesized that deficits in the amygdala lead to a lack of feeling aversive behaviors, such as fear. Without experiencing these aversive emotions an individual may be inclined to behave in self-serving ways without fear of outcomes.

In order to assess the relationship between aggression and brain dysfunction, researchers examined individuals with brain dysfunction in one of the areas mentioned above. In addition, these individuals' histories of aggression were recorded and the individuals were classified according to what type of aggression they predominantly displayed. The results are presented as follows:

Figure 1 Aggression type in patients with prefrontal cortical dysfunction

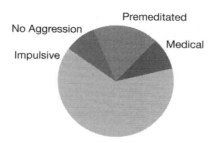

Prefrontal Cortex

Figure 2 Aggression type in patients with cingulate gyrus dysfunction

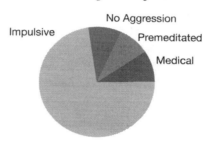

Anterior Cingulate Gyrus

Figure 3 Aggression type in patients with amygdalar dysfunction

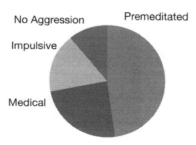

Amygdala

31. Why might those with amygdala deficits predominantly show the kind of aggression they do?
    A) Lack of social skills
    B) Lack of executive functioning skills
    C) Lack of fear-based learning
    D) Lack of memory

32. What would likely be another area in which an individual with impulsive aggression might have deficits?
    A) Immune functions
    B) Physical development
    C) Vestibular sense
    D) Language

33. Which of the following disorders could lead to problems with aggression via the temporal lobe?
    A) Schizoid Disorder
    B) Schizophrenia
    C) Epilepsy
    D) Anxiety

34. What type of intervention would not be helpful for an individual demonstrating aggression as a result of anterior cingulate gyrus dysfunction?
    A) Affect arousal modulation skill instruction
    B) Social skills training
    C) Weighing the pros and cons of engaging in deviant behavior
    D) Connecting thoughts, feelings, and behaviors

35. Why might an individual with impulsive aggression also have low scores on visuospatial tasks on an IQ test?
    A) There might be right prefrontal cortex damage
    B) There might be left prefrontal cortex damage
    C) There might be right temporal lobe damage
    D) There might be left temporal lobe damage

Passage 5 Explanation

Youth that **chronically perpetrate violence** may have **neurobiological issues**. It is first important to consider what type of aggression the individual primarily perpetrates. There are three main types of aggression. The first is **premeditated** aggression, in which the aggression is consciously planned and executed for some expected gain, such as a planned robbery. A second type of aggression is **medically related** aggression. This aggression is symptomatic of some medical condition. An example is that children with Down Syndrome may have trouble controlling their body and avoiding hitting others. A final type of aggression is **impulsive** aggression, which results from children having difficulty controlling their actions and reacting impulsively with aggression.

Key terms: chronic violence, neurobiological issues
Contrast: premeditated vs. medical vs. impulsive aggression

An area of the brain that is implicated in aggression is the **prefrontal cortex**, an area of the brain that controls many **executive functions** and other areas of the brain. An especially important function it controls is affect. Within the prefrontal cortex, the **left prefrontal cortex** primarily connects **words to emotional** experiences and encodes memories. The **right prefrontal cortex** controls the **retrieval of memory and visuospatial information**, both important in nonverbal problem solving. In normal human development, at about age 4 the **left prefrontal cortex** comes to **dominate** other areas of the brain, resulting in **good** interpretation of events and **decision making**. However, **dysfunction** in the prefrontal cortex can result in a number of dysfunctional behaviors, including inattention, impulsivity, and disorganization, among other conditions. The impact of this dysfunction can **result in aggression,** first, by making it difficult for the individual to choose non-aggressive responses. Second, having deficits in prefrontal cortex controlled processes, such as executive decision making, can lead a child to have a number of social problems. Children who demonstrate a number of these inappropriate behaviors, as listed above, can find themselves **ostracized** and unable to connect with peers. The result of this separation is a **lack of social skill building and peer support**. This predisposes this type of child to aggression because he has not learned alternative ways to handle conflicts or frustration and does not have social support to do so.

Key terms: executive function, prefrontal cortex
Cause and effect: deficiencies in the prefrontal cortex can lead to aggression and inappropriate behavior, which then leads to being socially ostracized and further behavioral problems.

Another area of the brain associated with aggressive behavior is the **anterior cingulate gyrus**. The anterior cingulate gyrus is a part of the **limbic system**, primarily involved with **processing emotional** experiences. The anterior cingulate gyrus connects the limbic system with the prefrontal cortex, and thus serves to **modulate** the processing of emotional information. The anterior cingulate gyrus helps the brain to shift attention to relevant stimuli. The anterior cingulate gyrus serves to modulate attention between affect and cognition. Thus when the anterior cingulate gyrus is **functioning properly** the individual is able to **encounter provocative situations** that may lead to feelings of frustration. However, this individual can then **reflect** back on internal controls and **modulate this arousal**. When the anterior cingulate gyrus is dysfunctional an individual may only be able to focus on his own feelings of frustration and be unable to focus on the social expectations of a peer group, for example. This can result in the individual being uninhibited by social constraints and perhaps reacting with aggression.

Key terms: anterior cingulate gyrus, limbic system
Cause and effect: when an individual encounters a situation that would provoke anger, the anterior cingulate gyrus lets them calm down and think about the situation.

A final area of the brain implicated in aggressive behaviors is the **temporal lobe**. The temporal lobe is involved with a host of bodily functions, including memory, mood, and perception, among others. Thus temporal lobe dysfunction can have far-reaching implications in terms of functioning. An area of the temporal lobe that is especially involved in aggression is the **<u>amygdala</u>**. The amygdala is primarily **<u>responsible for aversion emotions</u>**, such as fear or disgust. **<u>Low amygdala activity</u>** has been found in people with **<u>antisocial personality disorder</u>**. It is hypothesized that deficits in the amygdala lead to a lack of feeling aversive behaviors, such as fear. Without experiencing these aversive emotions an individual may be inclined to behave in self-serving ways **<u>without fear of outcomes</u>**.

Key terms: amygdala, temporal lobe, antisocial personality disorder
Cause and effect: the amygdala controls emotions like fear and disgust and people with antisocial personality disorder have low amygdalar function

In order to assess the relationship between aggression and brain dysfunction, **<u>researchers examined individuals with brain dysfunction in one of the areas mentioned above</u>**. In addition, these individuals' histories of aggression were recorded and the individuals were classified according to what type of aggression they predominantly displayed. The results are presented as follows:

Figure 1 Aggression type in patients with prefrontal cortical dysfunction

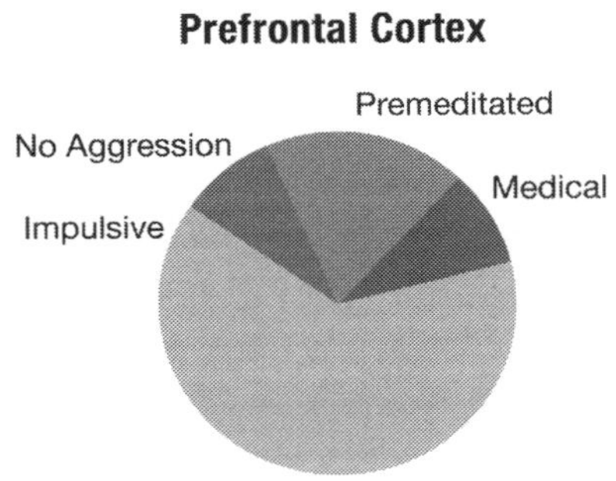

Prefrontal Cortex

Figure 2 Aggression type in patients with cingulate gyrus dysfunction

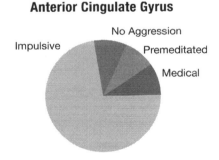

Anterior Cingulate Gyrus

Figure 3 Aggression type in patients with amygdalar dysfunction

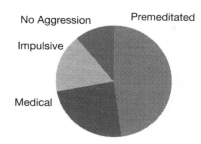

Amygdala

Figures 1 through 3 show us the type of aggression exhibited by patients with various brain dysfunctions, with impulsive being the most common, except for those with amygdalar dysfunction who display more premeditated aggression.

31. Why might those with amygdala deficits predominantly show the kind of aggression they do?
   A) Lack of social skills
   B) Lack of executive functioning skills
   C) **Lack of fear-based learning**
   D) Lack of memory

   Answer: C – The amygdala is responsible for experiencing aversion responses, including fear. Without feeling fear, an individual may commit premeditated aggression without concern.

32. What would likely be another area in which an individual with impulsive aggression might have deficits?
   A) Immune functions
   B) Physical development
   C) Vestibular sense
   D) **Language**

   Answer: D – According to the data, individuals with impulsive aggression likely have trouble with the prefrontal cortex or anterior cingulate gyrus. The prefrontal cortex also regulates language, therefore there could be a deficit in both language and impulsive aggression.

33. Which of the following disorders could lead to problems with aggression via the temporal lobe?
   A) Schizoid Disorder
   B) Schizophrenia
   C) **Epilepsy**
   D) Anxiety

   Answer: C – Epilepsy can affect the temporal lobe. Aggression can result due to dysfunction in the temporal lobe, as described in the passage.

34. What type of intervention would not be helpful for an individual demonstrating aggression as a result of anterior cingulate gyrus dysfunction?
   A) Affect arousal modulation skill instruction
   B) Social skills training
   C) **Weighing the pros and cons of engaging in deviant behavior**

D) Connecting thoughts, feelings, and behaviors

Answer: C – This type of intervention would be useful with someone who demonstrated premeditated aggression, not a type of aggression associated with anterior cingulate gyrus dysfunction.

35. Why might an individual with impulsive aggression also have low scores on visuospatial tasks on an IQ test?
    A) **There might be right prefrontal cortex damage**
    B) There might be left prefrontal cortex damage
    C) There might be right temporal lobe damage
    D) There might be left temporal lobe damage

    Answer: A – Right prefrontal cortex damage is associated with both.

This page intentionally left blank.

CHAPTER III
Timed Section Practice

Section 1: 59 Questions, 95 Minutes

Passage 1

Weber's law presents an interesting exception in the case of sound. While other sorts of stimuli will have a constant just-noticeable difference (jnd) across the full range of perceptible stimuli (the change in stimulus intensity as a fraction of the original intensity is a constant), for sound this does not always hold true.

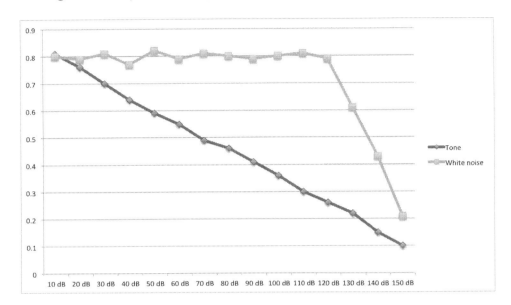

Figure 1 The jnd as a function of intensity for a single pure tone and for white noise

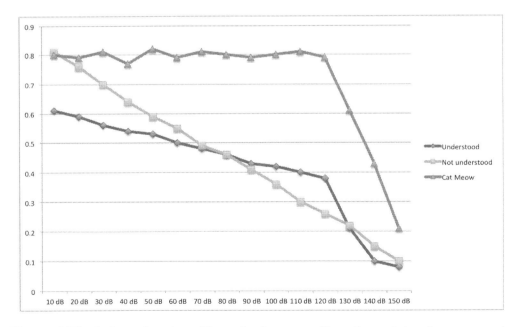

Figure 2 The jnd as a function of intensity for a recording of speech in a language understood by the listener, one not understood by the listener, and a recognizable non-speech sound (a cat's meow)

1. In studies of the just-noticeable difference, perception is measured in what way?
   A) Sensation
   B) Discrimination
   C) Magnitude estimation
   D) Signal transduction

2. For the especially loud noises, subjects often report negative emotions such as anger after hearing several of the loud sounds. The James-Lange theory would posit that this emotional response:
   A) precedes and causes a person to experience physiological arousal which then contributes to further unpleasant affect.
   B) occurs simultaneously and independently of the physiological arousal stimulated by the loud sounds.
   C) is a result of both physiological arousal and a cognitive appraisal of that arousal.
   D) follows from and is caused by the physiological arousal experienced as a result of the loud sounds.

3. For nearly every type of sound played, the just-noticeable difference dropped significantly near or above 130 dB. Which of the following is the most likely reason?
   A) Above a certain intensity level, sound perception also occurs as a result of signal transduction directly through the skull rather than solely through the ossicles and organ of Corti.
   B) The threshold of pain is near or above 130 dB and the jnd for pain is much lower than for many other types of stimuli.
   C) Study participants were more attentive to the especially loud sounds as a result of the physiological arousal those sounds created.
   D) The distracting nature of the especially loud sounds made it more difficult for study participants to detect changes in stimulus intensity.

4. The just-noticeable difference for response to different intensity electric shocks is presented below. Which of the following is most likely true?

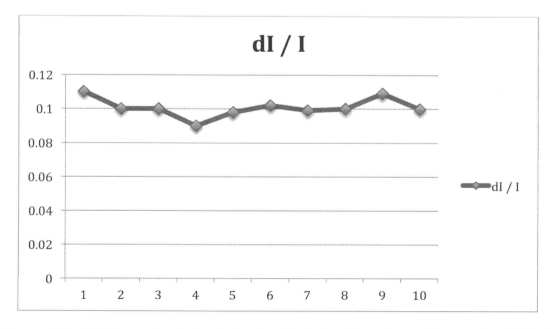

Figure 3 The jnd for a series of electric shocks with the shock intensity scaled as a series of 10 arbitrary but equal-value units

A) Nociceptors are significantly more sensitive to variations in pain intensity than the auditory system is to variations in loudness.

B) Unlike auditory perception of white noise sound intensity, the perception of pain intensity generally follows Weber's law at lower levels.

C) The signal transduction mechanisms by which pain is experienced do not rely on the same ion-channel triggers as do those for sound.

D) An 11% increase or decrease in shock intensity will generally not be noticed by a person.

5. The experiment involved playing noises loud enough that some study participants may have experienced discomfort or even pain. For the experiment to be approved by the researchers' institutional review board, they must have done all of the following EXCEPT:

A) Keeping the sound intensity well below the level at which each individual study participant will experience discomfort

B) Determining the least harmful or invasive protocol to achieve the study's results

C) Obtaining informed consent from the study participants prior to beginning the study

D) Treating study participants equally regardless of factors such as socioeconomic status, race, or gender

This page intentionally left blank.

Passage 2

The following advice was given by an expert in memory about how to better remember other peoples' names.

"First of all, it is important to pay attention and hear the other person's name being spoken. Many people forget names because they are not truly processing the person's name because they are doing other things. They may be focusing on their own feelings and thoughts at the time, especially how they are appearing to the other person. While you are focusing on the other person, once you hear their name a good thing to do is then repeat their name three times, while you are looking at them."

"A good strategy for remembering names is to involve all of your senses in the effort. First of all, try to integrate your sense of vision. To do this, try to imagine that you can see the person's name written on his forehead. Furthermore, try to imagine it is written in your favorite color. This will make the name stand out more."

"Another sense that can be integrated to assist in remembering is the sense of touch. You can imagine that you are actually writing down the name of the person. Try to imagine what it would feel like to write the person's name, feeling the pencil and the paper. You can even gently move you finger's micro-muscles as you are imagining writing. This will help ingrain the name in your memory even more."

"If you are meeting a group of people and are trying to remember several names, a good strategy is to remember them in groups. For example, you might group together the names of couples or group the names in the order in which you heard them. Repeating the names aloud as they are saying them to you can be helpful for remembering them. Finally, it can be helpful to use a mnemonic device for remembering names, such as grouping their names with an object that begins with the same letter."

"While it may be difficult to utilize all of these strategies for remembering names at once, with practice it can become easier and soon you should be able to remember peoples' names much easier than before. In a study, participants were instructed to use each of these techniques and then were introduced to 20 people. The participants then had another task that they were to perform for 20 seconds. Upon completing the task, the participants were queried on the number of names they were able to recall 30 seconds later."

Figure 1 Number of names recalled

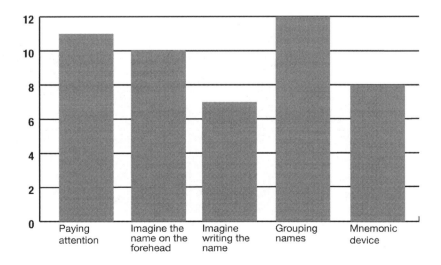

6. What flaw in the research design of the study would cause there to be serious doubts of the validity of the results?
   A) Having the participants use all techniques in the same order
   B) Having different participants use different techniques
   C) Having a control group
   D) Recording participant demographic characteristics

7. Participants were queried a month after the study about names they recalled. This type of memory primarily involves what part of the brain?
   A) Brain stem
   B) Corpus callosum
   C) Hippocampus
   D) Orbitofrontal cortex

8. In a follow-up study participants were brought back two days later and either asked to simply recall as many names as possible (group 1) or presented with a list of 50 names and asked to select names from the list that had been among the original 20 names presented (group 2). Which of the following is most likely true about this follow-up study?
   A) Both groups will correctly identify approximately the same number of names as in the original study since the memory techniques discussed improve both long-term and short-term memory.
   B) To have any external validity the participants must be required to perform the same twenty second intervening task at the start of this second recall attempt.
   C) Both groups will correctly identify fewer names two days later, but group 1 will correctly identify close to the same number of names whereas group 2 will likely mis-identify more names than are correctly identified, given that the new list has more incorrect than correct names available.
   D) While long-term memory is likely to involve some forgetting for both groups, group 2 will correctly identify more names.

9. Using all of the memory techniques listed in the passage helps improve memory through what process?
   A) Multi-tasking
   B) Parallel processing
   C) Diversification
   D) Neuroplasticity

Passage 3

Attachment theory is based on the work begun by Baumrind, in which she demonstrated that there is a relationship between the early patterns of interactions of parents and children and later child development. Baumrind initially classified three patterns of child behaviors. The first type she termed Pattern I and is characterized by children being secure, self-reliant, and explorative. The second type was known as Pattern II, in which children tend to withdraw, are distrustful, and are discontent. The third type, Pattern III, consists of children who have little self-control, tend to retreat from novel experiences, and tend to lack self reliance.

Baumrind postulated that parenting styles lead to children developing one of these patterns. Baumrind and colleagues first classified a number of preschool children as belonging to one of the above types based on five criteria: self-control, approach-avoidance tendency, self-reliance, subjective mood, and peer affiliation.

These children were then observed interacting with their parents. Parenting behavior was considered and coded in the following areas: parental control, parental maturity demands, parent-child communication, and parental nurturance. The following associations emerged: Parents of Pattern I children tended to be high on all parental behavior dimensions. These parents were consistent with their children, respected the child's independence, but held the children to a position once decided, demonstrated control of the children, were supportive, and communicated clearly. This type of parenting became to be later termed Authoritative parenting. Pattern II children's parents were characterized by being highly controlling of the children, providing little nurturance, not using reasoning with the children, and not encouraging the children to communicate. This style of parenting became to be known later as Authoritarian parenting. The parents of Pattern III children were not controlling of the children, were less organized, were more insecure about parenting, and tended to use withdrawal of love as a consequence for child behavior. This parenting style was later termed Permissive parenting.

Because children who exhibited Pattern I behavior tend to be viewed as having the healthiest developmental behaviors, efforts have been made to foster this style in children. A study was conducted in which researchers aimed to teach parents Authoritative parenting skills. The researchers assessed the parents' parenting styles before and after the intervention and assigned each parent into one parenting style. The results of the study are presented as follows:

Figure 1 Parenting styles before and after training

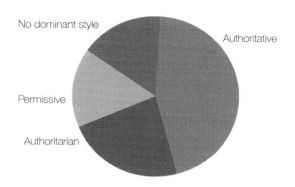

10. It can be expected that after the training children will begin to demonstrate what type of Pattern of behavior more than before the training?
    A) Pattern I
    B) Pattern II
    C) Pattern III
    D) Pattern IV

11. An infant who demonstrates Pattern I behavior and whose parents' parenting style is Authoritative probably has what type of attachment style with his parent?
    A) Anxious-Ambivalent
    B) Avoidant
    C) Disorganized
    D) Secure

12. What could be a reason for research that found that Authoritarian parenting may be a healthier parenting style in some instances?
    A) Different cultural norms
    B) Pattern II behavior is healthier
    C) Attachment style changes frequently over time
    D) Long-term outcomes aren't associated with early attachment

13. Authoritative parents are probably best able to help their child resolve what first Eriksonian developmental stage?
    A) Intimacy v. Isolation
    B) Trust v. Mistrust
    C) Formal operations v. Concrete operations
    D) Oedipal v. Latency

14. If a child does not have a secure attachment with his caregivers and later is unable to form secure attachments, he may have missed what period of time for learning to develop attachments?
    A) Attachment period
    B) Latency period
    C) Imprinting period
    D) Post-natal period

These questions are **NOT** related to a passage.

15. In which of the following scenarios is the subject most clearly exhibiting cognitive dissonance?
    A) A wealthy businessman who never got a college degree pushes his daughter to attend an expensive private university.
    B) An oncologist who knows the dangers of smoking nonetheless continues to experience pleasure when smoking.
    C) A successful attorney feels pride when her daughter is admitted to a top law school.
    D) A grief counselor feels guilt after the death of a loved one because he chooses not to seek help for the significant negative effects of his grief.

16. The social phenomenon of groupthink is characterized by all of the following EXCEPT:
    A) a significant over-rating of the decision-making abilities of members of the ingroup.
    B) a decrease in the creativity of individual group members in contributing to solutions the ingroup wants to achieve.
    C) high loyalty and group cohesiveness causing members to feel safe raising controversial issues and proposing alternative solutions.
    D) an effort to minimize conflict and ensure consensus.

17. According to attachment theory, which of the following children is most likely to attach to a male psychologist, previously unknown to the child, in the course of a psychological study?
    A) A two month old female infant raised in a safe, stable environment
    B) A five month old male infant raised in a safe, stable environment
    C) An eight month old male infant raised by a single caregiver who frequently neglects the child
    D) A thirteen month old female infant raised by two caregivers who occasionally neglect the child

18. Each of the following are aspects of the McDonaldization of Society EXCEPT:
    A) rationalization of decisions into cost/benefit analysis structures and away from traditional modes of thinking
    B) bureaucratic organization that formalizes well-establish division of labor and impersonal structures
    C) a dissolution of heirarchical modes of authority into collaborative team-based decision protocols
    D) an intense effort on achieving sameness across diverse markets

This page intentionally left blank.

Passage 4

There are factors which uniquely impact the mental health of women of retirement age in Japan. Japanese women typically decrease their volunteer work in their community as they arrive at retirement age. Reasons for this include that women most frequently volunteer through their children's schools and as their children graduate there are fewer opportunities for this. Lessening volunteer work is correlated with higher levels of depression. In addition, due to cultural norms many Japanese women of retirement age are also supporting an elder family member in their homes, which may require a great deal of time. The relationship between women caretakers and their elderly family members may be stressful, and can result in a number of conflicts.

To address these unique needs Japan has adopted programs to assist them. The Long-Term Care Initiative of 2000 strives to coordinate care resources for the elderly and provide psychosocial support for their caregivers. In Japan, seeking mental health services outside of the home is still taboo, especially among older individuals. To meet the need of women of retirement age, case managers first identify those in highest need. Those caregivers who are providing care for family members with high levels of health needs typically have the highest stress levels. Case managers target these caregivers as a priority, providing services such as social talk and educating about approaching and avoiding styles of care. Social talk consists of interactions between caregivers and case managers that provide an opportunity for caregivers to express themselves and their frustrations, much as might occur in a therapy session. Avoidance strategies consist of the caregiver taking space and time for herself in order to address her own needs. Approaching strategies consist of formulating ways for the caregiver to enlist the elderly in their own care. These interventions have been shown to reduce caregiver stress.

19. Which of the following is NOT a cultural factor described in the passage that might account for increased levels of stress among Japanese women of retirement age?
    A) Need to support elderly relatives
    B) Emphasis on education
    C) Reduced volunteerism
    D) Reluctance to access public mental health resources

20. Asking an elderly mother-in-law to assist in preparing breakfast is an example of what kind of strategy?
    A) Approaching strategy
    B) Social talk
    C) Care initiative
    D) Avoidance strategy

21. Which of the following is an example of an effective strategy to reduce stress associated with generational inequity?
    A) Providing extra resources for elderly individuals living with younger family members
    B) Increasing attachment among family members living with each other
    C) Encouraging women caregivers to take time to do activities they enjoy
    D) Helping women caregivers understand the developmental needs of elderly family members

22. What is a possible reason for taking care of elderly family members and avoiding mental health services outside of the home in Japan?
    A) Socialization
    B) Psychoanalytic drive
    C) Cognitive dissonance
    D) Altruism

Passage 5

Both Freud and Jung believed in the usefulness of analyzing dreams to understand the unconscious. They both viewed the unconscious as expressing itself in the forms and images of the dream and that it was important to attempt to understand the unconscious through dreams. However, they disagreed about the form and function of dreams and how to interpret them.

Both disagreed on what the dream represents. Freud viewed the dream as a disguised representation of a person's wishes. He stated that the dream is disguised because if the wish was presented in its natural form, it would be too disturbing for the person. Jung viewed the dream as a direct representation of the dreamer's mental state, represented in symbols. Jung believed that dreams represent the objective and subjective reality, both the events that happen and the person's interpretation of them. This contrasted with Freud, who viewed dreams as only representing an individual's wishes.

The way the dream presents itself is an area in which they disagreed. Jung viewed the dream as having a compensatory function, in which the dream represents an aspect of the person that is perceived as lacking. For example, a person who feels stifled may dream of flying. Freud viewed the dream as presenting both manifest and latent content. The manifest content consists mainly of "day residue," which is experiences that the person had during the day. The latent content is the unconscious wishes that the person has, which is disguised in the manifest content, often through condensation, or several aspects of the unconscious representing itself in similar forms.

Another difference between the two is in their method of interpreting dreams. Freud advocated for using free association to interpret, in which the patient talks about the dream and in so doing the significance of the dream comes to be realized. According to Freud, an analyst is necessary to assist in the interpretation. Jung believed that a person is able to interpret his own dreams and in fact encouraged this. He was focused more on the symbols present in the dream and encouraged patients to immediately record their dreams in a dream journal upon waking. This is not to say that Jung did not value the associations a person made with the dream, which he termed amplifications. He did believe these interpretations to be important; however, he wanted to focus more on the dream, whereas Freud would allow a patient's free associations to lead his thoughts wherever they might go.

23. It can be inferred that both Freud and Jung desired to bring the meaning of dreams into a person's:
    A) consciousness.
    B) free association.
    C) hypnogogic state.
    D) dream journal.

24. According to Freud, which of the following could be the latent meaning of a child's dream of a lake?
    A) The uniting force of mankind
    B) A lake the child saw on a map
    C) A desire to return to a favorite family vacation place
    D) Hysteria

25. Which of the following techniques might Jung advocate an individual do to process a dream?
    A) Attempt to forget unpleasant aspects of the dream
    B) Analyze the circadian rhythms of his sleep
    C) Summarize the dream into an audio recording device
    D) Wait until an analyst is available to recount the dream

26. Freud and Jung's approach to bring unconscious material to a person's awareness is a major tenet of which branch of psychology?
    A) Humanistic psychology
    B) Psychoanalytic psychology
    C) Cognitive Behavioral psychology
    D) Systems psychology

These questions are **NOT** related to a passage.

27. In an experiment of role-taking development, a four year old child is presented with the "Holly scenario": "Holly is an avid 8-year-old tree climber. One day, Holly falls off a tree, but does not hurt herself. Holly's father makes Holly promise that she will stop climbing trees, and Holly promises. Later, Holly and her friends find a kitten stuck in a tree. Holly is the only one who can climb trees to save the kitten, who may fall at any moment." The researcher then asks, "How will Holly's father react if he finds out Holly climbed the tree and saved the kitten?" Which of the following is the most likely response from the four year old?

    A) "The father will be mad at Holly because she broke her promise."
    B) "The father will not mind the disobedience because he likes kittens and the kitten will make him happy."
    C) "The father will be mad if Holly gets hurt but he will be happy if she saves the kitten."
    D) "The father will understand that saving a kitten is more important that keeping a promise not to climb trees."

28. A parent wishes to encourage her daughter to complete her homework every night without resorting to extrinsic motivation. Which of the following strategies would be best?

    A) Allow her daughter to set her own homework study schedule, and praise her effectiveness when she sticks to that schedule.
    B) Create an internal sense of competitiveness by fostering a competition between the daughter and the daughter's best friend who is in all of the same classes.
    C) Remind the daughter that getting good grades are their own reward, that good grades are the result of hard work doing the homework, and that good grades should generate a sense of accomplishment.
    D) Offer to increase the daughter's allowance if she completes her homework each week.

29. A psychologist conducts an experiment in which a dog is trained to roll over. The dog has a small device strapped to its back. Rolling over depresses a button on the device. If the dog rolls over in time, the button is pressed and the device does not shock the dog. This form of conditioning would best be described as:

    A) negative reinforcement through escape.
    B) negative punishment.
    C) negative reinforcement through avoidance.
    D) positive reinforcement.

30. A psychologist conducts an experiment in which subjects are asked to learn a series of "facts" which are actually statements that have been fabricated by the research team. The subjects consist of undergraduate students at the university where the experiment is being conducted. The subjects are randomly assigned to groups that are compensated either $10 or $20 for their participation, are given either 15 minutes or 30 minutes to learn the facts, and are asked to recall the facts either in the same room in which they learned the facts or in a very different, unfamiliar setting. Which of the following are dependent variables in this experiment?

  I. The amount the subjects were compensated.
  II. The gender of the subjects.
  III. The number of facts the subjects can recall.
  IV. The time the subjects were given to learn the facts.

    A) II only
    B) III only
    C) I and IV only
    D) I, III, and IV only

This page intentionally left blank.

Passage 6

Traditionally psychology has been practiced from a medical model, in which deficits in an individual's functioning are identified by practitioners and communicated to their patients. Because this norm has traditionally been dictated by the dominant culture, minorities have often been pathologized as a result of being compared to the norm. Thus, more recent efforts in psychology have emphasized practitioners developing multicultural competencies.

Some researchers espouse a culture-free view and contend that there are universal virtues that humans value, irrespective of culture. For these researchers culture serves to obfuscate these universal virtues. Other researchers endorse a culturally-embedded viewpoint. These researchers view virtues as being defined by culture. Further, these researchers contend that practitioners' own cultures influence their interpretation of other cultural virtues, so that culture must be recognized to properly understand others' cultures. For example, cultures have different views on the importance of happiness, with some cultures viewing it as one of the most important virtues and others viewing it as less important than enlightenment.

While defining cultural strengths might be elusive, there is a recognition that these strengths can have important beneficial effects on the individual, and are seen in a "strengths-based" approach. It is worthwhile to examine the factors that enable these individuals to do so and to promote these factors of resilience.

One way that salient factors might be identified is through the Four-Front Approach, a model of assessment that guides clinicians in obtaining culturally relevant information. Using this approach, clinicians gather information about the client in four areas: strengths of the client, deficiencies in the client, resources available in the client's environment, and deficiencies in the client's environment.

A way of using the Four-Front Approach can be illustrated by considering the following case. Juan is a 13 year old male in the seventh grade. He immigrated to the United States from Mexico with his family when he was 2 years old and his primary language is Spanish. His father is currently sick and unable to work. Juan has two younger siblings, who he frequently has to care for while his mother is at work. Juan has struggled academically this year at school. He has had difficulty interacting appropriately with his peers, frequently getting into fights and having difficulty when assigned to work together at school. Juan is able to get along with his peers when he plays soccer, an activity at which he excels. Juan and his family are Catholic and are very involved with their church.

Using this, a clinician used the Four-Front Approach to better understand Juan. The results are presented as follows:

Table 1 Results of patient assessment using Four-Front Approach

Front	Characteristics
Client strengths	-Bilingual –Good at soccer –Good caretaker of his siblings – Currently at age-appropriate grade level
Client deficiencies	-Academic difficulties –Social difficulties –Difficulties with English
Environmental strengths	-Church support –Mother is working –Father is present
Environmental deficiencies	-Lack of another caregiver for siblings –Lack of individual support at school

31. Emphasizing what Juan is good at and what resources are available to him to address his deficiencies is an example of what kind of approach to psychology?

A) Medical model

B) Strength-based approach

C) Culturally embedded approach

D) Cultural-free approach

32. How might Juan's social difficulties be viewed from a multicultural approach, rather than from the medical model approach?

A) Juan ought to practice his social skills in a group.

B) Juan was not taught social skills at a young age.

C) Juan's focus on taking care of his siblings has made it difficult to practice interacting with peers.

D) Juan's cognitive difficulties have made learning social skills difficult.

33. What is an example of a multicultural intervention to support Juan?

A) Exposing him exclusively to English language instruction

B) Involving child services to remove Juan and his siblings from the home to be placed with caretakers who can support them better

C) Attributing Juan's difficulties with school to the fact that he is bi-cultural

D) Using Juan's family's church to help with the caretaking of Juan's siblings

34. Which of the following would NOT be a beneficial result of normalizing Juan's caretaking of his siblings as being culturally appropriate to Juan?

A) Juan may feel self-esteem from behaving in a culturally virtuous way.

B) Juan may feel a greater sense of connection with his Mexican culture.

C) Juan may come to feel less connected with American culture.

D) Juan may learn to access cultural resources to help in the caretaking.

Passage 7

Eyewitness testimony is an area of forensic psychology that has been researched, especially within the past 30 years, in efforts to evaluate and improve its accuracy. Accuracy in eyewitness testimony is an important consideration because oftentimes individuals' freedom is at stake. The reliability of eyewitness testimony has come into question as researchers have found a number of instances in which eyewitness testimony has later proved to be untrue. Researchers have examined factors in eyewitness testimony that hinder its reliability and have formed recommendations for how to address these factors.

One of the first factors that can affect eyewitness testimony is suggestibility. Suggestibility refers to incorporating information learned after the event into the testimony about the event as if it actually occurred. Suggestibility is often introduced when the witness is asked about the event and information, or false cues, are introduced that are then incorporated into the memory. Suggestibility was demonstrated in an experiment in which participants viewed a picture of a car next to either a stop sign or a yield sign. When questioning the participants about what they saw the researchers purposely used the name of the type of sign that was opposite of what the participants actually saw. When questioned about what type of sign the participants saw the majority of participants stated that they had seen the opposite sign than what they actually saw, in accordance with what the researchers said. In the same experiment the participants were also shown a picture of a car accident. When the researchers used the word "smashed" in their questioning about the event, participants were more likely to report having seen broken glass than those who did not hear that word used. These findings and others about suggestibility have led to guidelines for professionals questioning witnesses that guard against introducing any suggestibility into the questioning. Questioners should ask open ended questions and avoid introducing any provocative words which may influence testimony.

Even if witnesses are questioned in an unbiased manner, the way the witnesses reconstruct the memory is subject to their own personal biases. When recounting a memory, researchers have found that witnesses will reconstruct a narrative that involves actual facts from the event, as well as incorporating their own schemas into the narrative. A schema is an individual's own representation of information and its relationship in context of other information. This has been seen in experiments in which participants were presented with a complicated story which they were then asked to retell. Researchers found that participants retold facts from the story, but also interjected their own understanding of how the facts were related. In addition, information which is inconsistent with an individual's schemas tends to be forgotten or omitted at a much greater rate than information which is consistent with schemas. To address the interference of schemas and other personal biases in an eyewitness's testimony, recommendations have been made to those hearing eyewitness testimony, such as juries, to consider individual factors of the eyewitness, such as his reliability and details of the content of the testimony that add or delete validity.

A final factor which affects eyewitness testimony is that once testimony about an event is initially recounted, the eyewitness tends to increase his belief in the veracity of the event the way he recounted it. He will tend to continue to incorporate facts he mistakenly introduced into the testimony in future retellings, and the facts will become consolidated with the memory. Examples of this has been observed in actual court cases in which a witness who initially identifies a suspect as being a perpetrator in a police line-up will continue to identify that individual as a perpetrator in subsequent line-ups, even when that individual is known to not be the actual perpetrator. To counter the effect of incorrect events being repeatedly recounted in testimony, efforts should be made to accurately record testimony of eyewitnesses at the initial recounting of the event before false memories can be interjected and solidified at subsequent retellings. Also, those questioning eyewitnesses should ask about details of the event in multiple ways to attempt to verify the veracity of the event.

In a study to evaluate the effect of the use of these recommendations on eyewitness testimony, participants were shown a video clip of a violent incident. The participants were then asked to recall the violent incident 48 hours later.

Half of the participants were asked to recall the events using the techniques described in this passage and half were asked to recall the event without any techniques being used. The number of accurate details recounted by the participants was recorded. The average number of accurate details for each of the two groups is presented as follows:

Table 1 The effect of careful interrogation technique on witness recall

Group	Average Number of Correct Details Recalled
Using Techniques	40.1
Without Using Techniques	28.2

The average number of details recalled by the two groups were compared using an independent samples t-test. The results indicated that there was a significant difference between the two groups ($p < .0001$).

35. What type of bias might be introduced by the question, "What type of gun did the man have?"
    A) Consolidated memory bias
    B) Suggestibility
    C) Schema bias
    D) Flashbulb memory bias

36. What fact, if true, might influence the following interpretation of the data: using the techniques discussed leads to more accurate eyewitness testimony overall?
    A) The eyewitnesses recalled the event 72 hours later, not 48
    B) There were demographic differences within the two groups of eyewitnesses
    C) There were a higher number of details recalled, both true and false, in the group in which techniques were used
    D) The control group sometimes used techniques in their interviews

37. Which of the following factors might increase the suggestibility of a comment made by an interviewer?
    A) If the comment is vague
    B) If the eyewitness is an adult, rather than a child
    C) If the interviewer is of the same ethnicity as the eyewitness
    D) If the interviewer is perceived to be an expert by the eyewitness

38. What is to be expected about the number of inaccurate facts both of the groups will incorporate in future retellings of the event?
    A) The group interviewed with techniques will tell as many or more inaccurate facts
    B) The group interviewed without techniques will tell as many or more inaccurate facts
    C) Both groups will tell as many or more inaccurate facts
    D) Neither group will tell as many or more inaccurate facts

39. What could be another interpretation of the results of the study?
    A) The group without techniques witnessed information that was different than their beliefs
    B) The group with techniques witnessed information that was different than their beliefs
    C) Erroneous facts the group without techniques recalled became consolidated in their memory
    D) Erroneous facts the group with techniques recalled became consolidated in their memory

This page intentionally left blank.

Passage 8

There is disagreement about what autism specifically is, but its features include: limited vocabulary, poor social interaction, and repetitive self-soothing movements. Some researchers contend that autism should not be considered a categorical condition, but rather a point along a continuum of pervasive developmental disturbances with similar symptomatology, with less severe conditions like Pervasive Developmental Disorder-Not Otherwise Specified (PDD-NOS) and Asperger's syndrome.

Researchers have attempted to provide explanations for the causes of the symptomatic behavior listed above. First, people with autism are overloaded with sensory stimulation. Many of the symptomatic behaviors they display are products of trying to deal with this overload. The repetitive behaviors are an attempt to focus on something while being flooded with stimuli.

The cause of autism continues to remain a mystery. There are various theories as to what causes it. Most studies agree that autism is a result of a combination of improper neurological, genetic, and cognitive functioning. For example, one study showed that among those with autism the pathways between the hippocampus and amygdala had abnormal microstructures. Scientists have additionally identified certain chromosomes which appear associated with autism. There have also been some environmental factors identified as contributing to the development of autism. One area of autism research that has been especially controversial lately is an alleged link between autism and vaccines. A study done 20 years previously showed there was no link between vaccines and autism, however a 2007 U.S. Federal court ruled in a lawsuit that a child who had received a vaccine and developed autism would receive a compensation settlement.

Tito, a 13 year old boy with autism, has been working with his mother and other professionals for a long time and has developed the capability to express himself through writing and typing. During an interview, when Tito was asked about why he flaps his hands and rocks, he replied that, "I just need to find my position in space... I forget that I have a body and it reminds me that I have one." Tito described how when he was younger he looked at a cloud and someone said banana and the cloud and the banana became permanently associated together forever. Tito's therapist described how Tito's senses come in waves. He sees parts before the whole. When asked about how to describe a door, he answers that he looks at the shape of the door then the colors and then subsequent details. However, if the door is then opened he has to start over.

Figure 1 Spectrum of Pervasive Developmental Disorders

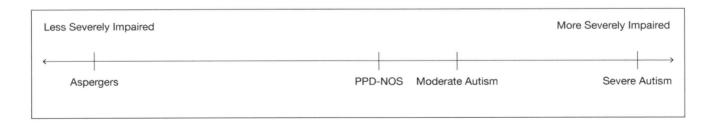

40. What would be an argument for considering Pervasive Developmental Disorders along a continuum of severity?
    A) Many disorders along the continuum have similar symptoms.
    B) The etiology of the disorders is the same.
    C) An individual can move from a more severe disorder to a less severe disorder.
    D) An individual can move from a less severe disorder to a more severe disorder.

41. What is a possible explanation for the increased prevalence of autism that has been found in recent years?
    A) Increased abnormal microstructures
    B) Increased vaccinations
    C) Increased recognition of symptoms
    D) Increased social contact

42. What is an explanation of a child with autism's repeated hand-clapping from a functionalist viewpoint?
    A) Neurological deficits lead to incorrect signaling of motor areas of the brain
    B) The clapping allows him to focus on only one stimulus
    C) The clapping is a response to a stimulus learned via operant conditioning
    D) Repeated movements, of which hand-clapping is an example, are symptoms of autism

43. Through therapy, when a person with a Pervasive Developmental Disorder learns that another person with raised eyebrows and an open mouth is surprised rather than happy, what type of associative learning has taken place?
    A) Generalization
    B) Discrimination
    C) Extinction
    D) Acquisition

These questions are **NOT** related to a passage.

44. When hungry, a person will seek food. According to drive theory, which of the following is (are) true about this behavior?
 I. The drive to eat will decrease over time.
 II. Eating is an attempt to reduce a homeostatic disturbance.
 III. Eating behavior and hunger operate on a negative feedback control system.
 A) I only
 B) II only
 C) II and III only
 D) I, II, and III

45. A child is born into a society with one majority ethnicity and two significant minority ethnicities. He is a member of the majority ethnicity. In the course of his early childhood, he hears comments by both his mother and his father expressing disparaging attitudes towards minority group one and laudatory attitudes towards minority group two. The child then grows into an adult and maintains those same attitudes, which reflect attitudes held by the plurality of members of the majority ethnicity. Which of the following accurately describes this scenario?
 A) The attitudes he developed were a result a secondary socialization because he took on the attitudes and beliefs of his larger society.
 B) The attitudes he developed were a result of primary socialization because he took on the attitudes and beliefs of his parents as a young child.
 C) As a member of the majority ethnicity, the attitudes he developed were a result of both socialization influences and genetic influences.
 D) The attitudes he developed as a result of primary socialization were held strongly enough to persist in the face of opposing secondary socialization.

46. A soldier who has lost his lower leg due to a battlefield injury complains of repeated painful feelings in that now-amputated lower leg, describing this sensation as "phantom pain". Which somatoform disorder is the soldier experiencing?
 A) Hypochondriasis
 B) Conversion disorder
 C) Body dysmorphic disorder
 D) The soldier is not experiencing a somatoform disorder.

47. Which of the following best describes the negative feedback loop which regulates appetite levels and adipose tissue levels?
 A) Decreasing levels of adipose tissue result in lower concentrations of leptin hormones in the bloodstream, which stimulates appetite until increased adipose mass causes higher concentrations of leptin hormones in the bloodstream and appetite decreases.
 B) Decreasing levels of adipose tissue result in higher concentrations of leptin hormones in the bloodstream, which stimulates appetite until increased adipose mass causes lower concentrations of leptin hormones in the bloodstream and appetite decreases.
 C) GABA is produced by adipose tissue, makes its way into the brain, and stimulates production of glutamate, which decreases appetite, causing less adipose tissue and less GABA production, after which appetite increases.
 D) Glutamate is produced by adipose tissue, makes its way into the brain, and stimulates production of GABA, which decreases appetite, causing less adipose tissue and less glutamate production, after which appetite increases.

This page intentionally left blank.

Passage 9

There is an overrepresentation of English Language Learning students (ELL students) in special education. One possible reason for this disparity is that differences in students' education experiences in their country of origin and their current American academic experiences may create difficulties in learning with methods utilized at their American school. Another possibility is that due to English language deficiencies, these students appear to have learning disabilities and are misdiagnosed as such. It is important to distinguish whether a student is struggling with reading in general or learning the second language.

There is evidence, however, that children who have difficulty learning another language may do so because they have an underlying Reading Disability (RD). Difficulties with Working Memory (WM) have been found among struggling ELL students and those with an RD. WM involves the rehearsal of verbal and visuo-spatial information, skills that are involved in phonological processing, a task involved in reading and language acquisition. The relationship between WM deficits and difficulties with both tasks is further supported by findings that WM deficits are associated with less vocabulary knowledge and with risk for later development of RD among both ELL students and English as a First Language students (EFL students).

There is also a strong connection between first language literacy skills and second language acquisition. A majority of researchers found that strong first language literacy skills were associated with better second language acquisition. On the other hand, it was indicated in other research that literacy is likely more complicated than simply decoding language. In addition to this skill, there are a variety of cultural issues involved, such as understanding shared cultural topics, cultural communication, and understanding social contexts. While these aspects appear to accentuate semantic understanding and nuanced understanding of language, the preponderance of studies indicate that first language literacy is correlated with second language acquisition, strengthening the support for RD and ELL difficulties being related.

A program which taught first language literacy skills to struggling ELL students was evaluated. The average reading grade level of fifth grade students who received the instruction were compared with a control group. The results are presented in the following table:

Table 1 Effects of EFL literacy program

	Students in literacy program	Control students
Pre-program	2.1	2.2
Post-program	4.3	3.8

A repeated measures ANOVA was used to compare the pre – to post – scores of both groups. The difference was found to be significant at $p < .0001$.

48. All of the following are possible explanations for ELL students struggling to learn English and NOT having an RD, EXCEPT:

    A) differences in learning styles.

    B) lack of exposure to cultural issues.

    C) misdiagnosis.

    D) difficulty with working memory.

49. If, during the study, all the students knew if they were in the reading instruction group or in the control group, what could be a confounding factor that biased the results?

    A) Placebo effect

    B) Inclusive fitness

    C) Fundamental attribution error

    D) Cultural factors

50. Students with strong first language skills would likely do well with reading and pronouncing what type of word compared to students with weak first language skills?

    A) A sight word that is not pronounced phonetically

    B) A phonetic word that can be pronounced according to phonetic rules

    C) A word that have first heard pronounced by another person

    D) A word that sounds similar to a word in their first language

51. Why is having a pre-program score for each group important for the research design?

    A) To acclimatize the students to the task

    B) To assess for RD

    C) To control for differences between the two groups

    D) To improve the reliability of the findings

52. A struggling ELL student, without an RD, would likely have trouble understanding what type of reading passage?

    A) A passage with metaphors unique to countries with English as a first language

    B) A passage with many phonetic words

    C) A passage that is first read aloud to him

    D) A passage with a number of short words

Passage 10

Eysenck viewed neuroticism as varying along a continuum from being primarily calm at one end to being primarily neurotic, or nervous, at the other. Because Eysenck viewed personality as deriving primarily from genetic causes, he viewed neuroticism as controlled by the sympathetic nervous system (SNS). The SNS responds to perceived stimuli and prepares our body to emotionally respond, primarily through production of epinephrine. Eysenck viewed the SNS as responding differently in different people, with some individuals having more sensitive SNS's than others.

When the SNS of an individual responds in an overly-sensitive manner, then this individual typically displays neuroticism, which can take the form of neurotic disorders. An example of a type of neurotic symptom that is displayed when the SNS is too responsive is a panic attack. A panic attack can be viewed somewhat like a feedback loop, similar to what happens when a microphone is placed too closely to a speaker, resulting in an ever-increasing feedback loop. In terms of the SNS during a panic attack, the individual initially perceives some potentially bothersome stimuli, such as a presentation in front of a group. The individual then perceives himself to be reacting overly-sensitively to this stimulus, perhaps via somatic displays, such as sweating or blushing. This reaction then becomes a stimulus itself, causing the individual to have further embarrassment and displaying further reactions. This feedback loop continues in a worsening cycle until the individual is incapacitated via a panic attack.

Eysenck also researched the temperament dimension of extraversion-introversion. This dimension refers to an individual's propensity for engaging with others versus valuing his own time alone. Extraverted people tend to enjoy being around others, engaging in social activities, and working in groups. Introverted people tend to enjoy solitary activities and are more reserved in groups. While other researchers have considered this dimension, Eysenck focused on what was the reason an individual displayed more of one trait than the other. He stated that the reason individuals display one style over the other is due to their preferred arousal level, with extraverts preferring to be more aroused and introverts less aroused.

The way in which Eysenck derived these dimensions of personality was through factor analysis of individuals' responses to questionnaires. Eysenck looked for items which tended to be endorsed together and formed categories of temperament from them. An example of this is given as follows, in which the following participants rated the extent to which they agreed with the following statements on a scale from 1 to 5 with 1 indicating they did not agree at all up to 5 indicating that they completely agreed:

Table 1 Sample responses to a temperament questionnaire

	Participant Rating		
Statement	*Joe*	*Katherine*	*Sally*
I enjoy attending parties.	5	2	1
I get nervous in groups.	1	5	5
I sometimes feel as if I'm having a panic attack.	1	4	5
I enjoy doing activities alone.	2	5	4

53. Based on the limited information provided, which participants appear to have an introverted style?
    A) Joe & Katherine
    B) Katherine & Sally
    C) Sally & Joe
    D) None

54. Eysenck viewed personality as primarily deriving from what?
    A) Nature
    B) Nurture
    C) Exogenous factors
    D) Both B and C

55. To conclude that because Joe likes to attend parties thus he likes to attend all social gatherings is to commit what kind of error?
    A) Availability heuristic
    B) Self-fulfilling prophecy
    C) Mental short-cut heuristic
    D) Fundamental attribution error

56. Which theoretical view of personality does NOT contrast with the view that personality is derived from temperamental dimensions?
    A) Behaviorism
    B) Psychoanalytic
    C) Five Factor View of Personality
    D) Neurobiological

These questions are **NOT** related to a passage.

57. A hunter puts on camouflage that is designed to "break up" the visual outline border between himself and his surrounding environment. What effect does this have on the visual processing of a person who looks at the camouflaged hunter?

    A) Activity of feature detector neurons in his optical nerve decreases.

    B) Activity of feature detector neurons in his visual cortex decreases.

    C) Activity of rods in his retina decreases.

    D) Activity of cones in his retina decreases.

58. During which of Jean Piaget's stages of development do children begin to realize that their thoughts and feelings, rather than being shared by others, are unique to them?

    A) Sensorimotor Stage

    B) Preoperational Stage

    C) Concrete Operational Stage

    D) Formal Operational Stage

59. What is the difference between vestibular sense and kinesthetic sense?

    A) Vestibular sense allows balance by detecting body movement; kinesthetic sense allows detection of where a person's body parts are positioned even without looking.

    B) Vestibular sense allows the detection of pain; kinesthetic sense allows the detection of temperature changes.

    C) Vestibular sense detects smells and scents; kinesthetic sense detects motion or acceleration.

    D) Vestibular sense detects empty spaces; kinesthetic sense detects enclosed spaces.

This page intentionally left blank.

Section 1 Answers and Explanations

Key					
1	B	21	C	41	C
2	D	22	A	42	B
3	B	23	A	43	B
4	A	24	C	44	C
5	A	25	C	45	B
6	A	26	B	46	D
7	C	27	B	47	A
8	D	28	A	48	D
9	D	29	C	49	A
10	A	30	B	50	B
11	D	31	B	51	C
12	A	32	C	52	A
13	B	33	D	53	B
14	C	34	C	54	A
15	D	35	B	55	D
16	C	36	C	56	C
17	A	37	D	57	B
18	C	38	C	58	C
19	B	39	A	59	A
20	A	40	A		

Passage 1 Explanation

Weber's law presents an interesting **exception** in the case of **sound**. While other sorts of stimuli will have a **constant just-noticeable difference** (jnd) across the full range of perceptible stimuli (the change in stimulus intensity as a fraction of the original intensity is a constant), for **sound** this does **not always** hold true.

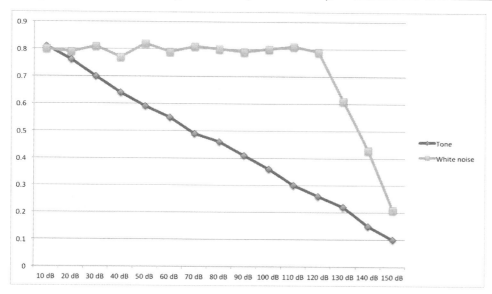

Figure 1 The jnd as a function of intensity for a single pure tone and for white noise

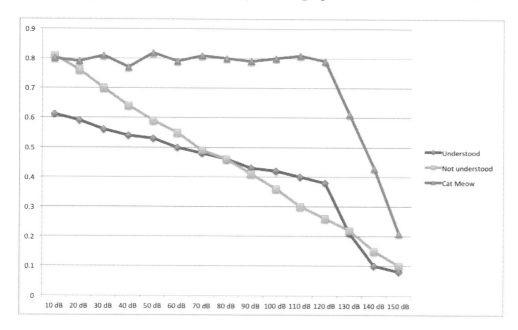

Figure 2 The jnd as a function of intensity for a recording of speech in a language understood by the listener, one not understood by the listener, and a recognizable non-speech sound (a cat's meow)

1. In studies of the just-noticeable difference, perception is measured in what way?
    A) Sensation
    B) <u>Discrimination</u>
    C) Magnitude estimation
    D) Signal transduction

Weber's law asks a person to perceive two stimuli and then determine whether or not they are the same or different. Perceiving differences between two stimuli is discrimination.

A, D: Sensation and signal transduction refer to the raw physical process of taking in external stimuli, whereas Weber's law relates to making judgments about them.
C: Magnitude estimation would involve playing a single tone and asking the person to estimate its loudness. Weber's law, however, concerns itself with the difference between two tones.

2. For the especially loud noises, subjects often report negative emotions such as anger after hearing several of the loud sounds. The James-Lange theory would posit that this emotional response:
    A) precedes and causes a person to experience physiological arousal which then contributes to further unpleasant affect.
    B) occurs simultaneously and independently of the physiological arousal stimulated by the loud sounds.
    C) is a result of both physiological arousal and a cognitive appraisal of that arousal.
    D) <u>follows from and is caused by the physiological arousal experienced as a result of the loud sounds.</u>

The James-Lange theory of emotion asserts that emotions start from the body (physiological arousal) and that those bodily sensations cause our emotions.

B: This is closer to the Cannon-Bard theory of emotion.
C: This is closer to the Schacter-Singer theory of emotion.

3. For nearly every type of sound played, the just-noticeable difference dropped significantly near or above 130 dB. Which of the following is the most likely reason?
    A) Above a certain intensity level, sound perception also occurs as a result of signal transduction directly through the skull rather than solely through the ossicles and organ of Corti.
    B) <u>The threshold of pain is near or above 130 dB and the jnd for pain is much lower than for many other types of stimuli.</u>
    C) Study participants were more attentive to the especially loud sounds as a result of the physiological arousal those sounds created.
    D) The distracting nature of the especially loud sounds made it more difficult for study participants to detect changes in stimulus intensity.

The level of sound intensity that will cause pain varies by individual, but typically around 130-140 dB is the pain threshold. At that point, participants are experiencing auditory and pain inputs, so their ability to discriminate between stimuli is going to change.

A: Human sound perception always goes through the hair cells of the organ of Corti.
C, D: We have to reason to suspect that the louder sounds are making the study participants more or less attentive to the sounds themselves.

4. The just-noticeable difference for response to different intensity electric shocks is presented below. Which of the following is most likely true?

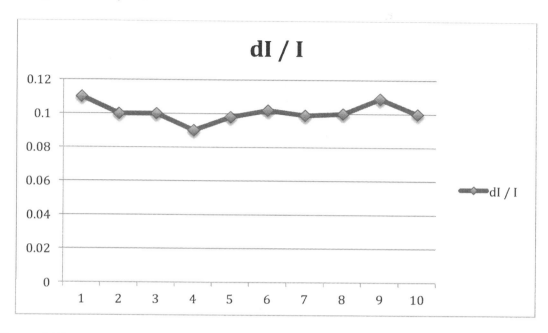

Figure 2 The jnd for a series of electric shocks with the shock intensity scaled as a series of 10 arbitrary but equal-value units

A) <u>**Nociceptors are significantly more sensitive to variations in pain intensity than the auditory system is to variations in loudness.**</u>
B) Unlike auditory perception of white noise sound intensity, the perception of pain intensity generally follows Weber's law at lower levels.
C) The signal transduction mechanisms by which pain is experienced do not rely on the same ion-channel triggers as do those for sound.
D) An 11% increase or decrease in shock intensity will generally not be noticed by a person.

Notice the y-axis here; the jnd for pain is hovering just over 0.1 which is much less than that given on the y-axis in the sound studies. Thus it is reasonable to conclude that people are much more sensitive to variations in pain intensity.

B, C, D: These are all opposite statements. White noise sound detection does follow Weber's law at lower levels (note the relatively flat slope in figure 1), 11% is detectable (note the jnd for pain hovers right around 0.11), and signal transduction for perceptions does rely on changes in ion-channel transport.

5. The experiment involved playing noises loud enough that some study participants may have experienced discomfort or even pain. For the experiment to be approved by the researchers' institutional review board, they must have done all of the following EXCEPT:

A) Keeping the sound intensity well below the level at which each individual study participant will experience discomfort

B) Determining the least harmful or invasive protocol to achieve the study's results

C) Obtaining informed consent from the study participants prior to beginning the study

D) Treating study participants equally regardless of factors such as socioeconomic status, race, or gender

Choices B, C, and D are all classic examples of the ethical principles that must guide experiments using human subjects. Non-maleficence (B), respect for autonomy (C), and respect for justice (D) are all requirements of ethical research. Human experimentation may involve some discomfort or even pain for the subjects, so choice A is not an absolute requirement, so long as researchers have absolutely minimized the pain involved.

Passage 2 Explanation

The following advice was given by an **expert in memory** about how to better **remember other peoples' names**.

"First of all, it is important to **pay attention** and hear the other person's name being spoken. Many people forget names because they are not truly processing the person's name because they are **doing other things**. They may be focusing on their own feelings and thoughts at the time, especially how they are appearing to the other person. While you are focusing on the other person, once you hear their name a good thing to do is then **repeat their name three times**, while you are looking at them."

Opinion: To memorize a name, pay attention and repeat the name

"A good strategy for remembering names is to involve all of your senses in the effort. First of all, try to integrate your sense of **vision**. To do this, try to imagine that you can see the **person's name written on his forehead**. Furthermore, try to imagine it is written in your favorite color. This will make the name stand out more."

Opinion: Use vision to help memorizing names

"Another sense that can be integrated to assist in remembering is the **sense of touch**. You can imagine that you are actually **writing down the name of the person**. Try to imagine what it would feel like to write the person's name, feeling the pencil and the paper. You can even gently move you finger's micro-muscles as you are imagining writing. This will help ingrain the name in your memory even more."

Opinion: It's good to imagine writing the name as a way to memorize it

"If you are meeting a group of people and are trying to remember **several names,** a good strategy is to **remember them in groups**. For example, you might group together the names of couples or group the names in the order in which you heard them. Repeating the names aloud as they are saying them to you can be helpful for remembering them. Finally, it can be helpful to **use a mnemonic device** for remembering names, such as grouping their names with an **object** that begins with the same letter."

Opinion: A good way to remember names in groups of people is by putting groups of the names together

"While it may be difficult to utilize all of these strategies for remembering names at once, with practice it can become easier and soon you should be able to remember peoples' names much easier than before. In a study, participants were instructed to **use each of these techniques and then were introduced to 20 people**. The participants then had another task that they were to perform for 20 seconds. Upon completing the task, the participants were queried on the number of names they were able to recall 30 seconds later."

Key terms: experiment done to assess effectiveness

Figure 1 Number of names recalled

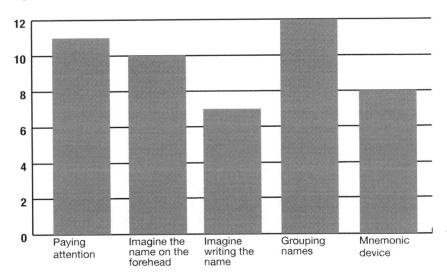

Figure 1 Here we see the results of the study. While there is no control group, we see that each of the techniques produced some recall: at least 7 names. The most successful were simply paying attention and grouping names.

6. What flaw in the research design of the study would cause there to be serious doubts of the validity of the results?
    A) <u>**Having the participants use all techniques in the same order**</u>
    B) Having different participants use different techniques
    C) Having a control group
    D) Recording participant demographic characteristics

    Answer: A – Having the participants use the techniques in the same order would lead to ordering effects as there would likely be some benefit from using previous techniques when being assessed for later techniques.

7. Participants were queried a month after the study about names they recalled. This type of memory primarily involves what part of the brain?
    A) Brain stem
    B) Corpus callosum
    C) <u>**Hippocampus**</u>
    D) Orbitofrontal cortex

    Answer: C – The hippocampus is the brain area primarily involved in long-term memory.

8. In a follow-up study participants were brought back two days later and either asked to simply recall as many names as possible (group 1) or presented with a list of 50 names and asked to select names from the list that had been among the original 20 names presented (group 2). Which of the following is most likely true about this follow-up study?
    A) Both groups will correctly identify approximately the same number of names as in the original study since the memory techniques discussed improve both long-term and short-term memory.
    B) To have any external validity the participants must be required to perform the same twenty second intervening task at the start of this second recall attempt.
    C) Both groups will correctly identify fewer names two days later, but group 1 will correctly identify close to the

same number of names whereas group 2 will likely mis-identify more names than are correctly identified, given that the new list has more incorrect than correct names available.

D) **<u>While long-term memory is likely to involve some forgetting for both groups, group 2 will correctly identify more names.</u>**

Answer: D – Recognition is typically much easier than recall, so the group that simply had to pick the correct names out of the list would be much more likely to correctly identify more names. Both groups, however, will recall fewer names since all types of memory degrade over time (often called the "curve of forgetting").

9. Using all of the memory techniques listed in the passage helps improve memory through what process?
    A) Multi-tasking
    B) Parallel processing
    C) Diversification
    D) **<u>Neuroplasticity</u>**

Answer: D – Neuroplasticity refers to the brain's ability to form multiple synaptic connections in regards to information. Using all of the senses forms multiple connections to the information to be memorized through neuroplasticity.

Passage 3 Explanation

Attachment theory is based on the work begun by **Baumrind**, in which she demonstrated that there is a relationship between the early patterns of interactions of parents and children and later child development. Baumrind initially classified three patterns of child behaviors. The first type she termed **Pattern I** and is characterized by children being **secure**, self-reliant, and explorative. The second type was known as **Pattern II**, in which children tend to **withdraw**, are distrustful, and are discontent. The third type, **Pattern III**, consists of children who have **little self-control**, tend to retreat from novel experiences, and tend to lack self reliance.

Key terms: Attachment theory, Baumrind
Opinion: Baumrind has three categories of child behavior

Baumrind postulated that **parenting styles lead to children developing one of these patterns**. Baumrind and colleagues first classified a number of **preschool children** as belonging to one of the above types based on five criteria: **self-control, approach-avoidance tendency, self-reliance, subjective mood, and peer affiliation**.

Opinion: Baumrind thinks parenting style creates certain child behaviors and studied 5 criteria

These children were then **observed interacting with their parents**. Parenting behavior was considered and coded in the following areas: **parental control, parental maturity demands, parent-child communication, and parental nurturance**. The following associations emerged: Parents of **Pattern I** children tended to be high on all parental behavior dimensions. These parents were consistent with their children, respected the child's independence, but held the children to a position once decided, demonstrated control of the children, were supportive, and communicated clearly. This type of parenting became to be later termed **Authoritative** parenting. **Pattern II** children's parents were characterized by being **highly controlling** of the children, providing little nurturance, not using reasoning with the children, and not encouraging the children to communicate. This style of parenting became to be known later as **Authoritarian parenting**. The parents of **Pattern III** children were **not controlling** of the children, were less organized, were more **insecure about parenting**, and tended to use withdrawal of love as a consequence for child behavior. This parenting style was later termed Permissive parenting.

Cause and effect: Authoritative parenting leads to Pattern I child behavior, Authoritarian parenting leads to Pattern II child behavior, and Permissive parenting leads to Pattern III child behavior.

Because children who exhibited **Pattern I** behavior tend to be viewed as having the **healthiest** developmental behaviors, efforts have been made to foster this style in children. A study was conducted in which researchers aimed to **teach parents Authoritative parenting skills**. The researchers assessed the parents' parenting styles before and after the intervention and assigned each parent into one parenting style. The results of the study are presented as follows:

Opinion: Pattern I is the healthiest behavior so parents are taught Authoritative parenting

Figure 1 Results of parenting styles before and after training

Parenting Styles Before Training   **Parenting Styles After Training**

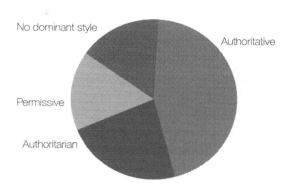

Figure 1 shows us that the training leads to a significant increase in Authoritative parenting behavior, small decreases in Permissive and No Dominant Style and a larger decrease in Authoritarian parenting.

10. It can be expected that after the training children will begin to demonstrate what type of Pattern of behavior more than before the training?
    A) **Pattern I**
    B) Pattern II
    C) Pattern III
    D) Pattern IV

    Answer: A – Pattern I behavior is associated with Authoritative parenting style, the style of behavior that increased from before to after training.

11. An infant who demonstrates Pattern I behavior and whose parents' parenting style is Authoritative probably has what type of attachment style with his parent?
    A) Anxious-Ambivalent
    B) Avoidant
    C) Disorganized
    D) **Secure**

    Answer: D – Secure attachment style is characterized by Pattern I type behavior and authoritative parenting behavior.

12. What could be a reason for research that found that Authoritarian parenting may be a healthier parenting style in some instances?
    A) **Different cultural norms**
    B) Pattern II behavior is healthier
    C) Attachment style changes frequently over time
    D) Long-term outcomes aren't associated with early attachment

    Answer: A – In some cultures, having an Authoritarian parenting style may lead to healthier results for children. Particularly in unsafe environments, Authoritarian parenting has been found to keep children safer.

13. Authoritative parents are probably best able to help their child resolve what first Eriksonian developmental stage?
    A) Intimacy v. Isolation
    B) **Trust v. Mistrust**
    C) Formal operations v. Concrete operations
    D) Oedipal v. Latency

    Answer: B – According to Erikson, trust v. mistrust is the first stage that infants must address. Having authoritative parents helps ensure the infant is able to successfully negotiate this stage.

14. If a child does not have a secure attachment with his caregivers and later is unable to form secure attachments, he may have missed what period of time for learning to develop attachments?
    A) Attachment period
    B) Latency period
    C) **Imprinting period**
    D) Post-natal period

    Answer: C – During imprinting periods, children are sensitive for learning certain things. If this period passes and the child did not learn what he was supposed to learn, he may be unable to learn this item at a later time.

These questions are **NOT** related to a passage.

15. In which of the following scenarios is the subject most clearly exhibiting cognitive dissonance?
    A) A wealthy businessman who never got a college degree pushes his daughter to attend an expensive private university.
    B) An oncologist who knows the dangers of smoking nonetheless continues to experience pleasure when smoking.
    C) A successful attorney feels pride when her daughter is admitted to a top law school.
    D) **A grief counselor feels guilt after the death of a loved one because he chooses not to seek help for the significant negative effects of his grief.**

Cognitive dissonance asserts that people will feel distress when they hold conflicting attitudes or beliefs, or when the exhibit behavior that is inconsistent with their beliefs. In this question, the grief counselor in (D) is experiencing cognitive dissonance (guilt). He is a grief counselor himself, but chooses not to seek out the help such counselors can provide, which leads to mental distress.

A: We don't know whether the businessman believes that education is valuable or not and we don't know how he feels about sending his daughter to an expensive private university.
B: The oncologist has conflicting beliefs and behaviors, but here we're told he continues to experience pleasure, rather than distress.
C: The attorney's beliefs and attitudes are consonant here. With no dissonance between beliefs, there is no cognitive dissonance.

16. The social phenomenon of groupthink is characterized by all of the following EXCEPT:
    A) a significant over-rating of the decision-making abilities of members of the ingroup.
    B) a decrease in the creativity of individual group members in contributing to solutions the ingroup wants to achieve.
    C) **high loyalty and group cohesiveness causing members to feel safe raising controversial issues and proposing alternative solutions.**
    D) an effort to minimize conflict and ensure consensus.

Groupthink is a phenomenon that occurs when highly cohesive and loyal groups of people end up valuing consensus over clear decision-making and confronting ingroup conflicts. This high cohesiveness leads people to avoid raising controversial issues or propose alternatives to the group's desired solution. Thus (C) is false and because this is an EXCEPT question, it's the right answer. The remaining choices are all apt descriptions of groupthink.

17. According to attachment theory, which of the following children is most likely to attach to a male psychologist, previously unknown to the child, in the course of a psychological study?
    A) **A two month old female infant raised in a safe, stable environment**
    B) A five month old male infant raised in a safe, stable environment
    C) An eight month old male infant raised by a single caregiver who frequently neglects the child
    D) A thirteen month old female infant raised by two caregivers who occasionally neglect the child

Attachment theory describes a series of steps that infants will progress through as they grow. During the first three months of life, an infant will indiscriminately attach to any person and will respond equally to any caregiver. Thus (A) is an apt description of attaching to a previously unknown adult.

Around 4 to 6 months babies will begin to recognize certain caregivers but will still accept care from anyone. Thus in (B) the baby will probably accept care from the psychologist, but the infant in (A) is much more likely to attach to the psychologist.

From 6 to 9 months a baby will exhibit a strong attachment preference for a single caregiver, although the pattern of that attachment will vary based on the relationship that has developed between the caregiver and the child. Despite the neglect, the child in (C) will still have a preference for a single caregiver.

After 9 months, children slowly develop increasing independence and will slowly form multiple attachments. The child in (D) will thus begin to develop attachments to both caregivers, but not to the psychologist, who is a stranger.

18. Each of the following are aspects of the McDonaldization of Society EXCEPT:
    A) rationalization of decisions into cost/benefit analysis structures and away from traditional modes of thinking.
    B) bureaucratic organization that formalizes well-establish division of labor and impersonal structures.
    C) **a dissolution of hierarchical modes of authority into collaborative team-based decision protocols.**
    D) an intense effort on achieving sameness across diverse markets.

Sociologist George Ritzer coined the term McDonaldization to describe the modern form of the social phenomenon of rationalization discussed by Max Weber at the end of the nineteenth century. The rationalization of society involves a shift in social structures towards rational means/ends tests (like choice A) a focus on efficiency and formal methods of social control. The classic example of a rational social structure is bureaucracy (as described in B) that aims to create a uniformity of outcomes (as described in D).

The correct answer (C) is not a part of McDonaldization, which would focus on strongly hierarchical methods of control.

Passage 4 Explanation

There are factors which uniquely impact the **mental health of women of retirement age** in Japan. Japanese women typically **decrease their volunteer work** in their community as they arrive at retirement age. Reasons for this include that women most frequently volunteer through their **children's schools** and as their children graduate there are fewer opportunities for this. **Lessening volunteer** work is correlated with higher levels of **depression**. In addition, due to **cultural norms** many Japanese women of retirement age are also **supporting an elder family member** in their homes, which may require a great deal of time. The relationship between women caretakers and their elderly family members may be stressful, and can result in a number of conflicts.

Cause and effect: detachment from schools causes reduced volunteerism which causes depression; cultural norms cause Japanese women to spend time caring for elderly relatives.

To address these unique needs, Japan has adopted programs to assist them. The **Long-Term Care Initiative of 2000** strives to coordinate care resources for the elderly and provide psychosocial support for their caregivers. In Japan, seeking **mental health services** outside of the home is still **taboo**, especially among older individuals. To meet the need of women of retirement age, case managers first identify those in highest need. Those caregivers who are providing care for family members with **high levels of health needs** typically have the highest **stress** levels. Case managers target these caregivers as a priority, providing services such as social talk and educating about approaching and avoiding styles of care. **Social talk** consists of interactions between caregivers and case managers that provide an opportunity for caregivers to **express themselves** and their frustrations, much as might occur in a therapy session. **Avoidance** strategies consist of the caregiver taking space and **time for herself** in order to address her own needs. **Approaching** strategies consist of formulating ways for the caregiver to **enlist the elderly in their own care**. These interventions have been shown to **reduce caregiver stress**.

Key terms: long term care initiative, social talk, avoidance, approaching
Opinion: mental health service is taboo
Cause-and-effect: caring for someone with lots of health needs causes stress; interventions reduce stress.

19. Which of the following is NOT a cultural factor described in the passage that might account for increased levels of stress among Japanese women of retirement age?
    A) Need to support elderly relatives
    B) **Emphasis on education**
    C) Reduced volunteerism
    D) Reluctance to access public mental health resources

    Answer: B – Education is mentioned in the passage, but it is not described as a reason that elderly Japanese women might experience increased stress at retirement age, while the other factors are all described.

20. Asking an elderly mother-in-law to assist in preparing breakfast is an example of what kind of strategy?
    A) **Approaching strategy**
    B) Social talk
    C) Care initiative
    D) Avoidance strategy

    Answer: A – According to the passage, the purpose of approaching strategies is to get elderly family members actively involved in their own care, an example of which is to ask for help preparing breakfast.

21. Which of the following is an example of an effective strategy to reduce stress associated with generational inequity?
   A) Providing extra resources for elderly individuals living with younger family members
   B) Increasing attachment among family members living with each other
   C) **<u>Encouraging women caregivers to take time to do activities they enjoy</u>**
   D) Helping women caregivers understand the developmental needs of elderly family members

   Answer: C – Generational inequity is the view that elderly individuals are allocated an unfairly excessive amount of resources. A strategy which addresses this would help non-elderly receive their own resources. Answer C is an example of an avoidance strategy, a type of strategy discussed in the passage, which has been found helpful in reducing stress and encourages caregivers to allocate resources to themselves.

22. What is a possible reason for taking care of elderly family members and avoiding mental health services outside of the home in Japan?
   A) **<u>Socialization</u>**
   B) Psychoanalytic drive
   C) Cognitive dissonance
   D) Altruism

   Answer: A – As mentioned in the passage, both taking care of elderly family members and avoiding mental health services are based on social norms. These norms influence individuals' behavior through socialization.

Passage 5 Explanation

Both **Freud** and **Jung** believed in the **usefulness of analyzing dreams** to understand the unconscious. They both viewed the unconscious as expressing itself in the forms and images of the dream and that it was important to attempt to understand the unconscious through dreams. However, they **disagreed** about the **form and function** of dreams and how to **interpret** them.

Key terms: Freud, Jung
Opinion: Freud, Jung agree dreams are useful
Contrast: Freud, Jung disagree on nature of dreams and their interpretation

They disagreed on what the dream represents. **Freud** viewed the dream as a disguised representation of a **person's wishes**. He stated that the dream is **disguised** because if the wish was presented in its natural form, it would be too **disturbing** for the person. **Jung** viewed the dream as a direct representation of the dreamer's **mental state**, represented in symbols. Jung believed that dreams represent the objective and subjective reality, both the **events** that happen and the **person's interpretation** of them. This contrasted with Freud, who viewed dreams as **only** representing an individual's **wishes**.

Contrast: Freud vs. Jung; Freud said dreams only represent the desires of the dreamer but Jung said dreams show both facts and desires
Cause and effect: Because a person's desires can be disturbing, they disguise their desires in dreams

The way the dream presents itself is an area in which they disagreed. **Jung** viewed the dream as having a **compensatory** function, in which the dream represents an aspect of the person that is perceived as lacking. For example, a person who feels stifled may dream of flying. **Freud** viewed the dream as presenting both manifest and latent content. The manifest content consists mainly of **"day residue,"** which is experiences that the person had during the day. The **latent content** is the **unconscious wishes** that the person has, which is disguised in the manifest content, often through **condensation**, or several aspects of the unconscious representing itself in similar forms.

Contrast: Freud vs. Jung; Freud said dreams present manifest and latent content but Jung said dreams present compensations for the dreamer's own shortcomings
Key terms: condensation, day residue

Another difference between the two is in their method of interpreting dreams. **Freud** advocated for using **free association** to interpret, in which the patient talks about the dream and in so doing the significance of the dream comes to be realized. According to Freud, an **analyst** is **necessary** to assist in the interpretation. **Jung,** believed that a person is able to interpret his **own** dreams and in fact encouraged this. He was focused more on the **symbols** present in the dream and encouraged patients to immediately record their dreams in a **dream journal** upon waking. This is not to say that Jung did not value the associations a person made with the dream, which he termed **amplifications**. He did believe these interpretations to be important; however, he wanted to focus more on the dream, whereas Freud would allow a patient's free associations to lead his thoughts wherever they might go.

Contrast: Freud vs. Jung; Freud interprets dreams through free association, requiring a therapist but Jung lets people interpret their own dreams and uses symbols and dream journals.
Key terms: amplifications

23. It can be inferred that both Jung and Freud desired to bring the meaning of dreams into a person's:
    A) **consciousness.**
    B) free association.
    C) hypnogogic state.
    D) dream journal.

    Answer: A – As stated in the passage, both Jung and Freud desired to make a person aware of their unconscious, as expressed in the dream. This awareness is known as consciousness.

24. According to Freud, which of the following could be the latent meaning of a child's dream of a lake?
    A) the uniting force of mankind
    B) a lake the child saw on a map
    C) **a desire to return to a favorite family vacation place**
    D) hysteria

    Answer: C – According to Freud, the latent content of a dream is the dream's disguised meaning and Freud asserted that dreams represented the wishes of the dreamer. A dream of a lake might represent a wish to return to a favorite family vacation place.

25. Which of the following techniques might Jung advocate an individual do to process a dream?
    A) Attempt to forget unpleasant aspects of the dream.
    B) Analyze the circadian rhythms of his sleep.
    C) **Summarize the dream into an audio recording device.**
    D) Wait until an analyst is available to recount the dream.

    Answer: C – Jung advocated that an individual attempt to understand his own dream. He also encouraged a person to record his dream immediately after waking in a dream journal. An audio recording could be one form of a dream journal.

26. Freud and Jung's approach to bring unconscious material to a person's awareness is a major tenet of which branch of psychology?
    A) Humanistic psychology
    B) **Psychoanalytic psychology**
    C) Cognitive Behavioral psychology
    D) Systems psychology

    Answer: B – Both Freud and Jung were pioneers in psychoanalytic psychology. In addition, psychoanalytic psychology emphasizes focus on unconscious material.

These questions are **NOT** related to a passage.

27. In an experiment of role-taking development, a four year old child is presented with the "Holly scenario": "Holly is an avid 8-year-old tree climber. One day, Holly falls off a tree, but does not hurt herself. Holly's father makes Holly promise that she will stop climbing trees, and Holly promises. Later, Holly and her friends find a kitten stuck in a tree. Holly is the only one who can climb trees to save the kitten, who may fall at any moment." The researcher then asks, "How will Holly's father react if he finds out Holly climbed the tree and saved the kitten?" Which of the following is the most likely response from the four year old?

  A) "The father will be mad at Holly because she broke her promise."
  B) **"The father will not mind the disobedience because he likes kittens and the kitten will make him happy."**
  C) "The father will be mad if Holly gets hurt but he will be happy if she saves the kitten."
  D) "The father will understand that saving a kitten is more important to Holly than keeping a promise not to climb trees."

Role-taking theory posits that children develop an ability to understand the perspectives and feelings of others as they mature. This ability starts with a child unable to distinguish between his own desires and the desires of others, moves to an ability to understand that others have different desires, to ultimately being able to predict the behaviors of others based on an understanding of the motivations of others. A four year old child would still be in the first stage of development, Egocentric Role-Taking, in which the child cannot understand that others have a different perspective than his own. Thus (B) is the most likely answer, as the child is unable to separate his own fondness for kittens from either Holly or the father's perspectives.

A, C: These statements reflect the next stage of development, Subjective Role-Taking, in which a child can understand that others have different points of view and that those perspectives can different from the child's own point of view. Subjective Role-Taking begins around age 7-8.
D: This statement reflects either Self-reflective Role-Taking or the subsequent stage, Mutual Role-Taking, because now the child is able to understand that the points of view of other people can relate to each other, both outside of the child's own view. By acknowledging that the father understands Holly's point of view, the child is demonstrating a development at stage 3 or 4. Stage 3, Self-reflective Role-Taking, begins roughly age 8-10, and stage 4, Mutual Role-Taking is roughly ages 10 to 12.

28. A parent wishes to encourage her daughter to complete her homework every night without resorting to extrinsic motivation. Which of the following strategies would be best?

  A) **Allow her daughter to set her own homework study schedule, and praise her effectiveness when she sticks to that schedule.**
  B) Create an internal sense of competitiveness by fostering a competition between the daughter and the daughter's best friend who is in all of the same classes.
  C) Remind the daughter that getting good grades are their own reward, that good grades are the result of hard work doing the homework, and that good grades should generate a sense of accomplishment.
  D) Offer to increase the daughter's allowance if she completes her homework each week.

Intrinsic motivation is generated by an enjoyment of the activity itself, rather than by external rewards. It can be fostered when a person has a sense of their own autonomy over an action and when they believe they can be effective in meeting their own goals. Choice (A) describes a way to foster that sort of motivation.

B: Competition is inherently extrinsic, since the goal is to win rather than enjoy the task itself.

C: Completing homework in order to get good grades is extrinsic – the grades are outside the act of doing the homework itself.

D: Doing an activity for money is extrinsic motivation – the money is outside the activity itself.

29. A psychologist conducts an experiment in which a dog is trained to roll over. The dog has a small device strapped to its back. Rolling over depresses a button on the device. If the dog rolls over in time, the button is pressed and the device does not shock the dog. This form of conditioning would best be described as using:

    A) negative reinforcement through escape.

    B) negative punishment.

    C) **negative reinforcement through avoidance.**

    D) positive reinforcement.

Here the MCAT is testing your knowledge of operant conditioning. When a subject is presented with the removal of a negative stimulus, the subject is experiencing negative reinforcement. Remember reinforcement is used to encourage or increase a behavior. Here, the researcher is reinforcing the behavior of rolling over. This is negative reinforcement because the rolling over behavior is being reinforced through the removal of a negative stimulus. Because the dog is avoiding the shock entirely, choice (C) is the correct answer.

A: Escape requires that the subject actually experience the noxious stimulus and the correct behavior then removes the noxious stimulus. For example, the dog would receive a mild shock and the shock would stop upon rolling over.

B: Punishment is used to stop a behavior. Here we are trying to encourage the behavior of rolling over.

D: Positive reinforcement is providing a positive stimulus to encourage a behavior. Here, the dog is not receiving any positive stimulus: instead it is merely avoiding a negative one.

30. A psychologist conducts an experiment in which subjects are asked to learn a series of "facts" which are actually statements that have been fabricated by the research team. The subjects consist of undergraduate students at the university where the experiment is being conducted. The subjects are randomly assigned to groups that are compensated either $10 or $20 for their participation, are given either 15 minutes or 30 minutes to learn the facts, and are asked to recall the facts either in the same room in which they learned the facts or in a very different, unfamiliar setting. Which of the following are dependent variables in this experiment?

  I. The amount the subjects were compensated.

  II. The room in which the subjects were asked to recall facts.

III. **The number of facts the subjects can recall.**

IV. The time the subjects were given to learn the facts.

    A) II only

    B) **III only**

    C) I and IV only

    D) I, III, and IV only

In experimental design, the dependent variable is the variable being tested as a possible effect or output, whereas the independent variables are those that are controlled by the experimenters and tested as possible causes.

Here, the experimenters controlled the compensation amount, the time to learn, and the room in which the subjects were asked to recall the information. Thus, I, II, and IV are independent variables. The dependent variable here is III, the measured recall rate of the facts.

Passage 6 Explanation

Traditionally **psychology** has been practiced from a **medical model**, in which deficits in an individual's functioning are identified by practitioners and communicated to their patients. Because this norm has traditionally been dictated by the dominant culture, minorities have often been pathologized as a result of being compared to the norm. Thus, more recent efforts in psychology have emphasized practitioners **developing multicultural competencies**.

Key terms: medical model, pathological
Opinion: Psychologists need to develop multicultural competency to avoid pathologizing different cultures.

Some researchers espouse a culture-free view and contend that there are **universal virtues** that humans value, irrespective of culture. For these researchers culture serves to obfuscate universal virtues. **Other researchers** endorse a **culturally-embedded viewpoint**. These researchers view virtues as being defined by culture. Further, these researchers contend that **practitioners' own cultures influence their interpretation** of other cultural virtues, so that culture must be recognized to properly understand others' cultures. For example, cultures have **different views on the importance of happiness**, with some cultures viewing it as one of the most important virtues and others viewing it as **less important than enlightenment**.

Key terms: universal virtues, happiness, enlightenment
Contrast: Values that are universal across all cultures vs. values understood in the context of a given culture.
Opinion: Psychologists' own views are affected by the culture they are in.

While defining **cultural strengths** might be elusive, there is a recognition that these strengths can have important beneficial effects on the individual, as seen in a **"strengths-based" approach**. It is worthwhile to **examine the factors** that enable these individuals to do so and to promote these factors of **resilience**.

Key terms: strengths-based approach
Opinion: We should be examining the aspects of culture that promote resilience.

One way that salient factors might be identified is through the **Four-Front Approach**, a model of assessment that **guides clinicians in obtaining culturally relevant information**. Using this approach, clinicians gather information about the client in four areas: strengths of the client, deficiencies in the client, resources available in the client's environment, and deficiencies in the client's environment.

Key terms: Four-Front Approach
Opinion: The Four-Front Approach helps psychologists assess both the patient and the patient's culture.

A way of using the Four-Front Approach can be illustrated by considering the following **case**. **Juan** is a 13 year old male in the **seventh grade**. He immigrated to the United States from Mexico with his family when he was 2 years old and his **primary language is Spanish**. His father is currently sick and unable to work. Juan has two younger siblings, who he frequently has to care for while his mother is at work. Juan has **struggled academically** this year at school. He has had **difficulty** interacting appropriately with his **peers**, frequently getting into fights and having difficulty when assigned to work together at school. **Juan is able to get along** with his peers when he plays **soccer**, an activity at which he excels. Juan and his family are **Catholic** and are very involved with their church.

Key terms: Juan – we are given information about his case

Using this information, a clinician used the Four-Front Approach to better understand Juan. The results are presented as follows:

Table 1 Results of patient assessment using Four-Front Approach

Front	Characteristics
Client strengths	-Bilingual –Good at soccer –Good caretaker of his siblings – Currently at age-appropriate grade level
Client deficiencies	-Academic difficulties –Social difficulties –Difficulties with English
Environmental strengths	-Church support –Mother is working –Father is present
Environmental deficiencies	-Lack of another caregiver for siblings –Lack of individual support at school

Table 1 shows us information about Juan's assessment using the Four-Front Approach.

31. Emphasizing what Juan is good at and what resources are available to him to address his deficiencies is an example of what kind of approach to psychology?
    A) Medical model
    B) **Strength-based approach**
    C) Culturally embedded approach
    D) Cultural-free approach

    Answer: B – In a strengths-based approach, individual strengths are emphasized.

32. How might Juan's social difficulties be viewed from a multicultural approach, rather than from the medical model approach?
    A) Juan ought to practice his social skills in a group.
    B) Juan was not taught social skills at a young age.
    C) **Juan's focus on taking care of his siblings has made it difficult to practice interacting with peers.**
    D) Juan's cognitive difficulties have made learning social skills difficult.

    Answer: C – This answer illustrates how cultural factors may have led Juan to exhibit his current pattern of functioning.

33. What is an example of a multicultural intervention to support Juan?
    A) Exposing him exclusively to English language instruction
    B) Involving child services to remove Juan and his siblings from the home to be placed with caretakers who can support them better
    C) Attributing Juan's difficulties with school to the fact that he is bi-cultural
    D) **Using Juan's family's church to help with the caretaking of Juan's siblings**

    Answer: D – This intervention uses strengths in Juan's environment to support him.

34. Which of the following would NOT be a beneficial result of normalizing Juan's caretaking of his siblings as being culturally appropriate to Juan?

    A) Juan may feel self-esteem from behaving in a culturally virtuous way.

    B) Juan may feel a greater sense of connection with his Mexican culture.

    C) **Juan may come to feel less connected with American culture.**

    D) Juan may learn to access cultural resources to help in the caretaking.

Answer: C – This would not necessarily be a benefit for Juan.

Passage 7 Explanation

Eyewitness testimony is an area of forensic psychology that has been researched, especially within the past 30 years, in efforts to evaluate and **improve its accuracy**. Accuracy in eyewitness testimony is an important consideration because oftentimes individuals' freedom is at stake. The **reliability** of eyewitness testimony has **come into question** as researchers have found a number of instances in which eyewitness testimony has **later proved to be untrue**. Researchers have examined factors in eyewitness testimony that hinder its reliability and have formed recommendations for how to address these factors.

Key terms: eyewitness testimony
Opinion: Eyewitness testimony has proven false in the past, bringing its reliability into question

One of the first factors that can affect eyewitness testimony is **suggestibility**. Suggestibility refers to incorporating **information learned after the event into the testimony** about the event as if it actually occurred. Suggestibility is often introduced when the witness is asked about the event and information, or **false cues**, are introduced that are then incorporated into the memory. Suggestibility was demonstrated in an experiment in which participants viewed a picture of a car next to either a stop sign or a yield sign. When questioning the participants about what they saw the researchers purposely used the name of the type of sign that was opposite of what the participants actually saw. When questioned about what type of sign the participants saw **the majority of participants stated that they had seen the opposite sign** than what they actually saw, in accordance with what the researchers said. In the same experiment the participants were also shown a picture of a car accident. When the researchers used **the word "smashed"** in their questioning about the event, participants were **more likely to report having seen broken glass** than those who did not hear that word used. These findings and others about suggestibility have led to guidelines for professionals questioning witnesses that guard against introducing any suggestibility into the questioning. Questioners **should ask open ended questions** and avoid introducing any provocative words which may influence testimony.

Key terms: suggestibility
Cause and effect: using leading questions with false cues can introduce false facts into a memory
Opinion: Questioners should use open-ended questions to avoid contaminating a witness's recall.

Even if witnesses are questioned in an unbiased manner, the way the witnesses reconstruct the memory is subject to their own **personal biases**. When recounting a memory, researchers have found that witnesses will reconstruct a narrative that involves actual facts from the event, as well as **incorporating their own schemas** into the narrative. A schema is an individual's own representation of information and its relationship in context of other information. This has been seen in experiments in which participants were presented with a complicated story which they were then asked to retell. Researchers found that **participants retold facts** from the story, but also **interjected their own understanding** of how the facts were related. In addition, **information which is inconsistent** with an individual's schemas tends to be **forgotten** or omitted at a much greater rate than information which is consistent with schemas. To address the interference of schemas and other personal biases in an eyewitness's testimony, recommendations have been made to those hearing eyewitness testimony, such as juries, to **consider individual factors of the eyewitness**, such as his reliability and details of the content of the testimony that add or delete validity.

Cause and effect: Eyewitness testimony can be wrong because people will inject their own biases and forget facts which don't fit their views.
Opinion: Those listening to eyewitness testimony have to be careful about the credibility of the witness.

A final factor which affects eyewitness testimony is that once testimony about an event is initially recounted, **the**

eyewitness tends to increase his belief in the veracity of the event the way he recounted it. He will tend to continue to incorporate **facts he mistakenly introduced** into the testimony in future retellings, and the facts will become **consolidated** with the memory. Examples of this has been observed in actual court cases in which a witness who initially identifies a suspect as being a perpetrator in a police line-up will continue to identify that individual as a perpetrator in subsequent line-ups, even when that individual is known to not be the actual perpetrator. To counter the effect of incorrect events being repeatedly recounted in testimony, efforts should be made to **accurately record testimony of eyewitnesses at the initial recounting** of the event before false memories can be interjected and solidified at subsequent retellings. Also, those questioning eyewitnesses should ask about details of the event in multiple ways to attempt to verify the veracity of the event.

Cause and effect: Eyewitness testimony can be made more strongly incorrect when the witness incorrectly includes a wrong fact and then consolidates that wrong fact into the memory. Opinion: Testimony should be carefully recorded at the initial telling to avoid mistakes introduced later.

In a study to evaluate the effect of the use of these recommendations on eyewitness testimony, participants were shown a video clip of a violent incident. The participants were then asked to recall the violent incident 48 hours later. Half of the participants were asked to recall the events using the techniques described in this passage and half were asked to recall the event without any techniques being used. **The number of accurate details recounted by the participants was recorded**. The average number of accurate details for each of the two groups is presented as follows:

Table 1 The effect of careful interrogation technique on witness recall

Group	Average Number of Correct Details Recalled
Using Techniques	40.1
Without Using Techniques	28.2

The average number of details recalled by the two groups were compared using an independent samples t-test. The results indicated that there was a significant difference between the two groups ($p<.0001$).

Table 1 shows us that when interviewers are aware of how eyewitness testimony can be made inaccurate and use techniques to avoid contaminating the recollection, witnesses are able to successfully recall many more correct facts.

35. What type of bias might be introduced by the question, "What type of gun did the man have?"
   A) Consolidated memory bias
   B) **Suggestibility**
   C) Schema bias
   D) Flashbulb memory bias

   Answer: B – In suggestibility, facts that are introduced might become incorporated into the memory, so suggesting that there is a gun might lead the witness to recall there was a gun even if there wasn't one.

36. What fact, if true, might influence the following interpretation of the data: using the techniques discussed leads to

more accurate eyewitness testimony overall?

A) The eyewitnesses recalled the event 72 hours later, not 48
B) There were demographic differences within the two groups of eyewitnesses
C) **There were a higher number of details recalled, both true and false, in the group in which techniques were used**
D) The control group sometimes used techniques in their interviews

Answer: C – If there were more accurate and inaccurate facts recalled in one group then the conclusion that the eyewitness testimony is more accurate overall cannot be made.

37. Which of the following factors might increase the suggestibility of a comment made by an interviewer?

A) If the comment is vague
B) If the eyewitness is an adult, rather than a child
C) If the interviewer is of the same ethnicity as the eyewitness
D) **If the interviewer is perceived to be an expert by the eyewitness**

Answer: D – Research has shown that people place more credence in statements made by those who appear to be experts.

38. What is to be expected about the number of inaccurate facts both of the groups will incorporate in future retellings of the event?

A) The group interviewed with techniques will tell as many or more inaccurate facts
B) The group interviewed without techniques will tell as many or more inaccurate facts
C) **Both groups will tell as many or more inaccurate facts**
D) Neither group will tell as many or more inaccurate facts

Answer: C – According to the passage in future retellings of eyewitness testimony inaccurate facts tend to be incorporated into the story and remain in the narrative. This is true for all people.

39. What could be another interpretation of the results of the study?

A) **The group without techniques witnessed information that was different than their beliefs**
B) The group with techniques witnessed information that was different than their beliefs
C) Erroneous facts the group without techniques recalled became consolidated in their memory
D) Erroneous facts the group with techniques recalled became consolidated in their memory

Answer: A – According to the data, the group without techniques was not able to recall information as accurately as the group with techniques. A possible reason given in the passage is that when schemas and events are different participants may recall according to their schemas, or beliefs.

Passage 8 Explanation

There is **disagreement** about what **autism** specifically is, but its features include: **limited vocabulary, poor social interaction, and repetitive self-soothing movements**. Some researchers contend that autism should not be considered a categorical condition, but rather a point along a **continuum** of pervasive developmental disturbances with similar symptomatology, with less severe conditions like Pervasive Developmental Disorder-Not Otherwise Specified (PDD-NOS) and Asperger's syndrome.

Key terms: autism, limited vocabulary, poor social interaction, self-soothing movements
Opinion: autism is a point on a spectrum with other disorders

Researchers have attempted to provide explanations for the **causes** of the **symptomatic behavior** listed above. First, people with autism are **overloaded with sensory** stimulation. Many of the symptomatic behaviors they display are products of trying to deal with this overload. The repetitive behaviors are an attempt to focus on something while being flooded with stimuli.

Cause and effect: the overload of sense information causes autism symptoms

The **cause of autism continues to remain a mystery**. There are various theories as to what causes it. Most studies agree that autism is a result of a combination of improper neurological, genetic, and cognitive functioning. For example, one study showed that among those with autism the **pathways between the hippocampus and amygdala had abnormal microstructures**. Scientists have additionally identified certain **chromosomes** which appear associated with autism. There have also been some environmental factors identified as contributing to the development of autism. One area of autism research that has been especially **controversial** lately is an alleged link between autism and vaccines. A study done 20 years previously showed there was no link between **vaccines and autism.** However a 2007 U.S. Federal court ruled in a lawsuit that a child who had received a vaccine and developed autism would receive a compensation settlement.

Key terms: abnormal microstructures, vaccines
Opinion: causes of autism are unknown and related to brain structures, genetic factors and possibly environmental factors.

Tito, a 13 year old boy with autism, has been working with his mother and other professionals for a long time and has developed the capability to express himself through **writing and typing**. During an interview, when Tito was asked about why he **flaps his hands and rocks**, he replied that, "I just need to find my position in space… I **forget that I have a body** and it reminds me that I have one." Tito described how when he was younger he looked at a cloud and someone said banana and the cloud and the banana became permanently associated together forever. Tito's therapist described how Tito's **senses come in waves**. He sees **parts before the whole**. When asked about how to describe a door, he answers that he looks at the shape of the door then the colors and then subsequent details. However, if the door is then opened he has to start over.

Key terms: Tito

Opinion: Tito's repetitive motions help link him to his body, he senses parts before the whole

Figure 1 Spectrum of Pervasive Developmental Disorders

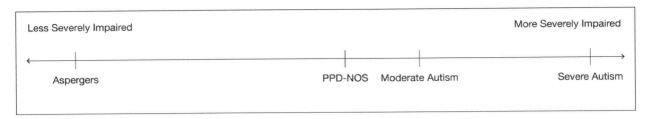

Figure 1 The scale provided offers no units, so there are no numbers to analyze. Instead, we can see the general trend. Asperger's is much less severe than the other disorders, with PPD-NOS falling between Asperger's and autism.

40. What would be an argument for considering Pervasive Developmental Disorders along a continuum of severity?
    A) **<u>Many disorders along the continuum have similar symptoms.</u>**
    B) The etiology of the disorders is the same.
    C) An individual can move from a more severe disorder to a less severe disorder.
    D) An individual can move from a less severe disorder to a more severe disorder.

    Answer: A – The passage states that the disorders have similar symptoms, though of differing levels of severity. Having a continuum allows the disorders to be considered together.

41. What is a possible explanation for the increased prevalence of autism that has been found in recent years?
    A) Increased abnormal microstructures
    B) Increased vaccinations
    C) **<u>Increased recognition of symptoms</u>**
    D) Increased social contact

    Answer: C – It is likely that the increased prevalence of autism has come from an increased recognition of the symptoms of autism that lead to a correct diagnosis.

42. What is an explanation of a child with autism's repeated hand-clapping from a functionalist viewpoint?
    A) Neurological deficits lead to incorrect signaling of motor areas of the brain
    B) **<u>The clapping allows him to focus on only one stimulus</u>**
    C) The clapping is a response to a stimulus learned via operant conditioning
    D) Repeated movements, of which hand-clapping is an example, are symptoms of autism

    Answer: B – Behavior is explained in functionalism in terms of the effect the behavior has. The effect repeated movements have in autism is to help the individual focus on one stimulus, instead of being overwhelmed by multiple stimuli.

43. Through therapy, when a person with a Pervasive Developmental Disorder learns that another person with raised eyebrows and an open mouth is surprised rather than happy, what type of associative learning has taken place?
    A) Generalization
    B) **<u>Discrimination</u>**
    C) Extinction
    D) Acquisition
    Answer: B – Learning that the facial expression means one type of feeling, rather than another, is an example of discrimination.

These questions are **NOT** related to a passage.

44. When hungry, a person will seek food. According to drive theory, which of the following is (are) true about this behavior?
   I. The drive to eat will decrease over time.
   II. **Eating is an attempt to reduce a homeostatic disturbance.**
   III. **Eating behavior and hunger operate on a negative feedback control system.**
      A) I only
      B) II only
      C) **II and III only**
      D) I, II, and III

Drive theory explains behaviors in terms of psychological drives. A drive is an aroused state caused by the person being disturbed from a homeostatic rest position. In this case, (II) is true because hunger is caused by a drive to eat and thus reduce the disturbance from homeostasis. When drives are satisfied, the person relaxes and that relaxation reduces the drive to continue the behavior. Thus, the drive and the behavior operate on negative feedback, making (III) also true.

(I) is false because drive theory posits that drives increase over time until they are fulfilled.

45. A child is born into a society with one majority ethnicity and two significant minority ethnicities. He is a member of the majority ethnicity. In the course of his early childhood, he hears comments by both his mother and his father expressing disparaging attitudes towards minority group one and laudatory attitudes towards minority group two. The child then grows into an adult and maintains those same attitudes, which reflect attitudes held by the plurality of members of the majority ethnicity. Which of the following accurately describes this scenario?
   A) The attitudes he developed were a result a secondary socialization because he took on the attitudes and beliefs of his larger society.
   B) **The attitudes he developed were a result of primary socialization because he took on the attitudes and beliefs of his parents as a young child.**
   C) As a member of the majority ethnicity, the attitudes he developed were a result of both socialization influences and genetic influences.
   D) The attitudes he developed as a result of primary socialization were held strongly enough to persist in the face of opposing secondary socialization.

Primary socialization is the process of socialization we learn from parents and close family members. In this case, the prejudices were learned as a part of primary socialization. Secondary socialization is associated with adolescents and adults.

A: The person described in the passage had already taken on the prejudiced beliefs of his parents, so while secondary socialization may have reinforced those beliefs, he did not originally develop them in response to secondary socialization

C: Ethnic prejudice does not have a genetic component.

D: The scenario describes a majority ethnicity that reinforces, rather than opposes, his attitudes.

46. A soldier who has lost his lower leg due to a battlefield injury complains of repeated painful feelings in that now-amputated lower leg, describing this sensation as "phantom pain". Which somatoform disorder is the soldier experiencing?
    A) Hypochondriasis
    B) Conversion disorder
    C) Body dysmorphic disorder
    D) **The soldier is not experiencing a somatoform disorder.**

Phantom pain caused by an amputation is not currently classified as a somatoform disorder, as somatoform disorders are concerned with symptoms that cannot be explained by a general medical condition. This makes (D) the best answer.

A: Hypochondriasis is characterized by a person worrying that he or she has a serious illness. The soldier here is simply experiencing pain, not worrying about an illness.
B: Conversion disorder occurs when excessive anxiety causes loss of body function, which is not happening here.
C: Body dysmorphic disorder occurs when a subject perceives a defect in the appearance of part of his or her body, and becomes excessively preoccupied with this defect.

47. Which of the following best describes the negative feedback loop which regulates appetite levels and adipose tissue levels?
    A) **Decreasing levels of adipose tissue result in lower concentrations of leptin hormones in the bloodstream, which stimulates appetite until increased adipose mass causes higher concentrations of leptin hormones in the bloodstream and appetite decreases.**
    B) Decreasing levels of adipose tissue result in higher concentrations of leptin hormones in the bloodstream, which stimulates appetite until increased adipose mass causes lower concentrations of leptin hormones in the bloodstream and appetite decreases.
    C) GABA is produced by adipose tissue, makes its way into the brain, and stimulates production of glutamate, which decreases appetite, causing less adipose tissue and less GABA production, after which appetite increases.
    D) Glutamate is produced by adipose tissue, makes its way into the brain, and stimulates production of GABA, which decreases appetite, causing less adipose tissue and less glutamate production, after which appetite increases.

Choice (A) describes the negative feedback loop used for appetite and adipose tissue regulation.

B: This is the reverse of the correct answer.
C: GABA originates in the brain, not in adipose tissue, and does not pass through the blood-brain barrier. Additionally, neither GABA nor glutamate has the connection to appetite levels that leptin does.
D: Glutamate, in its neurotransmitter form, is not involved in appetite regulation.

Passage 9 Explanation

There is an **overrepresentation of English Language Learning students (ELL students) in special education**. One possible reason for this disparity is that **differences in students' education experiences** in their country of origin and their current American academic experiences may create difficulties in learning with methods utilized at their American school. Another possibility is that due to English language deficiencies, these students appear to have learning disabilities and are **misdiagnosed** as such. It is important to distinguish whether a student is struggling with reading in general or learning the second language.

Key terms: English Language Learners
Opinion: ELL kids are overrepresented in special ed
Cause and effect: some of the overrepresentation is due to misdiagnosis

There is evidence, however, that children who have **difficulty learning another language** may do so because they have an **underlying Reading Disability (RD)**. **Difficulties with Working Memory (WM)** have been found among struggling ELL students and those with an RD. WM involves the **rehearsal** of verbal and visuo-spatial **information**, skills that are involved in phonological processing, a task involved in reading and language acquisition. The relationship between WM deficits and difficulties with both tasks is further supported by findings that **WM deficits are associated with less vocabulary knowledge** and with risk for later development of RD among both ELL students and English as a First Language students (EFL students).

Cause and effect: problems with working memory can cause reading disabilities, difficulties learning a new language, and smaller vocabularies

There is also a strong connection between **first language literacy skills and second language acquisition**. A majority of researchers found that strong first language literacy skills were associated with better second language acquisition. On the other hand, it was indicated in other research that literacy is likely more complicated than simply decoding language. In addition to this skill, there are a **variety of cultural issues involved**, such as understanding shared cultural topics, cultural communication, and understanding social contexts. While these aspects appear to **accentuate** semantic understanding and nuanced understanding of language, the **preponderance** of studies indicate that **first language literacy is correlated with second language acquisition**, strengthening the support for **RD and ELL difficulties being related**.

Opinion: Culture matters in language, but RD and ELL are still probably related

A program which taught first language literacy skills to struggling ELL students was evaluated. The **average reading grade level of fifth grade students** who received the instruction were compared with a control group. The results are presented in the following table:

Cause and effect: a study was done to assess a general reading program on language skills

Table 1 Effects of EFL literacy program

	Students in literacy program	Control students
Pre-program	2.1	2.2
Post-program	4.3	3.8

A repeated measures ANOVA was used to compare the pre – to post – scores of both groups. The difference was found to be significant at $p<.0001$.

Table 1 shows us the effects of the literacy program. We see that all students in the study were reading below grade level (grade 5) but the students in the literacy program were brought up nearly to grade level.

48. All of the following are possible explanations for ELL students struggling to learn English and NOT having an RD, EXCEPT:
    A) differences in learning styles.
    B) lack of exposure to cultural issues.
    C) misdiagnosis.
    D) **difficulty with Working Memory.**

    Answer: D – There have been findings of WM deficits among those struggling with RD and struggling to learn English. The other factors are cultural causes for struggling.

49. If, during the study, all the students knew if they were in the reading instruction group or in the control group, what could be a confounding factor that biased the results?
    A) **Placebo effect**
    B) Inclusive fitness
    C) Fundamental attribution error
    D) Cultural factors

    Answer: A – If students knew they were getting instruction but the other group was not, they might have expected to do better and had better performance as a result, with the opposite effect for the control group. Difference in results being attributable to expectations is the placebo effect.

50. Students with strong first language skills would likely do well with reading and pronouncing what type of word compared to students with weak first language skills?
    A) A sight word that is not pronounced phonetically
    B) **A phonetic word that can be pronounced according to phonetic rules**
    C) A word that they first have first heard pronounced by another person
    D) A word that sounds similar to a word in their first language

    Answer: B – According to the passage, phonetic decoding skills have found to be transferable to another language. Sight words would not be able to be decoded by any student until they have received direct instruction in it. Having a word pronounced first and being similar to a word in the first language would likely benefit both groups of students equally.

51. Why is having a pre-program score for each group important for the research design?
    A) To acclimatize the students to the task
    B) To assess for RD
    C) **To control for differences between the two groups**
    D) To improve the reliability of the findings

    Answer: C – By comparing the change from the initial reading level to the reading level at post-program any differences between students' initial reading level is controlled for.

52. A struggling ELL student, without an RD, would likely have trouble understanding what type of reading passage?
    A) **A passage with metaphors unique to countries with English as a first language**
    B) A passage with many phonetic words
    C) A passage that is first read aloud to him
    D) A passage with a number of short words

    Answer: A – A struggling ELL, without an RD, would likely have trouble understanding the meaning of metaphors.

Passage 10 Explanation

Eysenck viewed neuroticism as varying along a **continuum** from being primarily **calm** at one end to being primarily neurotic, or **nervous**, at the other. Because Eysenck viewed personality as deriving primarily from **genetic** causes, he viewed neuroticism as **controlled by the sympathetic nervous system** (SNS). The SNS responds to perceived stimuli and prepares our body to emotionally respond, primarily through production of **epinephrine**. Eysenck viewed the SNS as responding differently in different people, with some individuals having more sensitive SNS's than others.

Opinion: Eysenck asserts that anxiety is genetic
Cause and effect: nervous responses are the SNS using epinephrine to control the body

When the SNS of an individual responds in an **overly-sensitive** manner, then this individual typically displays **neuroticism**, which can take the form of neurotic disorders. An example of a type of neurotic symptom that is displayed when the SNS is too responsive is a **panic attack**. A panic attack can be viewed somewhat like a **feedback loop**, similar to what happens when a microphone is placed too closely to a speaker, resulting in an ever-increasing feedback loop. In terms of the SNS during a panic attack, the individual initially perceives some potentially bothersome stimuli, such as a presentation in front of a group. The individual then perceives himself to be reacting overly-sensitively to this stimulus, perhaps via somatic displays, such as sweating or blushing. This reaction then becomes a stimulus itself, causing the individual to have further embarrassment and displaying further reactions. This feedback loop continues in a **worsening cycle** until the individual is **incapacitated** via a panic attack.

Cause and effect: The nervousness a person feels makes them feel even more nervous leading to a panic attack

Eysenck also researched the temperament dimension of **extraversion-introversion**. This dimension refers to an individual's propensity for engaging with **others** versus valuing his own **time alone**. Extraverted people tend to enjoy being around others, engaging in social activities, and working in groups. Introverted people tend to enjoy solitary activities and are more reserved in groups. While other researchers have considered this dimension, Eysenck focused on what was the reason an individual displayed more of one trait than the other. He stated that the reason individuals display one style over the other is due to their **preferred arousal level**, with extraverts preferring to be more aroused and introverts less aroused.

Cause and effect: A person's desire to be less aroused makes them an introvert and the opposite for extroverts

The way in which Eysenck derived these dimensions of personality was through factor analysis of individuals' responses to **questionnaires**. Eysenck looked for items which tended to be endorsed together and formed categories of temperament from them. An example of this is given as follows, in which the following participants rated the extent to which they agreed with the following statements on a scale from 1 to 5 with 1 indicating they did not agree at all up to 5 indicating that they completely agreed:

Opinion: Eysenck's opinions were formulated by using questionnaires

Table 1 Sample responses to a temperament questionnaire

Statement	Participant Rating		
	Joe	Katherine	Sally
I enjoy attending parties.	5	2	1
I get nervous in groups.	1	5	5
I sometimes feel as if I'm having a panic attack.	1	4	5
I enjoy doing activities alone.	2	5	4

Table 1: We see the ratings offered by three different test subjects on a 1 to 5 scale. There are no units for the numbers provided. The noticeable trend is that Katherine and Sally both gave high ratings to nervousness and preferring alone time, whereas Joe was the reverse. We might guess that Joe would be considered an extrovert and Katherine and Sally introverts.

53. Based on the limited information provided, which participants appear to have an introverted style?
    A) Joe & Katherine
    B) **Katherine & Sally**
    C) Sally & Joe
    D) None

    Answer: B – Katherine and Sally both endorsed items which suggest they prefer to be alone and do not like being in groups.

54. Eysenck viewed personality as primarily deriving from what?
    A) **Nature**
    B) Nurture
    C) Exogenous factors
    D) Both B and C

    Answer: A – As stated in the passage, Eysenck viewed personality as being derived from within the organism, or from nature.

55. To conclude that because Joe likes to attend parties thus he likes to attend all social gatherings is to commit what kind of error?
    A) Availability heuristic
    B) Self-fulfilling prophecy
    C) Mental short-cut heuristic
    D) **Fundamental attribution error**

Answer: D – In the fundamental attribution error, an individual's underlying characteristics are ascribed too much importance and situational factors are not taken into account. In this example, Joe might only like parties, but not like other types of social events.

These questions are **NOT** based on a passage.

56. Which theoretical view of personality does NOT contrast with the view that personality is derived from temperamental dimensions?

    A) Behaviorism
    B) Psychoanalytic
    C) **Five Factor View of Personality**
    D) Neurobiological

Answer: C – The Five Factor View of Personality views that personality consists of 5 factors, remembered with the acronym OCEAN, Outgoingness, Conscientiousness, Extraversion, Agreeableness, and Neuroticism. Because these factors align with Eysenck's factors that affect temperament, the Five Factor view does not contrast with Eysenck's theories as described in the passage.

57. A hunter puts on camouflage that is designed to "break up" the visual outline border between himself and his surrounding environment. What effect does this have on the visual processing of a person who looks at the camouflaged hunter?

    A) Activity of feature detector neurons in his optical nerve decreases.
    B) **Activity of feature detector neurons in his visual cortex decreases.**
    C) Activity of rods in his retina decreases.
    D) Activity of cones in his retina decreases.

The visual cortex is where feature detection, such as detection of edges, is processed, and is also where feature detection-specific neurons are located. This makes choice (B) correct.

A: Feature detector neurons are not located in the optical nerve.
C: Rods in the retina detect light levels, and are not involved in feature detection processing.
D: Cones in the retina detect different colors, and are not involved in feature detection processing.

58. During which of Jean Piaget's stages of development do children begin to realize that their thoughts and feelings, rather than being shared by others, are unique to them?

    A) Sensorimotor Stage
    B) Preoperational Stage
    C) **Concrete Operational Stage**
    D) Formal Operational Stage

The concrete operational stage is when, according to Piaget, children develop the realization that there are viewpoints and perspectives besides their own. So (C) is correct.

A: In the sensorimotor stage, children are very egocentric and have the conception that their thoughts and feelings are shared by everyone.
B: In the preoperational stage, children are still significantly egocentric and believe that everyone else has the same viewpoint that they have.
D: Before the formal operational stage is reached, children have already realized that their thoughts and feelings, rather than being shared by everyone, are unique to them.

59. What is the difference between vestibular sense and kinesthetic sense?

    A) **Vestibular sense allows balance by detecting body movement; kinesthetic sense allows detection of where a person's body parts are positioned even without looking.**

    B) Vestibular sense allows the detection of pain; kinesthetic sense allows the detection of temperature changes.

    C) Vestibular sense detects smells and scents; kinesthetic sense detects motion or acceleration.

    D) Vestibular sense detects empty spaces; kinesthetic sense detects enclosed spaces.

Of the choices available, only choice (A) describes the features of both vestibular sense and kinesthetic sense correctly.

B: This describes nociception (pain) and thermoception (temperature).

C: This describes olfacoception (scent detection) and vestibular sense (motion).

D: There is no sense known that detects empty or enclosed spaces.

Section 2: 59 Questions, 95 Minutes

Passage 1

The implicit association test assesses for implicit attitudes through a categorization task. Participants are presented with a computer screen displaying two words on the left side of the screen and two words on the right. The middle of the screen then flashes a word or image and the participant must click a button to indicate the appropriate category as quickly as they can.

A typical set up involves putting the categories "good" and "bad" on the sides of the screen (left vs. right determined randomly) and then categories like "male" and "female" or "rich" and "poor". After going through several assignments, the category pairings are switched. So for example, a person might click the left button if an image is either "good or male" and the right button if the image is "bad or female" during round 1, and then have to click left for "good or female" and right for "bad or male" during round 2. The images or words presented unequivocally belong to one of these groups. For example, words like "disgust" or "agony" would be categorized as "bad" by 100% of participants, and the symbol for the men's bathroom would be categorized as "male" by 100% of participants.

Researchers hypothesize that faster response times indicate an implicit bias in favor of the grouping. That is, if a person is able to categorize an image as "good or male" more quickly than he is able to categorize an image as "good or female", this reveals an implicit sexism in favor of males.

The implicit assumption test was made available on the website of a prominent university and after several news stories, became very popular, with over 150,000 participants in the span of just a few months. The data showed the following results:

	Good	Bad			Good	Bad
Slim	751 ms	1003 ms		**Able**	833 ms	998 ms
Fat	1150 ms	633 ms		**Disabled**	1012 ms	710 ms

Table 1a and **1b** The average delay (in milliseconds) that a person took to correctly categorize an image.

1. Which of the following correctly identifies a limitation of the data set used?

    A) The size of the data set prevents the conclusions from having significant statistical power.

    B) Because the test works on implicit associations, it is unable to provide insight about those who are consciously biased.

    C) Recruitment through media discussion of the test, without the usual small payment to participants, means the data set would skew towards much higher ends of the socioeconomic ladder.

    D) The self-selection of participants prevents the data from being generalizable to any particular population.

2. The procedure described in the passage should also include each of the following EXCEPT:

    A) One or more training rounds in which the person only needs to categorize an image as "good" vs. "bad", rather than having to be aware of two distinct categorizations at once.

    B) Controls in which the two categories have no meaningful connection (implicit or otherwise), such as "up or red" vs. "down or green".

    C) Recruitment procedures to guarantee that equal numbers of male and female participants are gathered.

    D) Subsequent data analysis that discards outlying data points as irrelevant (e.g. a latency of 150,000 ms that suggests the person got up and left the computer in the middle of the test).

3. The results from the experiment indicate that:

    A) no implicit associations are associated with able-bodied versus disabled people.

    B) study participants demonstrated a stronger implicit preference for slimness than against able bodied people.

    C) a self-selected participant pool is more likely to have implicit biases than the general population.

    D) study participants demonstrated a stronger implicit preference against fat people than against disabled people.

4. If study participants feel a mild sensation of disgust in response to a word or image associated with disabled people, the Cannon-Bard theory of emotion would assert that:

    A) the physiological arousal and emotional sensation of disgust arise separately and independently in separated areas of the brain.

    B) the emotion is the result of the brain assessing the context of the physiological arousal experienced in the body.

    C) the emotion follows from and is directly caused by the physiological arousal experienced.

    D) the emotion is a cognitive response which then causes autonomic reflexes generating the feeling of the affect.

5. The test is assessing:

    A) unconscious discrimination.

    B) conscious discrimination.

    C) unconscious prejudice.

    D) conscious stereotypes.

Passage 2

Individuals may experience only a limited number of schizophrenic episodes, but a number go on to experience life-long schizophrenia. Schizophrenia represents only 2% of all mental health disorders, yet consumes 20-40% of mental health resources. Because of the far-reaching consequences of the disease, health professionals have sought strategies for managing schizophrenia early in its course, when it is hoped that long-term individual impairment and costs can be minimized. Researchers have attempted to identify individuals who can be targeted for early intervention. Some have proposed that there be a diagnosis called "Prodromal Schizophrenia" (PS) to identify individuals who meet criteria for being likely to go on to develop schizophrenia. Two physicians presented their views on the PS diagnosis.

Physician X: A PS diagnosis identifies people who may go on to develop full schizophrenia. By identifying these people early, there exists the potential to better treat them. There are a number of treatments that could help them in avoiding developing schizophrenia.

Brain imaging studies also provide support for the usefulness of this diagnosis. Brain studies have shown differences in the brains of those who later go on to develop schizophrenia from brains of those who don't. Specifically, there have been findings of decreased gray matter and hippocampal volume.

Physician Y: Many of those diagnosed with PS do not go on to develop full psychosis. Children exhibit symptoms which could be mistaken for symptoms of schizophrenia, including bizarre thoughts, mild hallucinations, and disorganized appearance. Diagnosing schizophrenia can be difficult as well, given that there are a variety of presentations, symptoms can be ambiguous, and those with the disorder may not be good informants. Clinicians typically rely on obtaining a history of individuals suspected of having schizophrenia and consider the presence of these symptoms over time. Given that the age of onset of schizophrenia is typically late adolescence and early adulthood, PS would likely emerge at an even younger age than that. That would result in clinicians being unable to obtain as full a history as when diagnosing schizophrenia and would also complicate distinguishing what might be age appropriate for youth from symptoms of fledgling schizophrenia.

For people who would not otherwise go on to develop schizophrenia, receiving a diagnosis like PS could be detrimental to their psychological well-being.

A study was conducted with 250 participants who had been referred for psychiatric treatment at a local hospital. The participants were interviewed and assessed for the presence of PS. The researchers did not inform the participants of the findings, but contacted them again 10 years later to ascertain if they had received a diagnosis of schizophrenia during that time.

Figure 1 Study results

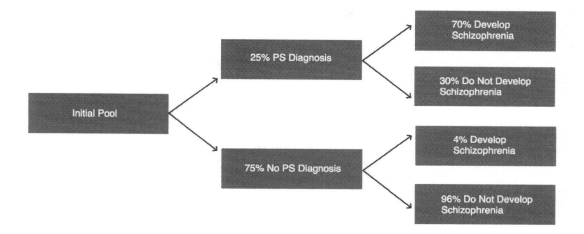

6. The 30% of the people in the study who received the PS diagnosis, but did not go on to develop schizophrenia represents what kind of error?
    A) Type I False Positive
    B) Type II False Negative
    C) Type III True Positive
    D) Type IV True Negative

7. What is the term for someone being given a label and then being more likely to become that label due to expectations?
    A) Cognitive dissonance
    B) Self-fulfilling prophecy
    C) Fundamental attribution error
    D) Stereotype threat

8. Which of the following is NOT an argument for the prodromal schizophrenia diagnosis?
    A) Potential long-term cost savings
    B) Diagnosing schizophrenia can be difficult
    C) There seems to be a biological path from PS to schizophrenia
    D) The number of early treatments available

9. In the study, the 70% of the participants who had received the PS diagnosis who then went on to develop schizophrenia refers to what aspect of a test?
    A) Sensitivity
    B) Specificity
    C) Reliability
    D) Validity

Passage 3

Anxiety is a disorder that is estimated to affect 10-20% of all children and adolescents. One subtype of anxiety is Generalized Anxiety Disorder (GAD). To meet the criteria for this disorder a person must exhibit excessive anxiety and worry for at least 6 months, find it difficult to control this worry, exhibit somatic symptoms, and be caused distress by the anxiety. Many children with GAD worry about topics, such as harm, that will befall them, their level of performance, or the future. These children are often self-conscious, over-estimate the likelihood of negative events occurring, and underestimate their ability to cope with difficulties.

In terms of the etiology of GAD, a number of factors may combine to dispose a child to develop the disorder. First, the child may have a heritable biological diathesis to developing GAD. This is supported by the higher incidence of family members of people with GAD also having GAD themselves. Parents who display an anxious style may influence the formation of anxiety in their children, as well, through modeling. The children may also come to share their parent's beliefs about the world being an insecure place. Parents may also influence their children developing anxiety through their attachment style. Parents exhibiting high control with little warmth or lack of parental care tended to have more anxious children.

Also, temperament plays a role in predisposing some to develop GAD. Children who display an inhibited style of temperament in which they are shy, quiet, and introverted tend to display this style throughout childhood. There is a significant correlation between inhibition and occurrence of GAD. In addition, children who tend to display negative affect and physiological hyperarousal as temperament characteristics tend to develop GAD later.

In terms of psychosocial risk factors among children with GAD, there tends to be a feeling of low control that mediates the relationship between stressful events and negative affect. This sequence may often develop as a result of experiencing many events that are uncontrollable in life. However, this feeling of uncontrollability is then learned and surfaces at later events that may be controllable. This sequence then perpetuates itself upon subsequent events with the child developing a learned helplessness style of interacting with the world.

Figure 1 Factors affecting GAD development

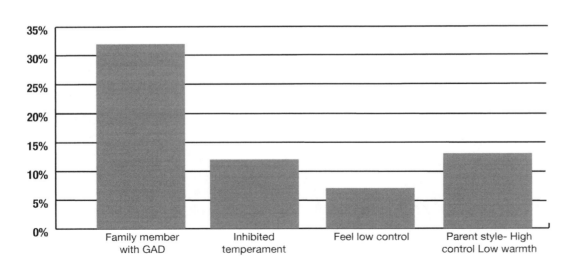

Percent of children with GAD with the presence of the following factors

10. Which of the following is NOT an environmental cause of GAD in children?
    A) Parental modeling of an anxious style
    B) The heritability of GAD from parents
    C) Low warmth in parenting
    D) Learned helplessness

11. What parenting style is associated with increased prevalence of GAD in children?
    A) Permissive
    B) Authoritarian
    C) Authoritative
    D) Ambivalent

12. All of the following evidence would further support that GAD is heritable EXCEPT:
    A) 33% prevalence among children whose biological parents have GAD and who are raised by foster parents
    B) Lessened prevalence of GAD amongst more distant family than immediate family
    C) Having a style of GAD that is very similar to one's parents
    D) Monozygotic twins having a higher correlation of GAD than dizygotic twins

13. What of the following findings would be supported in the relationship between stressful events and negative affect among children with GAD?
    A) A direct relationship – Stressful event and high negative affect
    B) A direct relationship – Stressful event and low negative affect
    C) An indirect relationship – Stressful event, feeling low control, and high negative affect
    D) An indirect relationship – Stressful event, being inhibited, and high negative affect

These questions are **NOT** related to a passage.

14. One limitation of the symbolic interactionism perspective is:
    A) disregard for use of symbols
    B) limited significance of face-to-face interactions
    C) lack of analysis on the macro level
    D) lack of analysis on the micro level

15. The following are all examples of social stratification EXCEPT:
    A) The son of a wealthy real estate developer finds it easy to gain an important position in the real estate industry.
    B) Senior citizens find that they prefer to associate with people their own age.
    C) An immigrant uses a college education to achieve a higher annual income level than her parents.
    D) A number of women executives who experience difficulty in rising through the ranks of a male-dominated corporation react by starting a company of their own.

16. A teenager who has recently moved to the tropics finds that he gets sunburned every time he walks home from school during midday, but not when he walks to school in the early morning. After a few weeks have gone by, he starts putting on sunscreen, both before he leaves for school in the morning and before he leaves for home at midday. The fact that he puts on sunscreen before his early-morning walk to school is an example of:
    A) Context stimuli affecting behavior.
    B) Discriminative stimuli affecting behavior.
    C) Generalization of an escape or avoidance stimulus.
    D) Discrimination response to an escape or avoidance stimulus.

17. Three brothers: Bob the accountant, Joe the plumber, and Dan the dot.com multi-millionaire, belong to which social strata:
    A) middle class, lower class, upper class
    B) middle class, middle class, middle class
    C) working class, lower class, middle class
    D) middle class, working class, upper class

This page intentionally left blank.

Passage 4

An advertising company has evaluated the performance of its advertising sales department.

Table 1 Company metrics from last quarter

Metric	Change over quarter
Employee Retention	-12%
Employee Motivation	-8%
Complaints Filed	+6%
Sales	-7%

To improve performance and increase productivity, an executive has proposed the following plan:

Dear colleagues,

To increase our competitiveness, I have devised the following plan to be implemented among the sales staff to increase performance. It is based on the following foundations to explain motivation:

Expectancy Theory: In this theory, employees are motivated when:
>   i. a certain amount of effort will lead to a certain level of performance;
>   ii. this performance level will lead to particular outcomes; and
>   iii. these outcomes are desirable.

Goal Setting Theory: Goal setting theory will help the department set goals that are productive for the employees. Goal setting theory states that effective goals should be difficult, specific, and relevant. It also emphasizes regular feedback.

Equity Theory: Finally, in order to balance performance with rewards, equity theory will be considered. It posits that an employee is motivated to achieve balance between work and reward relative to some referent. The individual considers an ideal work-reward balance and how to achieve that balance based on some referent. The referent could be a company policy or another individual. Equity is achieved when the employee's work-reward ratio is perceived to be congruent with his expected work-reward ratio based on the referent.

I suggest the following reward system be implemented:
>   i. Employees will each have a sales goal that managers will know, but the employees will not.
>   ii. Reward employees with a bonus only after they reach their goals, but randomly select which times to reward them, so as not to spend too much money rewarding them every time.
>   iii. The bonuses earned throughout the year will be paid at the end of the sales year.

18. What type of operant conditioning reinforcement procedure is being utilized in the proposed reward system?
   A) Positive reinforcement
   B) Negative reinforcement
   C) Positive punishment
   D) Negative punishment

19. Upon reviewing the performance from the previous to current quarter, it was found that employees were paid a commission based solely on total sales dollars during the past quarter. In what way might this system have impacted performance?
   A) The commission policy was not a good referent
   B) Competition was increased, leading to decreased morale
   C) The rewards boosted productivity
   D) The feedback from the commissions were erratic

20. What type of reward system is proposed in the executive's plan?
   A) Fixed interval
   B) Variable interval
   C) Fixed ratio
   D) Variable ratio

21. If the executive's plan works and the employees become motivated by his plan, what could be the effect of reducing the incentives later, compared with rewarding the employees after every time they met a goal?
   A) Productivity will drop quicker
   B) Productivity will drop slower
   C) Productivity will increase quicker
   D) Productivity will increase slower

Passage 5

People's approach to death has been an increasingly studied topic in psychology, with the goal of making this transition more comfortable for individuals. Culture has a large impact on how death is viewed by an individual. A culture's death ethos, or approach and attitude towards death, can be inferred from observing that culture's rituals, such as art and traditions that are related to death. A salient aspect of a culture's death ethos is that culture's view of death's desirability, whether it is considered sacred or profane, or welcome or unwanted. Throughout the West, the meaning of death has fluctuated over time, with death viewed primarily as an end of life during the scientific-minded Renaissance Age. During the Romantic Age in the 1800's, death was glorified and there was an emphasis on achieving a noble death. More recently, in the 20th century death came to be something to be avoided, with much focus on medical methods to prolong life.

Kubler-Ross conceptualized the 5 stages of dying. In the first stage, the individual experiences denial upon realizing he will soon die. The individual then experiences the second stage, anger. During this stage the individual understands that he will die, but feels cheated out of remaining life. This leads to the third stage, bargaining, in which the individual attempts to negotiate prolonged life with God or whatever other entity the individual feels is responsible. The fourth stage is depression, in which the death is recognized as being inevitable. The individual experiences a sense of loss of his own unrealized experiences. The final stage is acceptance. During this stage the individual comes to realize that death is a natural process. This acceptance may provide comfort and relief during the final stages.

The conceptualization of dying in this process lends to the formulation of interventions to assist the dying individual through the process. Kubler-Ross emphasized that the dying person should be allowed to talk openly through the process with cared persons and health care professionals. The emotions that become prominent during each stage should be allowed to be expressed in order for the individual to fully address the themes of each stage. The 5 stages of dying model is not intended to be taken as an invariant process. Individuals may proceed through the stages in varying manners, skipping some stages or going through others in different sequences.

Bereavement is the process individuals experience as they process the death of a loved one. Researchers assessed levels of depression, via a depression inventory, which produced a z-score of depression level. Individuals were assessed before they became widowed and at 6 and 13 months after they became widowed. The researchers found patterns in bereavement among the individuals that they studied, which they classified into 4 patterns of bereavement.

Figure 1 Bereavement styles and depression level

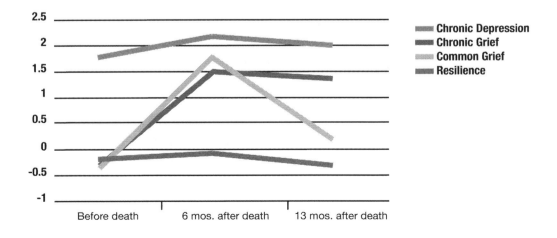

22. Which of the following bereavement styles might be more common in a culture which views death as a natural phenomenon?
- A) Chronic depression
- B) Chronic grief
- C) Resilience
- D) Culture doesn't impact bereavement

23. Individuals who have successfully resolved Erikson's ego integrity v. despair stage are more likely to have achieved what stage in the 5 stage model of dying?
- A) Anger
- B) Bargaining
- C) Depression
- D) Acceptance

24. How might the 5 stages of dying model be applied to assist those individuals in bereavement?
- A) Encourage bereaving individuals to talk about their experiences
- B) Encourage bereaving individuals to proceed through the 5 step model in sequence
- C) Encourage bereaving individuals to achieve ego integrity about the deceased individual
- D) Recognize that individuals with chronic depression are likely still in the depression stage

25. Individuals fearing death because they can easily recount sensational media accounts of disturbing deaths illustrate what process of conceptualizing information?
- A) Availability heuristic
- B) Fundamental attribution error
- C) Intuition
- D) Anchoring heuristic

These questions are **NOT** related to a passage.

26. Two adult siblings, who act and speak cordially to each other when in public, sometimes use raised voices and unrestrained behavior when the only observers present are family members. This is best explained by:
    A) The difference between front-stage and back-stage selves.
    B) The role of culture in shaping expression.
    C) The intersection of prestige with social status.
    D) Conflict theory as applied to the norms of a family's structural functionalism.

27. A group of adolescent males, who usually wear earth tones or other similar colors, snicker at and tease a group member who wears light purple shirts. Eventually, the group member switches to a more earth-toned wardrobe. What best describes this situation?
    A) Diversity as a cause of evolving norms and rituals.
    B) The role of class as a factor that contributes to prejudice.
    C) The effect of dramaturgical inclinations affecting behavior in different situations.
    D) The use of peer pressure and stigma to induce a change in deviant behavior.

28. In the classic series of children's books, "Where's Waldo?" the child is presented with a huge, colorful image filled with characters and objects, and must search through the image looking for a particular character wearing a red and white striped shirt. This exercise represents what sort of sensory processing set up?

    A) Unimodal stimuli and top-down processing
    B) Unimodal stimuli and bottom-up processing
    C) Multimodal stimuli and top-down processing
    D) Multimodal stimuli and bottom-up processing

This page intentionally left blank.

Passage 6

The process of encouraging individuals to initially utilize mental health services and continue to use them can be viewed as containing several steps and choices the client and his family make about whether or not to utilize services. Eysenbach applied a process Rogers formulated, regarding the general adaptation and use of innovations, to the utilization of mental health services within a community. This process consists of, first, a diffusion of awareness of the service to prospective clients, normally through change agents, or those people with contact with both the service and the community. An example of a change agent is a worker at a community mental health center, with ties to a particular neighborhood. This change agent might promote services available at his agency to the members of his community. Whether or not a community member decides to engage in mental health services may be influenced by key community figures or contact persons who recommend the services. These key figures may be the change agent, but may also be other key figures that the individual holds in regard, and who have perhaps utilized the services themselves.

This analysis of the people influencing an individual's decision of whether or not to engage in services suggests that promoting mental health services which are viewed favorably in a community may increase the initial use of these services. This suggests that creating programs which are consonant with community values may result in the recommendation of these programs throughout a community by figures who have become aware of these programs.

Once services have been initiated, the decision to continue to utilize services or not use them can be influenced by the manner in which the participant perceives the following characteristics: the relative advantage to continue using services versus not using them, the compatibility of the services with existing personal values, the degree of complexity of the services, and how observable the impact of the services is to others. Some of these factors may be more salient to certain individuals than to others.

29. According to this passage, the manner by which individuals come to utilize mental health services can best be understood through:

    A) Social cognitive theory
    B) Elaboration Likelihood model
    C) Operant conditioning
    D) Social constructionism

30. According to this model for mental health service utilization, what would be an effective way to promote mental health service usage within an impoverished community?

    A) Educate doctors about possible services available
    B) Initiate a campaign on TV advertising available services
    C) Promote available services to community leaders
    D) Offer discounted services

31. How might Rogers' initial theory, which Eysenbach applied to mental health services, explain the reluctance of a community to adopt sanitary procedures for consuming water?

    A) The procedures were new to the community
    B) The procedures had multiple steps involved
    C) The procedures were those that would be typically done by someone who was unwell
    D) The entire community was not given specific instructions in the procedures

32. All of the following might encourage someone to continue attending psychotherapy EXCEPT:

    A) Incorporating the client's religious practices into the therapy
    B) Tracking client progress and presenting this progress to the client
    C) Challenging client resistance
    D) Explaining the purpose of techniques in clear language

33. How might the concepts described in this passage explain deviant behavior among youth?

    A) Neurobiological factors contribute to bad choices
    B) Youth with status in a group influence other youth
    C) Youth enjoy the "thrill" of misbehaving
    D) Developmentally, youth are not yet mature enough to make informed decisions

Passage 7

Self-injurious behavior (SIB) refers to a number of behaviors an individual may perpetrate upon himself that can result in harm and which seem to serve no apparent function. Two subtypes of SIB are Compulsive SIB, involving repetitive self-injurious behavior and normally considered an impulse control disorder, and Impulsive SIB, characterized by self-injurious behavior normally done to relieve tension.

Development may influence the way in which SIB arises and in what form it is expressed. For example, disruptions in parent care were associated with impulsive self-cutting behaviors, a type of Impulsive SIB, in children. It was postulated that in these children demonstrating Impulsive SIB, there was a large amount of anger, which could not safely be expressed towards the parents and was instead directed towards themselves. This was supported by the finding that Impulsive SIB tends to be associated with an increased amount of self-punitive ideation.

As an individual employs Impulsive SIB more frequently, it may come to take the form of Compulsive SIB, as behaviors initially performed for relief come to be performed out of a sense of compulsion. Neuroanatomically, it is hypothesized that in Compulsive SIB, much like in Obsessive Compulsive Disorder (OCD), there is dysregulation in the prefrontal cortex-basal ganglia-thalamus pathway. As in OCD, there may be a problem with basal ganglia functioning in those with Compulsive SIB, as supported by findings of smaller than average caudate nucleus in the basal ganglia. The basal ganglia forms a system with the frontal lobes known as the frontostriatal system. When there is perception of some distressing event, the basal ganglia signals the orbitofrontal cortex to address the situation. This system is reliant upon dopamine. Reduced dopamine levels, as has been found in Compulsive SIB, may result in dysfunction in the basal ganglia. In this condition, the basal ganglia does not recognize that the orbitofrontal cortex has been signaled and continues to signal the presence of disruptive stimuli.

In terms of the repetitive actions that are associated with OCD and Compulsive SIB, deficits in the putamen, a part of the basal ganglia also sensitive to dopamine and which has connections to the premotor strip in the frontal cortex, is not able to properly recognize that the motor area has been signaled, resulting in repetitive signals for movement and corresponding repetitive movements. Taken together, the disruptions in the path from the basal ganglia to the orbitofrontal cortex and premotor strip, result in an individual continuously perceiving disruptive stimuli and enacting repetitive behaviors in an attempt to relieve the associated distress. In an individual who has learned to relieve tension through self-injurious behavior, this takes the form of Compulsive SIB.

34. Based on information in the passage, which could be an effective medication to alleviate symptoms of Compulsive SIB?

   A) Dopaminergic antagonist
   B) Dopaminergic agonist
   C) Serotonergic antagonist
   D) Serotonergic agonist

35. Obsessive Compulsive Disorder (OCD) and Self-Injurious Behavior (SIB) share all of the following characteristics EXCEPT:

   A) depleted dopamine levels.
   B) repetitive behaviors.
   C) self-punitive ideation.
   D) basal ganglia dysfunction.

36. Which of the following treatments might be effective in addressing SIB, but not OCD?

   A) Teaching relaxation techniques
   B) Medication to manage brain dysregulation
   C) A behavioral plan to encourage alternative coping skills
   D) Early parent attachment training

37. Which of the following represent causal relationships?

   A) Impulsive SIB and Compulsive SIB
   B) Dopamine depletion and OCD
   C) Early parental abuse and Impulsive SIB
   D) None of the answers can be determined to have a causal relationship

Passage 8

Hallucinations frequently occur in psychotic disorders, such as schizophrenia, or when senses are otherwise altered, such as through drug use. A common cause of hallucinations is brain damage to sensory systems. In Charles Bonnet syndrome the individual has damage to the visual system or between the visual system and the central nervous system. Hallucinations have also been observed in other individuals with brain lesions in their sensory systems.

Hallucinations stemming from damage to sensory systems are different from the types of hallucinations that are experienced by those suffering from psychotic disorders. These types of hallucinations are seen most often in individuals with schizophrenia, who primarily experience auditory hallucinations. The brain area implicated is located on the dorsal superior temporal gyrus. The dorsolateral prefrontal cortex is associated with the sense of auditory awareness being voluntary or involuntary.

Neuroimaging studies consistently find decreased gray matter in the superior temporal gyrus and dorsolateral prefrontal cortex. Because these areas serve in understanding and interpreting language, it follows that dysfunction within them would lead to auditory misinformation in the form of hallucinations. Dysfunction of the dorsolateral prefrontal cortex causes the individual to have trouble distinguishing these perceived auditory stimuli from genuine stimuli.

Findings of reduced frontotemporal activity have been found in those with hallucinations. These individuals have broad deficits in being able to connect disparate information. A type of task that may be difficult for these individuals is being able to interpret the source of stimuli. For example, these individuals had difficulty correctly distinguishing between sensations of being tickled by another person and being tickled by themselves.

A relatively recent treatment to address auditory hallucinations in schizophrenics is transcranial magnetic stimulation (TMS). This procedure involves applying an electromagnetic stimulus to areas of the head to stimulate certain areas of the brain with a magnetic pulse. Researchers have had some success with applying TMS to areas of the temporal lobe to reduce the occurrence of auditory hallucinations.

Researchers investigated the effect TMS had on individuals with schizophrenia who were experiencing auditory hallucinations. They applied TMS to half of the group and used a placebo TMS with the other half. The percent of both groups who experienced auditory hallucinations after receiving treatment are presented as follows:

Table 1 Effect of TMS

Treatment – Received TMS	45%
Control – Didn't receive TMS	89%

The difference between the two groups was significant at $p < .0001$.

38. What hypothesis does the results of the study support?
    A) Temporal lobe defects are symptoms of auditory hallucinations
    B) Auditory hallucinations are symptoms of temporal lobe defects
    C) Auditory hallucinations and temporal lobe defects occur concurrently but are unrelated
    D) Auditory hallucinations are caused by lack of magnetic stimulation

39. What would likely be a distinguishing characteristic of hallucinations in Charles Bonnet syndrome and hallucinations in schizophrenia?
    A) Charles Bonnet syndrome hallucinations do not appear real
    B) An individual with Charles Bonnet hallucinations has difficulty determining if hallucinations are internal or external
    C) An individual with schizophrenic hallucinations may have difficulty determining if visual images are real or not
    D) Schizophrenic hallucinations do not involve damage to sensory processing centers

40. Including the results of the study, which would likely NOT be an effective treatment to address the auditory hallucinations in people with schizophrenia?
    A) TMS
    B) Antipsychotic medication
    C) Stimulant medication
    D) Cognitive Behavioral Therapy for coping with the hallucinations

41. What is NOT a condition in which an individual may experience hallucinations?
    A) Temporal lobe epilepsy
    B) Drug intoxication
    C) Neuroinfections
    D) Attention Deficit Hyperactivity Disorder

These questions are **NOT** related to a passage.

42. According to the functionalist perspective:
    A) aspects of society are interdependent and contribute to macro level functioning
    B) interdependent aspects of society allow micro level observations and conclusions
    C) social change is encouraged
    D) the rich and powerful control the functional aspects of society

43. An individual joins an Internet discussion group relating to Japanese animation. The current group members often post comments containing Japanese words. Eventually, the individual researches the meaning of several Japanese words and starts using them in his own posted comments. This is most closely an example of:
    A) arriving at an acceptance of multiculturalism.
    B) conforming to the norms of a subculture.
    C) group polarization resulting from the interplay between two different perspectives.
    D) an evolving definition of self-concept and identity.

44. The following are all examples of spatial inequality EXCEPT:
    A) The inhabitants of a sparsely populated country on the coast of Europe enjoy a higher standard of living than the inhabitants of an overpopulated country in sub-Saharan Africa.
    B) Lower land values near heavily polluting steel mills result in a lower-income population choosing to live there, which exposes them to greater health risks than those who can afford to live farther from the steel mills.
    C) Increasing crime levels in the central neighborhood of a city prompt higher-income residents to move to the outskirts of the city, or to the suburbs.
    D) A politician denounces undocumented immigrants living in his town's outskirts as being unequal to those living in the town who have legal immigration status.

45. At an elementary school, 12 students who play soccer together and wear the same warm-up jackets get into a schoolyard brawl with 11 students from an ice hockey team who all wear the same team winter coats. From the perspective of one of the soccer players, his teammates are:
    A) an in-group.
    B) an out-group.
    C) a bureaucracy.
    D) a polarized group.

This page intentionally left blank.

Passage 9

One view of ethnocentrism is that it is a natural process, whereby an individual comes to regard his own group with understanding and other groups with suspicion. Therefore, it is probably unrealistic to expect to eradicate ethnocentrism. A more productive goal then would be for people to recognize their ethnocentrism and how it influences them. An important distinction is between flexible ethnocentrism, in which the individual recognizes other viewpoints, and inflexible ethnocentrism, in which an individual cannot understand the viewpoints of others and remains influenced by his own perspective.

The findings of how contact with other cultures influences development of ethnocentrism has been mixed. Some researchers have found that exposure to another culture increases ethnocentrism, while others have found that increased exposure decreases ethnocentrism.

One group of factors that could mediate the relationship is sociocultural factors. Researchers have found that among cultures that value conformity ethnocentrism is typically higher, with individual views of conformity further correlating with individual ethnocentrism. An interesting finding is that feelings of socioeconomic and political security were negatively correlated with ethnocentrism. Thus, in cultures in which individuals don't feel secure there is a tendency to seek safety in an ethnocentric cultural group.

A possible product of ethnocentrism is stereotypes. One way in which stereotypes come to be formed is through selective attention. In selective attention individuals bring a certain amount of their own bias in choosing to what they attend. Often they choose to only attend to information which confirms views that they already have.

Another way in which the individual's views of other cultures is biased is through their moods, in a phenomenon termed mood-congruent bias. In a study, researchers induced happy, sad, or neutral moods in participants of different ethnicities. The participants then rated the mood of individuals of the same or different ethnicity interacting with each other. The ratings were from 1 to 10, with 1 being the saddest up to 10 being the happiest. The researchers found that the participants' mood had an effect on how they rated the interactions they observed, with the participants' moods and the interacting individuals' rating of moods tending to be congruent. This effect was especially pronounced when the individuals they observed interacting were of different ethnicities.

Finally, another factor influencing stereotypes and ethnocentrism is real-world events. Researchers examined the views of a particular ethnic group across three separate times, during peace between their countries, after one of the countries had attacked the other country, and again when the countries were at peace. Researchers evaluated the net number of positive and negative statements the individuals made and averaged them across individuals. The results are presented as follows:

Table 1 Effect of political hostility on ethnocentrism

Before attack	During attack	After attack
+3.5	-4.2	+1.2

46. The combination of Happiness Group membership and Ethnicity Group observed represent what kind of effect?
    A) A unilateral effect
    B) An interaction effect
    C) A nested effect
    D) A single-sided effect

47. Which of the following groups would likely feel the *least* amount of ethnocentrism?
    A) A group who just entered an armed conflict with another nearby group
    B) A group who has high socioeconomic status
    C) A group in which members wearing similar clothing is encouraged
    D) A group that has alternated having political representation with another group

48. The study from which the data in Table 1 is presented represents what kind of research design?
    A) Random controlled trial study
    B) Experimental design
    C) Longitudinal design
    D) Cross-sectional design

49. Which of the following is NOT a reason, in the study cited above, that a campaign in which the positive qualities of the opposite country are promoted would fail to reduce ethnocentrism during times of war?
    A) War permanently changes views
    B) War reduces feelings of security
    C) War changes individuals' moods
    D) Individuals likely will not focus on those messages during war

50. What could be an evolutionary psychology explanation for ethnocentrism?
    A) Group membership helps individuals survive
    B) Ethnocentrism takes many generations to develop
    C) Ethnocentrism is a conscious choice that people make
    D) Ethnocentrism encourages cooperation across groups ensuring better outcomes for all

Passage 10

The choice many adolescents have to join a gang or not join is representative of choices many adolescents must make and involves searching for peer groups, needing to feel safe, trying to establish identity, and making decisions. However, the difference in the choice between joining a gang and other adolescent choices, such as with what friends to associate, is that deciding to join a gang involves higher stakes with more potential for danger and other repercussions.

Joining a peer group is natural during adolescence. A peer group provides companionship and support. Henry Stack Sullivan contended that all people have basic social needs that a peer group serves to fulfill. For adolescents living in gang-infested neighborhoods, peer group options may be limited, thus necessitating joining a gang to meet social needs.

In addition, adolescents feel a need to be safe like anyone else. However, with their increasing autonomy from their parents and their increasing involvement in their neighborhood and with peers, adolescents may feel more of a need to take it upon themselves to provide that safety versus relying on their parents. In a dangerous neighborhood, individual protection may be insufficient; therefore a gang may provide protection for the adolescent.

As an adolescent tries to establish an identity for himself, a big part of his source of identity comes from his peer group. Gangs provide a strong source of identity, with their distinct dress, signals, initiation, and customs. With an individual who does not derive a strong sense of identity from his home, gang identity may prove to be a strong draw. Many people would rather be identified negatively than not be identified at all. In order to identify with the gang, the adolescent must adapt the behavior that the gang has established. Adapting the behavior of the gang might be especially pronounced among adolescents who are high in self-monitoring. Self-monitoring is a strategy individuals use to manage their impressions they give others, by considering how their behavior corresponds to the behavior of their group. Individuals high in self-monitoring will adopt the behavior of the group, even if it seems incongruent with their true beliefs.

In order to assess the presence of self-monitoring among gang members, a study was conducted in which adolescent gang members and non-gang members were rated on self-monitoring. The percent of those groups who were considered to be high self-monitors is presented as follows:

Table 1 Self-monitoring in gang members

Group	% Considered High Self-Monitors
Gang Members	58%
Non-Gang Members	32%

51. According to Kohlberg, what stage of moral development might an adolescent be in if the only deterrent to committing crimes with his gang that he considers is a legal sentence that he might receive?
    A) Obedience and punishment
    B) Interpersonal relationships
    C) Maintaining social order
    D) Social contract and individual rights

52. How might an adolescent view his own deviant behavior if he comes to view his gang as his reference group versus society in general?
    A) He would likely not change his view of his behavior
    B) He would likely view his behavior as more socially appropriate
    C) He would likely view his behavior as less socially appropriate
    D) He would likely not be able to judge his behavior

53. In the dramaturgical perspective, an adolescent behaving in a more aggressive manner when he is with his gang and more non-aggressively when he is at home is demonstrating what type of contrast?
    A) In-group v. out-group
    B) Ethnocentrism v. relativism
    C) Front-stage self v. back-stage self
    D) Central processing v. peripheral route processing

54. In the study in the passage, a chi-square test was used to compare the percent of high self-monitors among adolescents in gangs versus those not in gangs. There was found to be a significant difference. What conclusions can be drawn from this finding?
    A) There is no difference in the percent of self-monitors between adolescents in gangs versus those not in gangs
    B) There is a higher percent of self-monitoring gang members than non-gang members
    C) There is a higher percent of self-monitoring non-gang members than gang members
    D) It is not possible to determine the relationship between self-monitoring and gang status

55. If it was found that trauma is correlated with self-monitoring, what could be conclusively said about the relationship between gang membership and self-monitoring?
    A) There is no relationship between occurrence of trauma and gang membership status
    B) There is higher incidence of trauma among gang members
    C) There is higher incidence of trauma among non-gang members
    D) No conclusions can be made about the incidence of trauma and gang membership without further analysis

These questions are **NOT** related to a passage.

56. A scientist attempting to train a chimpanzee gives the chimpanzee some fruit and leaves to eat every time the chimpanzee organizes blocks into groups of matching color. The training is eventually successful. What role do the fruit and leaves play in this chimpanzee's behavioral training?
    A) Unconditioned stimulus component of classical conditioning.
    B) Conditioned stimulus component of classical conditioning.
    C) Primary reinforcement component of operant conditioning.
    D) Positive reinforcement component of operant conditioning.

57. Which of the following is a hypothesized biological basis of schizophrenia?
    A) Loss of acetylcholine-producing cells in the basal forebrain
    B) Excessive blocking of dopamine receptors
    C) Genetic mutations causing an abnormality in astrocyte glial cells
    D) Norepinephrine from the bloodstream crossing the blood-brain barrier

58. A nomad belongs to a tribal society which is characterized by a strong sense of honor, religious symbolism, and a close-knit nuclear family structure. He has lived his whole life in a desert climate, taking his tent from place to place along with the rest of the tribe and periodically re-assembling it. During his spare time, he sometimes considers whether water from oases can be used to efficiently irrigate the surrounding land. Which best characterizes, in order, what each of these three statements describes?
    A) Symbolic interactionism: Social reality, physical reality, unique reality.
    B) Symbolic interactionism: Unique reality, physical reality, social reality.
    C) Symbolic interactionism: Physical reality, social reality, unique reality.
    D) Symbolic interactionism: Unique reality, social reality, physical reality.

59. A researcher is attempting to teach a bird to flip a particular switch in response to a low tone. He does this by playing a constant, high-pitched tone which is irritating to the bird. When the low tone sounds, the bird may flip the switch. If it does so, the high-pitched tone ceases for five minutes. The researcher:
    A) will not be successful as conditioning requires positive rewards.
    B) is incorrectly applying a principle of positive punishment to train the bird.
    C) would achieve faster results by using a pulsed low-pitch tone rather than a single low-pitch tone.
    D) is using negative reinforcement to encourage the desired response.

This page intentionally left blank.

Section 2 Answers and Explanations

Key					
1	D	21	B	41	D
2	C	22	C	42	A
3	D	23	D	43	B
4	A	24	A	44	D
5	C	25	A	45	A
6	A	26	A	46	B
7	B	27	D	47	B
8	B	28	A	48	C
9	A	29	A	49	A
10	B	30	C	50	A
11	B	31	C	51	A
12	C	32	C	52	B
13	C	33	B	53	C
14	C	34	B	54	B
15	C	35	C	55	D
16	C	36	D	56	D
17	D	37	D	57	C
18	A	38	B	58	A
19	B	39	C	59	D
20	D	40	C		

Passage 1 Explanation

The **implicit association test** assesses for implicit attitudes through a categorization task. Participants are presented with a computer screen displaying **two words** on the left side of the screen and two words on the right. The middle of the screen then flashes a word or image and the participant must click a button to indicate the **appropriate category** as quickly as they can.

Key words: implicit association test, two words, category

A typical set up involves putting the **categories "good"** and **"bad"** on the sides of the screen (left vs. right determined randomly) and then categories like "male" and "female" or "rich" and "poor". After going through several assignments, the category pairings are switched. So for example, a person might click the left button if an image is either "good or male" and the right button if the image is "bad or female" during round 1, and then have to click left for "good or female" and right for "bad or male" during round 2. The **images or words** presented **unequivocally belong** to one of these groups. For example, words like "disgust" or "agony" would be categorized as "bad" by 100% of participants, and the symbol for the men's bathroom would be categorized as "male" by 100% of participants.

Key words: categories, images words

Contrast: contrasting categories, good vs. bad

Cause-and-effect: the words or images to be sorted 100% belong to one of the labels

Researchers hypothesize that **faster response** times indicate an **implicit bias** in favor of the grouping. That is, if a person is able to categorize an image as **"good or male" more quickly** than he is able to categorize an image as "good or female", this reveals an **implicit sexism in favor of males**.

Cause-and-effect: someone's implicit biases will make them react faster when they think the two words go together (e.g. if they are biased against females, they will react faster when "female or bad" are grouped).

The implicit assumption test was made available on the **website** of a prominent university and after several **news stories**, became very popular, with over **150,000 participants** in the span of just a few months. The data showed the following results:

Cause-and-effect: media coverage made the test really popular

	Good	Bad
Slim	751 ms	1003 ms
Fat	1150 ms	633 ms

	Good	Bad
Able	833 ms	998 ms
Disabled	1012 ms	710 ms

Table 1a and 1b The average delay (in milliseconds) that a person took to correctly categorize an image.

Tables 1a and 1b show us that the average response time was faster for "fat and bad" than it was for "fat and good" and that the average response time was faster for "disabled and bad" than it was for "disabled and good", revealing the implicit associations in the participant pool.

1. Which of the following correctly identifies a limitation of the data set used?
    A) The size of the data set prevents the conclusions from having significant statistical power.
    B) Because the test works on implicit associations, it is unable to provide insight about those who are consciously biased.
    C) Recruitment through media discussion of the test, without the usual small payment to participants, means the data set would skew towards much higher ends of the socioeconomic ladder.
    D) <u>The self-selection of participants prevents the data from being generalizable to any particular population.</u>

The study had a huge pool of self-selected participants. Because the researchers could not control for (or always know) the demographic data of the participants, it limits their ability to generalize the data to any particular subset or population.

A: The sample size was huge, making choice A the opposite of what happened.
B: While the test is not one of explicit biases, that is not a limitation in the study. A study of implicit biases is not obliged to also be a test of explicit biases.
C: We have no reason to think that participants were necessarily unusually high on the socioeconomic ladder.

2. The procedure described in the passage should also include each of the following EXCEPT:
    A) One or more training rounds in which the person only needs to categorize an image as "good" vs. "bad", rather than having to be aware of two distinct categorizations at once.
    B) Controls in which the two categories have no meaningful connection (implicit or otherwise), such as "up or red" vs. "down or green".
    C) <u>Recruitment procedures to guarantee that equal numbers of male and female participants are gathered.</u>
    D) Subsequent data analysis that discards outlying data points as irrelevant (e.g. a latency of 150,000 ms that suggests the person got up and left the computer in the middle of the test).

Choices A, B, and D all describe standard procedures that would be a part of a good study protocol. Since the test hinges on very fast reactions (measuring in milliseconds), participants must be trained on the basics of selecting left and right (choice A). In addition, good controls would allow researchers to ensure that any biases are not simply due to lateralization of the categories (choice B), and any outlier data points that don't demonstrate meaningful participant in the experiment should also be discarded (choice D).

A research protocol is not obliged to study exactly equal numbers of males and females (after all, it'd be hard to image a prostate cancer study involving any females!).

3. The results from the experiment indicate that:
    A) no implicit associations are associated with able-bodied versus disabled people.
    B) study participants demonstrated a stronger implicit preference for slimness than against able bodied people.
    C) a self-selected participant pool is more likely to have implicit biases than the general population.
    D) <u>study participants demonstrated a stronger implicit preference against fat people than against disabled people.</u>
The two tables show us that the participants had strong implicit biases against fat and disability. Looking at the numbers, we see that people responded faster to the "fat and bad" grouping than they did to the "disabled and bad" grouping. They also responded slower to "fat and good" than they did "disabled and good". Taken together, this data suggests a stronger negative implicit bias against fat than against disability.

4. If study participants feel a mild sensation of disgust in response to a word or image associated with disabled people, the Cannon-Bard theory of emotion would assert that:

    A) the physiological arousal and emotional sensation of disgust arise separately and independently in separated areas of the brain.

    B) the emotion is the result of the brain assessing the context of the physiological arousal experienced in the body.

    C) the emotion follows from and is directly caused by the physiological arousal experienced.

    D) the emotion is a cognitive response which then causes autonomic reflexes generating the feeling of the affect.

The Cannon-Bard theory of emotion posits that the physiological arousal associated with the emotion and the subjective feeling of the emotion itself arise from separate and independent areas of the brain. This most closely matches choice A.

B: This is more like the Schacter-Singer theory.
C: This is the James-Lange theory of emotion.

5. The test is assessing:

    A) unconscious discrimination.

    B) conscious discrimination.

    C) unconscious prejudice.

    D) conscious stereotypes.

Because the test is one of implicit biases, we can eliminate choices B and D right off the bat. Discrimination is a behavior, not an attitude or idea, making choice A wrong as well. By process of elimination, we're left with choice C.

Passage 2 Explanation

Individuals may experience only a limited number of schizophrenic episodes, but a number go on to experience lifelong schizophrenia. **Schizophrenia represents only 2% of all mental health disorders, yet consumes 20-40% of mental health resources**. Because of the far-reaching consequences of the disease, health professionals have sought strategies for managing schizophrenia early in its course, when it is hoped that **long-term individual impairment and costs can be minimized**. Researchers have attempted to identify individuals who can be targeted for **early intervention**. Some have proposed that there be a **diagnosis called "Prodromal Schizophrenia" (PS)** to identify individuals who meet criteria for being likely to go on to develop schizophrenia. Two physicians presented their views on the PS diagnosis.

Key terms: Schizophrenia, prodromal schizophrenia
Cause and effect: the overwhelming cost and debilitating nature of schizophrenia is leading people to seek earlier intervention.

Physician X: A PS diagnosis identifies people who may go on to develop full schizophrenia. **By identifying these people early, there exists the potential to better treat them**. There are a number of treatments that could help them in avoiding developing schizophrenia.

Brain imaging studies also provide support for the usefulness of this diagnosis. **Brain studies have shown differences in the brains** of those who later go on to develop schizophrenia from brains of those who don't. Specifically, there have been findings of **decreased gray matter and hippocampal volume**.

Opinion: Physician X believes PS should be a diagnosis because brain studies show a physical basis for schizophrenia and early treatment will be better.

Physician Y: Many of those diagnosed with PS **do not go on to develop full psychosis. Children** exhibit symptoms which **could be mistaken** for symptoms of schizophrenia, including bizarre thoughts, mild hallucinations, and disorganized appearance. Diagnosing schizophrenia can be difficult as well, given that there are a variety of presentations, symptoms can be ambiguous, and those with the disorder may not be good informants. Clinicians typically rely on obtaining a history of individuals suspected of having schizophrenia and consider the presence of these symptoms over time. Given that the age of onset of schizophrenia is typically late adolescence and early adulthood, **PS would likely emerge at an even younger age** than that. That would result in clinicians being unable to obtain as full a history as when diagnosing schizophrenia and would also complicate distinguishing what might be age appropriate for youth from symptoms of fledgling schizophrenia.

For people who would not otherwise go on to develop schizophrenia, receiving a diagnosis like PS could be detrimental to their psychological well-being.

Opinion: Physician Y thinks that diagnosing PS would be difficult and would cause big problems through false diagnoses.

A study was conducted with 250 participants who had been referred for psychiatric treatment at a local hospital. The participants were **interviewed and assessed for the presence of PS**. The researchers did not inform the participants of the findings, but **contacted them again 10 years later** to ascertain if they had received a diagnosis of schizophrenia during that time.

Figure 1 Study results

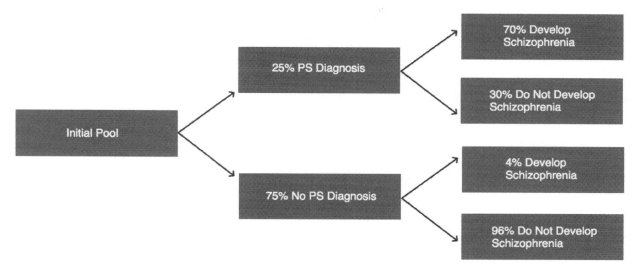

Figure 1 shows the results of the experiment. We see that when people do not receive the PS diagnosis, there is a 96% chance that they do not have the disease, but when 25% do receive the diagnosis, there is only a 70% that they will develop schizophrenia.

6. The 30% of the people in the study who received the PS diagnosis, but did not go on to develop schizophrenia represents what kind of error?

    A) **Type I False Positive**
    B) Type II False Negative
    C) Type III True Positive
    D) Type IV True Negative

    Answer: A – Concluding that there is a relationship, when in fact there is not, is a false positive. Concluding there is not a relationship, when there is, is a false negative.

7. What is the term for someone being given a label and then being more likely to become that label due to expectations?

    A) Cognitive dissonance
    B) **Self-fulfilling prophecy**
    C) Fundamental attribution error
    D) Stereotype threat

    Answer: B – Self-fulfilling prophecy, the expectation that someone has for himself can lead to him being more likely to become that

8. Which of the following is NOT an argument for the prodromal schizophrenia diagnosis?

    A) Potential long-term cost savings
    B) **Diagnosing schizophrenia can be difficult**
    C) There seems to be a biological path from PS to schizophrenia
    D) The number of early treatments available

Answer: B – The diagnostic confusion of schizophrenia is an argument against diagnosing PS as its criteria is likely even more unclear.

9. In the study, the 70% of the participants who had received the PS diagnosis who then went on to develop schizophrenia refers to what aspect of a test?

A) **<u>Sensitivity</u>**
B) Specificity
C) Reliability
D) Validity

Answer: A – Sensitivity refers to a test's ability to correctly identify those people that are intended to be identified, in this case those with PS who will go on to develop schizophrenia.

Passage 3 Explanation

Anxiety is a disorder that is estimated to affect 10-20% of all children and adolescents. One subtype of anxiety is **Generalized Anxiety Disorder (GAD)**. To meet the criteria for this disorder a person must exhibit **excessive anxiety** and worry for at least 6 months, find it **difficult to control** this worry, exhibit **somatic** symptoms, and be caused **distress** by the anxiety. Many children with GAD worry about topics, such as harm, that will befall them, their level of performance, or the future. These children are often **self-conscious**, over-estimate the likelihood of **negative events** occurring, and **underestimate** their ability to **cope** with difficulties.

Key terms: Generalized Anxiety Disorder (GAD)
Cause and effect: GAD makes it difficult to control excessive, distressing anxiety and leads to physical symptoms

In terms of the **etiology** of GAD, a number of factors may combine to dispose a child to develop the disorder. First, the child may have a **heritable** biological diathesis to developing GAD. This is supported by the higher incidence of family members of people with GAD also having GAD themselves. Parents who display an **anxious style** may influence the formation of anxiety in their children, as well, through **modeling**. The children may also come to share their **parent's beliefs** about the world being an insecure place. Parents may also influence their children developing anxiety through their attachment style. Parents exhibiting **high control with little warmth** or lack of parental care tended to have more anxious children.

Cause and effect: GAD is associated with genetics, modeling anxious style, taking up parent's beliefs, and with parents who are controlling

Also, **temperament** plays a role in predisposing some to develop GAD. Children who display an **inhibited** style of temperament in which they are shy, quiet, and introverted tend to display this style throughout childhood. There is a significant correlation between inhibition and occurrence of GAD. In addition, children who tend to display **negative affect and physiological hyperarousal** as temperament characteristics tend to develop GAD later.

Cause and effect: GAD is associated with inhibited temperament, negative affect, and physiological hyperarousal

In terms of **psychosocial** risk factors among children with GAD, there tends to be a feeling of low control that mediates the relationship between **stressful events and negative affect**. This sequence may often develop as a result of experiencing many events that are uncontrollable in life. However, this feeling of uncontrollability is then learned and surfaces at later events that may be controllable. This sequence then perpetuates itself upon subsequent events with the child **developing a learned helplessness** style of interacting with the world.

Cause and effect: Stressful events lead to feelings of low control which then cause negative emotions; repeated feelings of low control lead to helplessness

Figure 1 Factors affecting GAD development

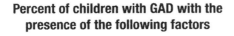

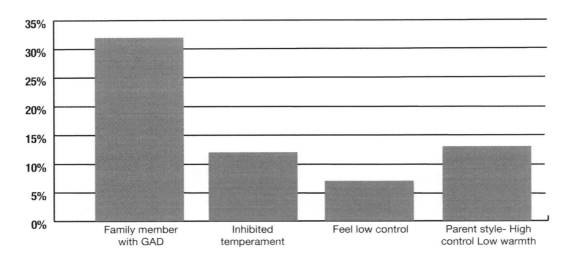

Percent of children with GAD with the presence of the following factors

10. Which of the following is NOT an environmental cause of GAD in children?
    A) Parental modeling of an anxious style
    B) **The heritability of GAD from parents**
    C) Low warmth in parenting
    D) Learned helplessness

    Answer: B – Heritability of disorders is an intrinsic cause of disorders. It is nature in the nature v. nurture debate.

11. What parenting style is associated with increased prevalence of GAD in children?
    A) Permissive
    B) **Authoritarian**
    C) Authoritative
    D) Ambivalent

    Answer: B – The authoritarian parenting style is characterized by high control and low warmth, factors related to the development of GAD.

12. All of the following evidence would further support that GAD is heritable EXCEPT:
    A) 33% prevalence among children whose biological parents have GAD and who are raised by foster parents
    B) Lessened prevalence of GAD amongst more distant family than immediate family
    C) **Having a style of GAD that is very similar to one's parents**
    D) Monozygotic twins having a higher correlation of GAD than dizygotic twins

    Answer: C – All of the other factors support the heritability of GAD. Having a similar style of GAD as one's parents could be learned.

13. What of the following findings would be supported in the relationship between stressful events and negative affect among children with GAD?

    A) A direct relationship – Stressful event and high negative affect

    B) A direct relationship – Stressful event and low negative affect

    C) **<u>An indirect relationship – Stressful event, feeling low control, and high negative affect</u>**

    D) An indirect relationship – Stressful event, being inhibited, and high negative affect

Answer: C – The passage states that feeling low control mediates the relationship between a stressful event and negative affect. Answer C illustrates this mediating relationship.

These questions are **NOT** related to a passage.

14. One limitation of the symbolic interactionism perspective is:
    A) disregard for use of symbols
    B) limited significance of face-to-face interactions
    C) **lack of analysis on the macro level**
    D) lack of analysis on the micro level

The symbolic interactionism perspective suggests that people attach meanings to symbols, and subsequent actions rely on interpretation of these symbols. Face-to-face interactions are a cornerstone of symbolic interaction. However, since the interactions are face-to-face, some critics argue that the perspective does not apply to macro-observations of society as a whole.

A: Symbols are integral to symbolic interactionism.
B: Face-to-face interactions are a cornerstone of symbolic interactionism.
D: In contrast with functionalism and conflict theory, symbolic interactionism focuses on the micro level.

15. The following are all examples of social stratification EXCEPT:
    A) The son of a wealthy real estate developer finds it easy to gain an important position in the real estate industry.
    B) Senior citizens find that they prefer to associate with people their own age.
    C) **An immigrant uses a college education to achieve a higher annual income level than her parents.**
    D) A number of women executives who experience difficulty in rising through the ranks of a male-dominated corporation react by starting a company of their own.

Rather than describing social stratification, choice (C) describes upward social mobility where an individual shifts from one class level to another.

A: This demonstrates a social status being passed from parent to child. This is an example of social reproduction, which is one aspect of social stratification.
B: This is an example of how people in the same age group may tend to remain in the same social groups as one another, and describes an intersection of social stratification with age.
D: This is an example of the intersection of gender with social stratification, and describes a situation that leads to increased social separation between gender groups.

16. A teenager who has recently moved to the tropics finds that he gets sunburned every time he walks home from school during midday, but not when he walks to school in the early morning. After a few weeks have gone by, he starts putting on sunscreen, both before he leaves for school in the morning and before he leaves for home at midday. The fact that he puts on sunscreen before his early-morning walk to school is an example of:
    A) Context stimuli affecting behavior.
    B) Discriminative stimuli affecting behavior.
    C) **Generalization of an escape or avoidance stimulus.**
    D) Discrimination response to an escape or avoidance stimulus.

An escape or avoidance stimulus is one which provokes an escape or avoidance behavior to end the stimulus – in this case, the behavioral response constitutes adding sunscreen to end the sunburning. Often, this escape or avoidance response can generalize to similar stimuli – in this case, to early-morning sun in addition to midday sun. (C) is therefore the correct answer.

A: Context stimuli are those which are present continuously during conditioning. Examples might be houses or landmarks that the teenager passes on his way to and from school, or the interior of his house while he is treating his sunburns. However, there is no indication here that his behavior is affected by any of these.
B: Discriminative stimuli are those which reinforce a particular response when present. Here, sunburns serve as a discriminative stimulus – however, the question asked only about why he puts on sunscreen before the early-morning walk, not why he puts on sunscreen at all. (C) is the better answer for this reason.
D: There is indeed an escape or avoidance stimulus, namely sunburning. However, a discrimination response would be one in which a specific stimulus provokes a given response while other stimuli do not provoke that response. Here, two different stimuli provoke the same response – putting on sunscreen.

17. Three brothers: Bob the accountant, Joe the plumber, and Dan the dot.com multi-millionaire, belong to which social strata:
   A) middle class, lower class, upper class
   B) middle class, middle class, middle class
   C) working class, lower class, middle class
   D) **middle class, working class, upper class**

The lower class is characterized by unemployment, poverty, and lack of education. The working class consists of less-educated people who may perform skilled or unskilled work, including blue collar workers and tradesmen; their work is often less prestigious than "middle class" work. The middle class consists of white collar workers who usually have more money and education than people from the working class, but less money than people from the upper class. The upper class are exceedingly rich with far more money than they could ever spend.

A: Joe the plumber is from the working class rather than the lower class.
B: Joe the plumber is from the working class and Dan the dot.com multi-millionaire is from the upper class.
C: Bob the accountant is from the middle class, Joe the plumber is from the working class, and Dan the dot.com multi-millionaire is from the upper class.

Passage 4 Explanation

An advertising company has evaluated the **performance** of its advertising **sales department**.

Table 1 Company metrics from last quarter

Metric	Change over quarter
Employee Retention	-12%
Employee Motivation	-8%
Complaints Filed	+6%
Sales	-7%

Table 1 shows us that the sales department's performance is poor. More complaints are being filed, and employee retention and motivation is down.

To **improve performance** and increase productivity, an **executive** has proposed the following plan:

Opinion: The execute believes he can improve company performance through a number of initiatives

Dear colleagues,

To increase our competitiveness, I have devised the following plan to be implemented among the sales staff to increase performance. It is based on the following foundations to explain motivation:

Expectancy Theory: In this theory, employees are motivated when:
    i. a certain amount of **effort** will lead to a certain level of **performance;**
    ii. this performance level will lead to **particular outcomes; and**
    iii. these outcomes are **desirable**

Key terms: the expectancy theory hinges on effort towards desirable outcomes

Goal Setting Theory: Goal setting theory will help the department set goals that are productive for the employees. Goal setting theory states that effective goals should be **difficult, specific, and relevant**. It also emphasizes regular **feedback**.

Key terms: The Goal Setting theory says that employees should be given difficult, specific, relevant goals with regular feedback.

Equity Theory: Finally, in order to balance performance with rewards, equity theory will be considered. It posits that an employee is motivated to achieve **balance between work and reward relative** to some referent. The individual considers an ideal work-reward balance and how to achieve that balance based on some referent. The referent could be a company policy or another individual. Equity is achieved when the **employee's work-reward ratio is perceived to be congruent with his expected work-reward ratio based on the referent.**

Key terms: Equity theory's balance between work and reward is based on reference to some benchmark (such as other employees).

I suggest the following reward system be implemented:
    i. Employees will each have a sales goal that **managers will know**, but the **employees will not**.
    ii. Reward employees with a bonus only **after they reach their goals**, but **randomly select which times** to reward them, so as not to spend too much money rewarding them every time.
    iii. The bonuses earned throughout the year will be **paid at the end of the sales year**.

Opinion: The sales executive thinks he will increase sales with a plan including these three aspects.

18. What type of operant conditioning reinforcement procedure is being utilized in the proposed reward system?
    A) **Positive reinforcement**
    B) Negative reinforcement
    C) Positive punishment
    D) Negative punishment

    Answer: A – Positive reinforcement occurs when some behavior (meeting the sales goal) is then rewarded with something reinforcing (being paid a bonus).19. Upon reviewing the performance from the previous to current quarter, it was found that employees were paid a straight commission during the past quarter. In what way might this system have impacted performance?

19. Upon reviewing the performance from the previous to current quarter, it was found that employees were paid a commission based solely on total sales dollars during the past quarter. In what way might this system have impacted performance?
    A) The commission policy was not a good referent
    B) **Competition was increased, leading to decreased morale**
    C) The rewards boosted productivity
    D) The feedback from the commissions were erratic

    Answer: B – It is likely that in this competitive environment, employees felt lowered morale from having to compete against each other, causing decreased productivity.

20. What type of reward system is proposed in the executive's plan?
    A) Fixed interval
    B) Variable interval
    C) Fixed ratio
    D) **Variable ratio**

    Answer: D – Giving rewards after a random amount of successes is a variable ratio reward system. An interval system consists of giving rewards after an amount of time, such as during certain holidays. Note that the bonuses are earned on a variable ratio schedule, even if the money itself isn't distributed until the end of the year, as point iii states.

21. If the executive's plan works and the employees become motivated by his plan, what could be the effect of reducing the incentives later, compared with a reduction following a system based on rewarding the employees after every time they met a goal?
    A) Productivity will drop quicker

B) **Productivity will drop slower**
C) Productivity will increase quicker
D) Productivity will increase slower

Answer: B – Productivity will drop when an incentive is phased out. However, it will drop slower when the reward is given after a variable ratio, compared with if the reward is given after a continuous reward schedule.

Passage 5 Explanation

People's approach to death has been an increasingly studied topic in psychology, with the goal of **making this transition more comfortable** for individuals. Culture has a large impact on how death is viewed by an individual. A culture's **death ethos**, or approach and attitude towards death, can be inferred from observing that culture's rituals, such as art and traditions that are related to death. A salient aspect of a culture's death ethos is that culture's view of **death's desirability**, whether it is considered sacred or profane, or welcome or unwanted. Throughout the West, the meaning of death has fluctuated over time, with death viewed primarily as an end of life during the scientific-minded **Renaissance Age**. During the **Romantic Age** in the 1800's, death was glorified and there was an emphasis on achieving a noble death. More recently, in the 20th century death came to be **something to be avoided**, with much focus on medical methods to prolong life.

Key terms: death ethos, Renaissance age, Romantic age, 20th century
Contrast: various ways death was viewed in different times and cultures

Kubler-Ross conceptualized the 5 stages of dying. In the first stage, the individual experiences **denial** upon realizing he will soon die. The individual then experiences the second stage, **anger**. During this stage the individual understands that he will die, but feels cheated out of remaining life. This leads to the third stage, **bargaining**, in which the individual attempts to negotiate prolonged life with God or whatever other entity the individual feels is responsible. The fourth stage is **depression**, in which the death is recognized as being inevitable. The individual experiences a sense of loss of his own unrealized experiences. The final stage is **acceptance.** During this stage the individual comes to realize that death is a natural process. This acceptance may provide comfort and relief during the final stages.

Key terms: Kubler-Ross
Opinion: Kubler-Ross constructed a five-stage process of dying/grief.

The conceptualization of dying in this process lends to the **formulation of interventions** to assist the dying individual through the process. Kubler-Ross emphasized that the dying person should be allowed to **talk openly** through the process with cared persons and health care professionals. The emotions that become prominent during each stage should be allowed to be expressed in order for the individual to fully address the themes of each stage. The 5 stages of dying model is **not** intended to be taken as an **invariant** process. Individuals may proceed through the stages in varying manners, skipping some stages or going through others in **different sequences**.

Opinion: Patients need to be allowed to express their emotions associated with dying; people can move through the Kubler-Ross stages in different sequences.

Bereavement is the process individuals experience as they process the death of a loved one. Researchers **assessed levels of depression**, via a depression inventory, which produced a z-score of depression level. Individuals were assessed before they became widowed and at 6 and 13 months after they became widowed. The researchers found patterns in bereavement among the individuals that they studied, which they classified into **4 patterns** of bereavement.

Opinion: Bereavement creates different patterns of grief and levels of depression.

Figure 1 Bereavement styles and depression level

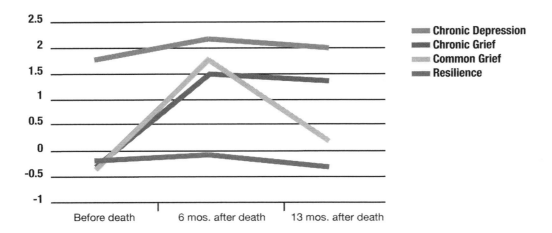

Figure 1 shows us the level of depression in each of the four styles of bereavement.

22. Which of the following bereavement styles might be most common in a culture which views death as a natural phenomenon?
    A) Chronic depression
    B) Chronic grief
    C) **Resilience**
    D) Culture doesn't impact bereavement

    Answer: C – In a culture in which dying is considered to be a natural process it is less likely that a death would lead to prolonged feelings of grief.

23. Individuals who have successfully resolved Erikson's ego integrity v. despair stage are more likely to have achieved what stage in the 5 stage model of dying?
    A) Anger
    B) Bargaining
    C) Depression
    D) **Acceptance**

    Answer: D – Those who have achieved ego integrity have reviewed their life and have found that they have lived a fulfilled life. These individuals have likely come to accept their own death.

24. How might the 5 stages of dying model be applied to assist those individuals in bereavement?
    A) **Encourage bereaving individuals to talk about their experiences**
    B) Encourage bereaving individuals to proceed through the 5 step model in sequence
    C) Encourage bereaving individuals to achieve ego integrity about the deceased individual
    D) Recognize that individuals with chronic depression are likely still in the depression stage

    Answer: A – The 5 stages of dying model is intended to be used as a framework for processing the experiences and emotions individuals have about dying.

25. Individuals fearing death because they can easily recount sensational media accounts of disturbing deaths illustrate what process of conceptualizing information?

    A) **<u>Availability heuristic</u>**
    B) Fundamental attribution error
    C) Intuition
    D) Anchoring heuristic

Answer: A – The availability heuristic refers to people more easily recalling information that is more prominent, such as if it has been sensationalized in media.

These questions are **NOT** related to a passage.

26. Two adult siblings, who act and speak cordially to each other when in public, sometimes use raised voices and unrestrained behavior when the only observers present are family members. This is best explained by:
    A) **The difference between front-stage and back-stage selves.**
    B) The role of culture in shaping expression.
    C) The intersection of prestige with social status.
    D) Conflict theory as applied to the norms of a family's structural functionalism.

Front-stage and back-stage theory states that persons will behave according to different sets of rules in different social settings; specifically, persons will shape their behavior differently depending on their "audience." This most closely matches choice (A).

B: This is not the ideal answer because it would assume that the siblings move between different cultures or sub-cultures when they switch between being in public and not being in public, which may not be the case. Additionally, the role of culture in shaping expression is usually more of a long-term phenomenon, and here the changes in the siblings' behavior take place here over the short term.

C: It is plausible that the siblings might be motivated by prestige or by the desire to retain social status; however, the prompt provides no specific evidence of this, and other factors such as introversion could be playing more of a role. Since information about the causes of their behavior is speculative, the only thing that is clear is that there are behavioral differences here between outside-the-family behavior and inside-the-family behavior. Choice A best describes this dynamic.

D: Conflict theory relates to the inequality between two groups in society, and the conflicts between these groups to which this inequality leads – no such two conflicting groups are described in the prompt. Also, structural functionalism theory indicates that certain structures, such as families, will help the different components of society to function together in a stable manner. Here, though, the siblings feel free to be less stable – not more – when in their family environment.

27. A group of adolescent males, who usually wear earth tones or other similar colors, snicker at and tease a group member who wears light purple shirts. Eventually, the group member switches to a more earth-toned wardrobe. What best describes this situation?
    A) Diversity as a cause of evolving norms and rituals.
    B) The role of class as a factor that contributes to prejudice.
    C) The effect of dramaturgical inclinations affecting behavior in different situations.
    D) **The use of peer pressure and stigma to induce a change in deviant behavior.**

Here, the deviant behavior in question – wearing a differently colored shirt than is the norm – is discouraged by the actions of the teen's peer group, specifically peer pressure to conform, and the creation of a stigma against the light purple-colored shirt.

A: Here, it is more the reverse – the group's norms remain in place, and they eventually cause conformity in behavior, which is the opposite of diverse behavior.

B: This is not correct because the prompt contains no information about whether or not the group members belong to different social or economic classes.

C: Dramaturgical inclinations would cause a difference between front-stage and back-stage behavior – essentially, different behaviors for different audiences. Here, though, the "audience" remains the same, so dramaturgical theory does not apply.

28. In the classic series of children's books, "Where's Waldo?" the child is presented with a huge, colorful image filled with characters and objects, and must search through the image looking for a particular character wearing a red and white striped shirt. This exercise represents what sort of sensory processing set up?

    A) <u>Unimodal stimuli and top-down processing</u>
    B) Unimodal stimuli and bottom-up processing
    C) Multimodal stimuli and top-down processing
    D) Multimodal stimuli and bottom-up processing

In a "Where's Waldo" book the stimuli are all visual, meaning the stimulus is a single mode. This lets us eliminate choices C and D. Since the child is taking in the visual image and processing it at a higher level, interpreting the information and seeking out a particular character, this would be top-down processing of sensory information. Thus choice A is correct.

Passage 6 Explanation

The process of **encouraging** individuals to initially **utilize mental health services** and continue to use them can be viewed as containing several steps and choices the client and his family make about whether or not to utilize services. **Eysenbach** applied a process **Rogers** formulated, regarding the general adaptation and use of innovations, to the utilization of mental health services within a community. This process consists of, **first, a diffusion of awareness** of the service to prospective clients, normally through **change agents**, or those people with contact with both the service and the community. An example of a change agent is a worker at a community mental health center, with ties to a particular neighborhood. This change agent might promote services available at his agency to the members of his community. Whether or not a community member decides to engage in mental health services may be influenced by key community figures or contact persons who recommend the services. These key figures may be the change agent, but may also be other key figures that the individual holds in regard, and who have perhaps utilized the services themselves.

Key terms: Eysenbach, Rogers, change agents
Cause and effect: to cause people to use mental health services you must first have a change agent or make people aware of those services

This analysis of the people influencing an individual's decision of whether or not to engage in services suggests that promoting mental health services which are **viewed favorably** in a community may increase the initial use of these services. This suggests that creating programs which are **consonant with community values** may result in the recommendation of these programs throughout a community by figures who have become aware of these programs.

Cause and effect: to get people to use mental health services, those services should be viewed favorably and should fit with the community's values

Once services have been initiated, the decision to **continue to utilize** services or not use them can be influenced by the manner in which the participant perceives the following characteristics: the relative **advantage** to continue using services versus not using them, the compatibility of the services with existing **personal values**, the degree of **complexity** of the services, and how observable the **impact** of the services is to others. Some of these factors may be more salient to certain individuals than to others.

Cause and effect: people will continue to use services based on a number of factors

29. According to this passage, the manner by which individuals come to utilize mental health services can best be understood through:
    A) **Social cognitive theory**
    B) Elaboration Likelihood model
    C) Operant conditioning
    D) Social constructionism

    Answer: A – Social cognitive theory suggests that people learn much of their behavior through observing individuals around them. Choosing to use mental health services because an individual sees another person using them is an example of this.

30. According to this model for mental health service utilization, what would be an effective way to promote mental health service usage within an impoverished community?
    A) Educate doctors about possible services available
    B) Initiate a campaign on TV advertising available services
    C) **Promote available services to community leaders**
    D) Offer discounted services

    Answer: C – According to this model, change agents or key community figures can be helpful in promoting mental health service usage in a community.

31. How might Rogers' initial theory, which Eysenbach applied to mental health services, explain the reluctance of a community to adopt sanitary procedures for consuming water?
    A) The procedures were new to the community
    B) The procedures had multiple steps involved
    C) **The procedures were similar to those that would be typically done by someone who was viewed as mentally unwell**
    D) The entire community was not given specific instructions in the procedures

    Answer: C – As specified in the passage, behaviors that are adopted by a community should be consonant with the community's values. In this situation, the new procedures would look like behaviors that the community associates with mental illness ("You want me to do what? That's what a crazy person does!"), which would lead to a reluctance in the community to adopt these procedures.

32. All of the following might encourage someone to continue attending psychotherapy EXCEPT:
    A) Incorporating the client's religious practices into the therapy
    B) Tracking client progress and presenting this progress to the client
    C) **Challenging client resistance**
    D) Explaining the purpose of techniques in clear language

    Answer: C – The last paragraph of the passage lists factors which are likely to contribute to a client continuing to use mental health services, which answers A,B, and D are examples of.

33. How might the concepts described in this passage explain deviant behavior among youth?
    A) Neurobiological factors contribute to bad choices
    B) **Youth with status in a group influence other youth**
    C) Youth enjoy the "thrill" of misbehaving
    D) Developmentally, youth are not yet mature enough to make informed decisions

    Answer: B – In this answer, the youth with status are the "change agents" that influence other group members to engage in deviant behavior.

Passage 7 Explanation

Self-injurious behavior (SIB) refers to a number of behaviors an individual may perpetrate upon himself that can result in harm and which seem to serve no apparent function. Two subtypes of SIB are **Compulsive** SIB, involving repetitive self-injurious behavior and normally considered an **impulse control** disorder, and **Impulsive** SIB, characterized by self-injurious behavior normally done to **relieve tension**.

Key Terms: Self-injurious behavior (SIB); Compulsive SIB, Impulsive SIB

Development may influence the way in which SIB arises and in what form it is expressed. For example, **disruptions in parent care** were associated with **impulsive self-cutting** behaviors, a type of Impulsive SIB, in children. It was postulated that in these children demonstrating Impulsive SIB, there was a large amount of **anger**, which could not safely be expressed towards the parents and was instead directed towards themselves. This was supported by the finding that Impulsive SIB tends to be associated with an increased amount of self-punitive ideation.

Cause and effect: anger and disruptions in parental care lead to self-cutting

As an individual employs **Impulsive** SIB **more frequently**, it may come to take the form of **Compulsive** SIB, as behaviors initially performed for relief come to be performed out of a sense of compulsion. Neuroanatomically, it is hypothesized that in Compulsive SIB, much like in Obsessive Compulsive Disorder (OCD), there is dysregulation in the **prefrontal cortex-basal ganglia-thalamus pathway**. As in OCD, there may be a problem with basal ganglia functioning in those with Compulsive SIB, as supported by findings of **smaller** than average **caudate nucleus** in the basal ganglia. The basal ganglia forms a system with the frontal lobes known as the **frontostriatal** system. When there is perception of some distressing event, the basal ganglia signals the orbitofrontal cortex to address the situation. This system is reliant upon dopamine. **Reduced dopamine** levels, as has been found in Compulsive SIB, may result in **dysfunction** in the basal ganglia. In this condition, the basal ganglia does not recognize that the orbitofrontal cortex has been signaled and **continues to signal** the presence of **disruptive** stimuli.

Key terms: prefrontal cortex, basal ganglia, caudate nucleus, dopamine
Cause and effect: frequent impulsive SIB can lead to compulsive SIB; low dopamine levels and a small caudate nucleus continue to send distress signals when they shouldn't, leading to SIB.

In terms of the **repetitive actions** that are associated with OCD and Compulsive SIB, the **putamen**, a part of the basal ganglia also sensitive to dopamine and which has connections to the **premotor strip** in the frontal cortex, is not able to properly recognize that the motor area has been signaled, resulting in repetitive signals for movement and corresponding repetitive movements. Taken together, the **disruptions in the path** from the basal ganglia to the orbitofrontal cortex and premotor strip, result in an individual **continuously perceiving disruptive stimuli and enacting repetitive behaviors** in an attempt to relieve the associated distress. In an individual who has learned to relieve tension through self-injurious behavior, this takes the form of Compulsive SIB.

Key terms: putamen, premotor strip
Cause and effect: problems with the link between the putamen and the premotor strip make a person engage in the repetitive behaviors of OCD and SIB

34. Based on information in the passage, which could be an effective medication to alleviate symptoms of Compulsive SIB?

    A) Dopaminergic antagonist
    B) **Dopaminergic agonist**
    C) Serotonergic antagonist
    D) Serotonergic agonist

Answer: B – According to the passage, lowered dopamine levels may result in disruption in the function of the basal ganglia, a mechanism involved in Compulsive SIB. Therefore, a medication which mimics elevated dopamine levels, a dopaminergic agonist, should be effective in alleviating this disorder.

35. Obsessive Compulsive Disorder (OCD) and Self-Injurious Behavior (SIB) share all of the following characteristics EXCEPT:

    A) depleted dopamine levels.
    B) repetitive behaviors.
    C) **self-punitive ideation.**
    D) basal ganglia dysfunction.

Answer: C – According to the passage, SIB is associated with increased self-punitive ideation, while not necessarily with OCD.

36. Which of the following treatments might be effective in addressing SIB, but not OCD?

    A) Teaching relaxation techniques
    B) Medication to manage brain dysregulation
    C) A behavioral plan to encourage alternative coping skills
    D) **Early parent attachment training**

Answer: D – According to the passage, SIB, especially Impulsive SIB, is associated with disruptions in parent care. Therefore, interventions which encourage effective parent care, such as healthy attachments, may lessen the likelihood of SIB developing.

37. Which of the following pairs of terms represent a cause and an effect (rather than correlations) as determined by the passage?

    A) Impulsive SIB and Compulsive SIB
    B) Dopamine depletion and OCD
    C) Early parental abuse and Impulsive SIB
    D) **None of the answers can be determined to have a causal relationship**

Answer: D – Although the passage described items in answer choices A-C as having associations, there was not conclusive evidence presented that causal relationships existed. Here, the MCAT is asking us to know the principle, "correlation does not prove causation". Don't confuse "cause and effect relationship" as a strategy for MCAT reading (where we look for linkages between terms in the passage) with an actual scientifically proven cause. In psychology and sociology, researchers much more often prove correlations rather than definitive causes.

Passage 8 Explanation

Hallucinations frequently occur in **psychotic disorders**, such as schizophrenia, or when senses are otherwise altered, such as through **drug use**. A common cause of hallucinations is **brain damage to sensory systems**. In **Charles Bonnet syndrome** the individual has damage to the visual system or between the visual system and the central nervous system. Hallucinations have also been observed in other individuals with brain lesions in their sensory systems.

Key terms: Hallucinations, psychotic disorders, drug use, brain damage, Charles Bonnet syndrome

Hallucinations stemming from damage to sensory systems are different from the types of hallucinations that are experienced by those suffering from psychotic disorders. These types of hallucinations are seen most often in individuals with **schizophrenia,** who primarily experience **auditory hallucinations**. The brain area implicated is located on the **dorsal superior temporal gyrus**. The **dorsolateral prefrontal cortex** is associated with the sense of auditory awareness being **voluntary or involuntary**.

Key terms: schizophrenia, dorsal superior temporal gyrus, dorsolateral prefrontal cortex
Contrast: Broca's (speaking) vs. Wernicke's (understanding speech)

Neuroimaging studies consistently find **decreased gray matter** in the **superior temporal gyrus and dorsolateral prefrontal cortex** have been consistently found. Because these areas serve in understanding and interpreting language, it follows that dysfunction within them would lead to auditory misinformation in the form of hallucinations. Dysfunction of the **dorsolateral prefrontal cortex** causes the individual to have trouble **distinguishing** these perceived auditory stimuli from **genuine stimuli**.

Cause and effect: decreased gray matter is associated with hallucinations; decreased gray matter in the dorsolateral prefrontal cortex makes it hard to tell real from hallucinatory sensations.

Findings of reduced **frontotemporal activity** have been found in those with hallucinations. These individuals have **broad deficits** in being able to connect disparate information. A type of task that may be difficult for these individuals is being able to **interpret the source of stimuli**. For example, researchers found that these individuals had difficulty correctly distinguishing between sensations of **being tickled by another person and being tickled by themselves**.

Cause and effect: Broad deficits in both frontal and temporal regions create difficulties in perceiving the source of stimuli (internal vs. external)

A relatively recent treatment to address auditory hallucinations in schizophrenics is **transcranial magnetic stimulation (TMS)**. This procedure involves applying an electromagnetic stimulus to areas of the head to **stimulate certain areas of the brain with a magnetic pulse**. Researchers have had some success with applying TMS to areas of the temporal lobe to **reduce the occurrence of auditory hallucinations**.

Key terms: transcranial magnetic stimulation
Cause and effect: Applying TMS to parts of the brain can reduce auditory hallucinations.

Researcher investigated the effect TMS had on individuals with schizophrenia who were experiencing auditory hallucinations. They applied TMS to half of the group and used a placebo TMS with the other half. The percent of both groups who experienced auditory hallucinations after receiving treatment are presented as follows:

Table 1 Effect of TMS

Treatment – Received TMS	45%
Control – Didn't receive TMS	89%

The difference between the two groups was significant at p<.0001.

Table 1 demonstrates that TMS cut the chance of experiencing auditory hallucinations almost in half.

38. What hypothesis does the results of the study support?
    A) Temporal lobe defects are symptoms of auditory hallucinations
    B) **<u>Auditory hallucinations are symptoms of temporal lobe defects</u>**
    C) Auditory hallucinations and temporal lobe defects occur concurrently but are unrelated Auditory hallucinations are caused by lack of magnetic stimulation

    Answer: B – It seems likely that auditory hallucinations are a result of temporal lobe defects, as addressing these defects ameliorates the hallucination symptoms.

39. What would likely be a distinguishing characteristic of hallucinations in Charles Bonnet syndrome and hallucinations in schizophrenia?
    A) Charles Bonnet syndrome hallucinations do not appear real
    B) An individual with Charles Bonnet hallucinations has difficulty determining if hallucinations are internal or external
    C) **<u>An individual with schizophrenic hallucinations may have difficulty determining if visual images are real or not</u>**
    D) Schizophrenic hallucinations do not involve damage to sensory processing centers

    Answer: C – Individuals with schizophrenia have trouble differentiating between real or perceived images, due to damage to the dorsolateral prefrontal cortex.

40. Including the results of the study, which would likely NOT be an effective treatment to address the auditory hallucinations in people with schizophrenia?
    A) TMS
    B) Antipsychotic medication
    C) **<u>Stimulant medication</u>**
    D) Cognitive Behavioral Therapy for coping with the hallucinations

    Answer: C – Stimulant medication would likely not help auditory hallucinations.

41. What is NOT a condition in which an individual may experience hallucinations?
    A) Temporal lobe epilepsy
    B) Drug intoxication
    C) Neuroinfections
    D) **<u>Attention Deficit Hyperactivity Disorder</u>**

Answer: D – ADHD is not characterized by experiences of hallucinations.

These questions are **NOT** related to a passage.

42. According to the functionalist perspective:

    A) **aspects of society are interdependent and contribute to macro level functioning**

    B) interdependent aspects of society allow micro level observations and conclusions

    C) social change is encouraged

    D) the rich and powerful control the functional aspects of society

Functionalism describes interdependent aspects of society contributing to functioning as a whole. This perspective allows macro level analysis.

B: Micro level analysis is a hallmark of the symbolic interactionist perspective. Functionalism and conflict theory allow macro level analysis.

C: Social change is a hallmark of conflict theory.

D: Conflict theory suggests that rich and powerful people force social order on the poor and weak.

43. An individual joins an Internet discussion group relating to Japanese animation. The current group members often post comments containing Japanese words. Eventually, the individual researches the meaning of several Japanese words and starts using them in his own posted comments. This is most closely an example of:

    A) arriving at an acceptance of multiculturalism.

    B) **conforming to the norms of a subculture.**

    C) group polarization resulting from the interplay between two different perspectives.

    D) an evolving definition of self-concept and identity.

Choice (B) is correct because the individual, while in the discussion group, notices the practices of current members and adjusts his practices to match the norms that have already been established within this subculture of Japanese animation fans.

A: This is not accurate because there is not any evidence that the individual's attitude about different cultures has undergone any changes, let alone a change from rejection to acceptance.

C: Polarization refers to the process wherein group members adopt opposing attitudes or viewpoints. Here, there is no development of opposing attitudes or conflicting viewpoints.

D: There is no evidence that the individual's identity is changing – only that he is changing his practices with the intent of matching what other people are doing.

44. The following are all examples of spatial inequality EXCEPT:

    A) The inhabitants of a sparsely populated country on the coast of Europe enjoy a higher standard of living than the inhabitants of an overpopulated country in sub-Saharan Africa.

    B) Lower land values near heavily polluting steel mills result in a lower-income population choosing to live there, which exposes them to greater health risks than those who can afford to live farther from the steel mills.

    C) Increasing crime levels in the central neighborhood of a city prompt higher-income residents to move to the outskirts of the city, or to the suburbs.

    D) **A politician denounces undocumented immigrants living in his town's outskirts as being unequal to those living in the town who have legal immigration status.**

Choice (D) is the only choice that does not relate to spatial inequality. Instead, it relates to a different form of inequality – specifically, an attempt to discriminate based on immigration status – which does not depend on the geographical location of the two groups, and so does not constitute spatial inequality.

A: This is an example of global inequality, a form of spatial inequality, and stems from the fact that different countries expose their inhabitants to conditions that are more likely to cause wealth or poverty.
B: This is an example of environmental injustice, a form of spatial inequality, and stems from the fact that lower-income people may be more likely than those with higher incomes to be located in areas with pollution or environmental damage.
C: This is an example of residential segregation, a form of spatial inequality which arises when events or social trends cause different groups to become located in different areas.

45. At an elementary school, 12 students who play soccer together and wear the same warm-up jackets get into a schoolyard brawl with 11 students from an ice hockey team who all wear the same team winter coats. From the perspective of one of the soccer players, his teammates are:

A) **an in-group.**
B) an out-group.
C) a bureaucracy.
D) a polarized group.

In-groups are characterized by loyalty, and the use of titles, dress, and external symbols to distinguish themselves from the out-group. From the perspective of a teammate, the team is an in-group. Furthermore, members of an in-group may express antagonism towards the out-group, the hockey players in this case.

B: In this scenario, the hockey players are the out-group.
C: A bureaucracy is characterized by written rules and regulations, an authority hierarchy, impersonal record-keeping, a paid administrative staff, and hiring of employees based on technical know-how and entrance exams. These traits are beyond the scope of an elementary school sports team.
D: Although it is possible that the group experiences some form of group polarization, that process relates more to decision-making after group deliberations. This is not relevant to the situation described in the question.

Passage 9 Explanation

One view of **ethnocentrism** is that it is a **natural process**, whereby an individual comes to regard his own group with understanding and other groups with suspicion. Therefore, it is probably unrealistic to expect to eradicate ethnocentrism. A more productive goal then would be for people to recognize their ethnocentrism and how it influences them. An important distinction, then, is between **flexible ethnocentrism**, in which individuals recognize other viewpoints, and **inflexible ethnocentrism**, in which an individual cannot understand others' viewpoints and remains influenced by his own perspective.

Key terms: ethnocentrism
Opinion: Ethnocentrism can't be eradicated, but flexible is better
Contrast: Flexible vs. inflexible ethnocentrism

The findings of how contact with other cultures influences development of ethnocentrism has been **mixed**. Some researchers have found that exposure to another culture increases ethnocentrism, while others have found that increased exposure decreases ethnocentrism.

Opinion: The findings have been mixed on the effect of cultural contact on ethnocentrism

One group of factors that could mediate the relationship is **sociocultural factors**. Researchers have found that among cultures that **value conformity ethnocentrism is typically higher**, with individual views of conformity further correlating with individual ethnocentrism. An interesting finding is that feelings of socioeconomic and political **security were negatively correlated with ethnocentrism**. Thus, in cultures in which individuals don't feel secure there is a tendency to **seek safety in an ethnocentric** cultural group.

Cause and effect: A conformist society has higher ethnocentrism and a politically secure country has low ethnocentrism.

A possible **product of ethnocentrism is stereotypes**. One way in which stereotypes come to be formed is through **selective attention**. In selective attention individuals bring a certain amount of their own bias in choosing to what they attend. Often they choose to only attend to information which confirms views that they already have.

Key terms: stereotype, selective attention

Cause and effect: ethnocentrism and selective attention lead to stereotype formation; people who think human behavior is a fixed thing will tend to notice information that confirms their views of other cultures.

Another way in which individual's views of other cultures is biased is through their **moods**, in a phenomenon termed **mood-congruent bias**. In a study, researchers induced happy, sad, or neutral moods in participants of different ethnicities. The participants then rated the mood of individuals of the same or different ethnicity interacting with each other. The ratings were from 1 to 10, with 1 being the saddest up to 10 being the happiest. The researchers found that the participants' mood had an effect on how they rated the interactions they observed, with the participants' moods and the interacting individuals' rating of moods tending to be congruent. This effect was **especially pronounced** when the individuals they observed interacting were of **different ethnicities**.

Key terms: mood-congruent bias

Cause and effect: Being in a particular mood (like happy) makes you only notice other people and other interactions that are also happy, and when observing people and interactions from another culture, this bias is bigger.

Finally, another factor influencing stereotypes and ethnocentrism is **real-world events**. Researchers examined the views of a particular ethnic group across three separate times, during peace between their countries, after one of the countries had attacked the other country, and again when the countries were at peace. Researchers evaluated the net number of positive and negative statements the individuals made and averaged them across individuals. The results are presented as follows:

Cause and effect: stereotypes and ethnocentrism are influenced by large political events.

Table 1 Effect of political hostility on ethnocentrism

Before attack	During attack	After attack
+3.5	-4.2	+1.2

Table 1 shows us that one country had a positive view of an outside country, but after political hostilities between them, the positive view that returned was much smaller.

46. The combination of Happiness Group membership and Ethnicity Group observed represent what kind of effect?
    A) unilateral effect
    B) **An interaction effect**
    C) A nested effect
    D) A single-sided effect

    Answer: B – There is a difference in the happiness ratings based on group membership. This effect is more pronounced depending on the sameness of the ethnicity observed. This combination of group membership and sameness of ethnicity represents an interaction effect.

47. Which of the following groups would likely feel the *least* amount of ethnocentrism?
    A) A group who just entered an armed conflict with another nearby group
    B) **A group who has high socioeconomic status**
    C) A group in which members wearing similar clothing is encouraged
    D) A group that has alternated having political representation with another group

    Answer: B – Groups that are economically, socially, and politically stable tend to have the least amount of ethnocentrism.

48. The study from which the data in Table 1 is presented represents what kind of research design?
    A) Random controlled trial study
    B) Experimental design
    C) **Longitudinal design**
    D) Cross-sectional design

    Answer: C – The group's attitudes are measured over time. This design is a longitudinal type study.

49. Which of the following is NOT a reason, in the study cited above, that a campaign in which the positive qualities of the opposite country are promoted would fail to reduce ethnocentrism during times of war?

    A) <u>**War permanently changes views**</u>
    B) War reduces feelings of security
    C) War changes individuals' moods
    D) Individuals likely will not focus on those messages during war

Answer: A – As can be seen from the results of the study, individuals' feelings of ethnocentrism are reduced after the war is finished, suggesting that the ethnocentrism is not permanent. Here, we're told that reduced feelings of security increase ethnocentrism. Thus (B) is a reason why ethnocentrism would increase and a campaign to reduce it would fail. Similarly, mood can influence ethnocentrism so (C) is a reason why such a campaign would fail. Finally (D) is a reason the campaign would fail; during war times any such campaign is not likely to command much attention.

50. What could be an evolutionary psychology explanation for ethnocentrism?

    A) <u>**Group membership helps individuals survive**</u>
    B) Ethnocentrism takes many generations to develop
    C) Ethnocentrism is a conscious choice that people make
    D) Ethnocentrism encourages cooperation across groups ensuring better outcomes for all

Answer: A – This reason explains how ethnocentrism can be beneficial to the individual's survival, a motivation in evolutionary psychology.

Passage 10 Explanation

The choice many adolescents have to join a gang or not join is representative of choices many adolescents must make and involves searching for **peer groups**, needing to feel **safe**, trying to **establish identity**, and making **decisions**. However, the difference in the choice between joining a gang and other adolescent choices, such as with what friends to associate, is that deciding to join a gang involves **higher stakes** with more potential for danger and other repercussions.

Contrast: normal peer groups vs. joining a gang, the gang is a search for safety and identity and is much riskier with higher stakes

Joining a **peer group is natural during adolescence**. A peer group provides companionship and support. **Henry Stack Sullivan** contended that all people have **basic social needs** that a peer group serves to fulfill. For adolescents living in gang-infested neighborhoods, peer group **options may be limited**, thus necessitating joining a gang to meet social needs.

Key terms: Henry Stack Sullivan
Opinion: Sullivan's view is that everyone has basic social needs so teenagers meet those needs by joining a gang

In addition, adolescents feel a need to be **safe** like anyone else. However, with their **increasing autonomy** from their parents and their increasing involvement in their neighborhood and with peers, adolescents may feel more of a need to take it upon **themselves to provide that safety** versus relying on their parents. In a **dangerous neighborhood**, individual protection may be insufficient; therefore a **gang may provide protection** for the adolescent.

Cause and effect: increasing autonomy means teenagers take control of their own need for safety and gangs are one source of safety.

As an adolescent tries to **establish an identity** for himself, a big part of his source of identity comes from his peer group. Gangs provide a strong source of identity, with their **distinct dress, signals, initiation, and customs**. With an individual who does not derive a strong sense of identity from his home, gang identity may prove to be a strong draw. Many people would rather be identified negatively than not be identified at all. In order to identify with the gang, the adolescent must adapt the behavior that the gang has established. Adapting the behavior of the gang might be especially pronounced among adolescents who are high in self-monitoring. **Self-monitoring** is a strategy individuals use to **manage their impressions they give others**, by considering how their behavior **corresponds to** the behavior of their **group**. Individuals high in self-monitoring will **adopt** the behavior of the **group**, even if it seems incongruent with their true beliefs.

Key terms: self-monitoring is presenting an identity that corresponds to the group
Cause and effect: the search for identity leads adolescents to take on the gang identity

In order to **assess the presence of self-monitoring among gang members**, a study was conducted in which adolescent gang members and non-gang members were rated on self-monitoring. The percent of those groups who were considered to be high self-monitors is presented as follows:

Table 1 Self-monitoring in gang members

Group	% Considered High Self-Monitors
Gang Members	58%
Non-Gang Members	32%

51. According to Kohlberg, in what stage of moral development might an adolescent be in if the only deterrent to committing crimes in his gang that he considers is a legal sentence that he might receive?
   A) **<u>Obedience and punishment</u>**
   B) Interpersonal relationships
   C) Maintaining social order
   D) Social contract and individual rights

   Answer: A – In the obedience and punishment stage of moral development an individual is motivated to comply with social order solely by a punishment that he might expect for non-compliance.

52. How might an adolescent view his own deviant behavior if he comes to view his gang as his reference group versus society in general?
   A) He would likely not change his view of his behavior
   B) **<u>He would likely view his behavior as more socially appropriate</u>**
   C) He would likely view his behavior as less socially appropriate
   D) He would likely not be able to judge his behavior

   Answer: B – If an adolescent comes to view his gang as his reference group, he would likely view his behavior as less deviant from the norm and thus view his behavior as being more socially appropriate.

53. In the dramaturgical perspective, an adolescent behaving in a more aggressive manner when he is with his gang and more non-aggressively when he is at home is demonstrating what type of contrast?
   A) In-group v. out-group
   B) Ethnocentrism v. relativism
   C) **<u>Front-stage self v. back-stage self</u>**
   D) Central processing v. peripheral route processing

   Answer: C – An individual demonstrates his front-stage self when he is present in front of a group and acts in a certain way. He demonstrates his back-stage self when he is not in front of a group and feels freer to act more naturally.

54. In the study in the passage, a chi-square test was used to compare the percent of high self-monitors among adolescents in gangs versus those not in gangs. There was found to be a significant difference. What conclusions can be drawn from this finding?
   A) There is no difference in the percent of self-monitors between adolescents in gangs versus those not in gangs
   B) **<u>There is a higher percent of self-monitoring gang members than non-gang members</u>**
   C) There is a higher percent of self-monitoring non-gang members than gang members
   D) It is not possible to determine the relationship between self-monitoring and gang status

   Answer: B – As indicated in the question, a significant difference was found in the chi-square test, indicating a difference in the percents of the two groups. Visual inspection reveals that the percent of self-monitoring gang members is higher than the non-gang members.

55. If it was found that trauma is correlated with self-monitoring, what could be conclusively said about the relationship between gang membership and self-monitoring?

    A) There is no relationship between occurrence of trauma and gang membership status

    B) There is higher incidence of trauma among gang members

    C) There is higher incidence of trauma among non-gang members

    D) **No conclusions can be made about the incidence of trauma and gang membership without further analysis**

Answer: D – While there may be a relationship between trauma and self-monitoring, to conclude that there is a relationship between trauma and gang membership would require further analysis.

These questions are **NOT** related to a passage.

56. A scientist attempting to train a chimpanzee gives the chimpanzee some fruit and leaves to eat every time the chimpanzee organizes blocks into groups of matching color. The training is eventually successful. What role do the fruit and leaves play in this chimpanzee's behavioral training?
   A) Unconditioned stimulus component of classical conditioning.
   B) Conditioned stimulus component of classical conditioning.
   C) Primary reinforcement component of operant conditioning.
   D) **Positive reinforcement component of operant conditioning.**

Positive reinforcement occurs when, after a subject completes a desired behavior, a stimulus with positive consequences is given to the subject or added to its environment. It is a component of operant conditioning, a form of learning that seeks to change a subject's behavior through positive and/or negative reinforcement, or positive and/or negative punishment. This makes (D) the correct answer.

A: An unconditioned stimulus refers to something which triggers a natural response in the absence of training.
B: A conditioned stimulus refers to an event which, although neutral, becomes associated in the subject's mind with an unconditioned stimulus, and will provoke a similar or identical response. This response is referred to as the "conditioned response."
C: Primary reinforcers are events which reward or encourage a behavior without conditioning being present – food encourages eating, air encourages breathing, bright light encourages closing of the eyelids.

57. Which of the following is a hypothesized biological basis of schizophrenia?
   A) Loss of acetylcholine-producing cells in the basal forebrain
   B) Excessive blocking of dopamine receptors
   C) **Genetic mutations causing an abnormality in astrocyte glial cells**
   D) Norepinephrine from the bloodstream crossing the blood-brain barrier

Here, (C) is correct – astrocytes, which are a type of glial support cells, are thought to play a role in causing schizophrenia when a genetic mutation causes abnormalities in them.

A: Loss of acetylcholine-producing cells in the basal forebrain has been implicated as a cause of Alzheimer's disease, not schizophrenia.
B: Blocking dopamine receptors will reduce schizophrenia symptoms, not increase them.
D: Norepinephrine cannot cross the blood-brain barrier.

58. A nomad belongs to a tribal society which is characterized by a strong sense of honor, religious symbolism, and a close-knit nuclear family structure. He has lived his whole life in a desert climate, taking his tent from place to place along with the rest of the tribe and periodically re-assembling it. During his spare time, he sometimes considers whether water from oases can be used to efficiently irrigate the surrounding land. Which best characterizes, in order, what each of these three statements describes?
   A) **Symbolic interactionism: Social reality, physical reality, unique reality.**
   B) Symbolic interactionism: Unique reality, physical reality, social reality.
   C) Symbolic interactionism: Physical reality, social reality, unique reality.
   D) Symbolic interactionism: Unique reality, social reality, physical reality.

The correct answer is (A). Social reality refers to a person's socially derived view of the world, as illustrated by the social constructs described in the first sentence. Physical reality refers to a person's physical, material surroundings in which he lives. Unique reality refers to the views and perspectives which set an individual apart from other individuals in his culture.

59. A researcher is attempting to teach a bird to flip a particular switch in response to a low tone. He does this by playing a constant, high-pitched tone which is irritating to the bird. When the low tone sounds, the bird may flip the switch. If it does so, the high-pitched tone ceases for five minutes. The researcher:
    A) will not be successful as conditioning requires positive rewards.
    B) is incorrectly applying a principle of positive punishment to train the bird.
    C) would achieve faster results by using a pulsed low-pitch tone rather than a single low-pitch tone.
    D) **is using negative reinforcement to encourage the desired response.**

Reinforcement is used when encouraging the subject to engage in a behavior. Here, the research is trying to get the bird to flip a switch. Reinforcement is negative when the reward is the removal of a noxious stimulus, and positive when the reward is being given a positive stimulus. Here, the removal of the high-pitched tone is a negative reinforcement. Thus, (D) is the correct answer.

A: Operant conditioning can use both positive and negative punishments as well as positive and negative reinforcement. Conditioning doesn't inherently require positive rewards.
B: Punishment is used to get the subject to stop doing something. Here, the researcher is trying to get the bird to do something – flip a switch.
C: The question tells us nothing about how birds respond to different types of tones, so we have no reason to assume that this is true.

This page intentionally left blank.

Section 3: 59 Questions, 95 Minutes

Passage 1

Risk attitudes are generally assessed under one of two frameworks: behavioral neuroscientists who assess personality traits of harm avoidance and novelty seeking, and behavioral economists who measure financial risk-taking decisions. In a study designed to evaluate these two frameworks, a group of 23 participants were given four different assessments. The following correlation matrix was developed:

	Novelty-Seeking	Harm Avoidance	Extraversion	Economic Risk-Taking
Novelty-Seeking	1	-0.65	-0.33	+0.02
Harm Avoidance	-0.65	1	-0.27	+0.05
Extraversion	-0.33	-0.27	1	-0.11
Economic Risk-Taking	+0.02	+0.05	-0.11	1

Table 1 Correlation matrix between three different temperament categories and one assessment of economic behavior

Higher dopaminergic activity is associated with increased novelty-seeking and risk-taking behaviors. This led researchers to investigate a particular gene for a dopamine receptor. Early studies suggested that a particular gene variant, the 7R allele, was correlated with increased risk-taking. However, a meta-study encompassing nearly 4,000 subjects found no significant correlation between variations in the dopamine receptor and either novelty-seeking or risk-taking behavior.

Given the lack of compelling results with the gene for this dopamine receptor, many researchers turned their attention to serotonergic activity. The SLC6A4 gene is involved in regulation of serotonin. One allele variant in this gene is a shorter version of the promoter region for the gene. This shorter promoter region results in decreased transcriptional efficiency. In a study, researchers found that those who were homozygous carriers of this shortened allele variant took 28% less risk in an economic exercise with real-money payouts. Such homozygous individuals were also more likely to demonstrate neuroticism and harm avoidance.

1. The data in table 1 suggest that if a psychiatrist is treating a patient who has made a number of very risky financial investments in life, the result of which leaves the patient in dire financial straits, the psychiatrist will also likely find that:

    A) the patient will score very high on assessments of novelty-seeking.

    B) there will be a positive correlation with assessments of extraversion.

    C) the patient may exhibit high or low scores in temperament inventories assessing novelty-seeking and extraversion.

    D) there is at least a somewhat elevated chance that the person does have the shorter promoter region in his SLC6A4 gene.

2. In the first study described in the passage:

    A) there is a methodological flaw in comparing three temperament measures but only one behavioral economic measure.

    B) the statistical power of the study is limited by the small number of study participants.

    C) demonstrates that there are different genetic bases of risk-taking behaviors in different life domains.

    D) is flawed because it failed to find the accepted strong positive correlation between novelty-seeking and harm avoidance.

3. Disorders related to the 7R allele that had been thought to be associated with increased risk-taking behavior could theoretically be associated with any of the following disorders EXCEPT:

    A) schizophrenia.

    B) Parkinson's disease.

    C) Korsakoff's syndrome.

    D) bipolar disorder.

4. A person who is homozygous for the shortened SLC6A4 promoter region gene variant would likely display which of the following temperaments?

    A) Higher than average novelty-seeking

    B) Slightly increased extraversion but lower than average novelty seeking

    C) Both decreased harm avoidance and decreased extraversion

    D) Novelty-seeking behaviors that could be higher or lower than average

5. The early studies that found a correlation between a particular dopamine receptor variant which was later disproven by the large meta-study could have made any of the following errors EXCEPT:

    A) an excess of effort placed on correctly establishing external validity.

    B) systematic error that incorrectly flagged participants as having a particular gene variant when they did not.

    C) a sample size that was too small to generate meaningful data.

    D) a methodological bias that failed to adequately screen for confounders.

Passage 2

During sleep, the brain passes through 5 distinct phases. These phases are characterized by the type of EEG wave pattern that occurs during each of them. The first phase of sleep is the pre-sleep, when the body and mind is relaxed and the brain is producing regular alpha waves. Next, comes phase I sleep, or sleep onset, when a person may experience imagery primarily drawn from information from that day, or hypnogogic imagery. The next phase is phase II sleep, which is a transition from the alpha waves to the larger and slower delta waves. Phase II sleep lasts about 10 to 30 minutes. Phase III and IV are known as slow-wave sleep, when delta wave patterns are observed. The body then begins REM sleep, the phase in which humans dream, about 15 to 30 minutes after beginning phase III and IV. In REM sleep, brain waves are short and rapid, similar to brain waves when awake. REM cycles occur about every 90 minutes, with the REM phases lasting longer and the delta wave phases being shorter as the night progresses.

The source of dream material is somewhat mysterious. Researchers have tried multiple methods to influence the content of dreams. Researchers have tried to provoke a sleeping subject with stimuli, such as water, a particular sound, or a particular image before or during sleep. These presentations of stimuli have been only moderately incorporated into dreams and not in any significant manner to affect thematic issues of the dream. In terms of the type of dream material, almost all involves visual material, about half contains some auditory material, and about 15 percent contains other sensory information.

It is clear, however, that REM sleep is essential. In a type of hereditary disease the afflicted persons' thalamus becomes damaged, leading them to become unable to enter REM sleep. The effects of the disease typically begin around middle age, causing extreme physical problems for the individuals and eventually leading to a coma and then death after several months without proper sleep. As to the purpose the REM sleep serves, an experiment was conducted in which the part of a cat's brain which causes its body to not move during sleep was altered, allowing the animal to move. When it began REM sleep, the cat behaved in a manner as if it were stalking prey. The researchers theorized that REM sleep is a time that animals rehearse strategies for it to function well.

For humans it appears that REM sleep serves to consolidate autobiographical memories and to attempt to make sense of them. The information stored in short-term memory in the hippocampus is reviewed and integrated to the prefrontal cortex. The neural circuits that connect this information are reinforced as the memories are rehearsed during REM sleep. This process was investigated in a study in which researchers examined the effect REM sleep had on visuospatial learning. Researchers showed participants a number of faces. Participants then went to sleep. The researchers allowed half of the participants to have REM sleep and prevented half from having REM sleep. The researchers then queried the participants on their ability to recall the faces the next day. The average number of faces recalled by the two groups is presented as follows:

Figure 1 Effect of REM sleep on recall

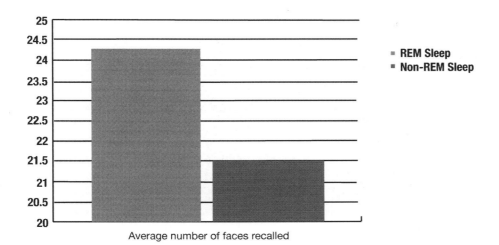

Average number of faces recalled

6. What could be a confounding factor in the study?
   A) Those without REM sleep moved less during the night.
   B) Those without REM sleep were more tired.
   C) Those without REM sleep weren't able to rehearse the faces.
   D) Those without REM sleep did not have hypnogogic imagery.

7. Which of the following does NOT support REM sleep functioning to help the brain rehearse important information?
   A) REM brain waves are similar to awake brain waves.
   B) Cats were observed performing in ways that are functional for them during REM.
   C) Those without REM performed less well on tasks than those with REM.
   D) A disordered thalamus impacts REM sleep negatively.

8. What could be a reason why infants spend many more hours in REM sleep than adults?
   A) Infants are learning much more new material and require REM to consolidate it.
   B) Infants are beginning to perceive color, which requires more REM.
   C) Infants don't actually enter REM sleep.
   D) If infants don't get REM sleep it can prove fatal.

9. What sleep pattern could be expected of study participants the first night after the study?
   A) Non-REM participants would begin REM sleep sooner than REM participants.
   B) Non-REM participants would remain in phase I sleep longer than REM participants.
   C) Non-REM participants would delay onset of REM as they did the previous night.
   D) Non-REM participants would demonstrate more delta waves than typical for them.

Passage 3

As adolescents look to distinguish themselves from their parents, some of their behaviors may go against the values of their parents. They often don't think about future consequences. For these reasons, many adolescents use drugs and alcohol during their adolescent years with their usage decreasing as they get older.

However, in some adolescents, drug and alcohol use can lead to abuse and then dependence. In these adolescents, drugs and alcohol become a problem and can have far-reaching consequences such as legal, health, psychological, and financial problems. The adolescents that come to abuse drugs or be dependent on drugs may have differences from their peers, who only use these substances recreationally, in that among adolescent heavy drug users there are the presence of risk factors, lack of protective factors, a biological predisposition, and psychological contributions.

Some risk factors that are associated with drug abuse include low parental involvement, peer pressure, and having problem-behaving friends. Some protective factors that adolescent problem users might be lacking include individual factors, such as appropriate intellectual functioning, family factors, such as close relationships with a parent figure, and extrafamilial context, such as connections to positive organizations.

Some adolescents may have some biological contributing factors such as having a genetic disposition to becoming substance users, lacking cognitive resources, or being more disposed to thrill seeking and less concerned with consequences. Just having these traits alone is not enough to become addicted to drugs or alcohol. However, these biological factors may contribute when in the presence of other factors.

To assess the contribution of each of these factors to adolescent drug abuse, a retrospective survey was taken of adolescents who were in treatment for substance use problems and a control group of adolescents. These adolescents were queried about having the presence of the factors addressed above. The percent of adolescents having these issues are presented as follows:

Figure 1 Effects of various factors on drug abuse

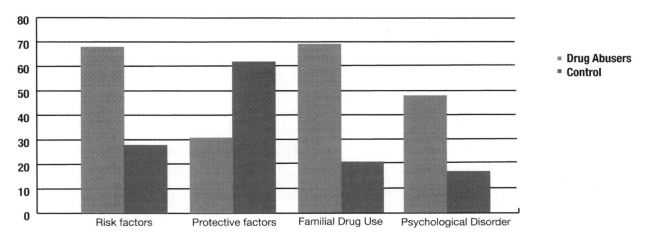

10. Which of the following is NOT a protective factor against adolescent drug abuse?
    A) High school achievement
    B) High Socio-economic status
    C) Involvement in school sports
    D) Parental substance use

11. Why do adolescents have difficulty making fully-informed decisions?
    A) Their frontal cortex has not fully developed.
    B) They are becoming more independent as adolescents.
    C) Their brainstem lacks certain neurotransmitters.
    D) There are psychological factors.

12. Which of the following is a factor that the control group had a higher level of than the drug abusing adolescents?
    A) Extra-familial support
    B) Peer groups with substance use issues
    C) Disorders, such as depression
    D) Substance use within the family

13. Why would an intervention like encouraging adolescents to "just say no to drugs" NOT be effective?
    A) It was not repeated enough.
    B) It was not shameful enough.
    C) It did not address the biopsychosocial factors involved with drug use.
    D) It did not account for adolescent cognitive immaturity.

These questions are **NOT** related to a passage.

14. Attribution of humanitarian efforts, democracy, and altruism to capitalist designs aimed at controlling the masses is an element of:
    A) functionalism.
    B) conflict theory.
    C) symbolic interactionism.
    D) the cross-cultural perspective.

15. After western societies abolished slavery, political leaders hoped that freed slaves moving to new cities and communities would experience:
    A) racism
    B) discrimination
    C) segregation
    D) assimilation

16. In George Orwell's novel, <u>1984</u>, the protagonist Winston Smith works as a historical revisionist for the totalitarian government. Such a government is characterized by:
  I. a single political party.
 II. propaganda and indoctrination of people.
III. a centrally planned economy.
    A) I only
    B) I and II only
    C) II and III only
    D) I, II and III

17. Ed earns $150k annually from salary and investments, is 56 years old, leads the local chapter of Toastmasters (a social group devoted to improvement of public speaking), and works as a policy-maker at the state government level. The primary characteristic defining Ed's social status is his:
    A) $150k annual salary.
    B) 56 years of age.
    C) verbal and oratory proficiency.
    D) government policy-making work.

This page intentionally left blank.

Passage 4

A manager of a car dealership would like to increase his dealership's sales. In order to do so, he has created a training program for his employees, which is presented as follows:

Dear employees,

First of all, there are some techniques that can be helpful in increasing sales. The first is called the "Foot-In-The-Door Technique." In this technique, one person asks another person for a small favor. After that favor is granted, the requestor then asks the requestee for a larger favor. Asking for that initial favor first increases a person's compliance in granting the second request.

Related to granting a first request, people that are told that other people have granted a first request will be more likely to grant a second request. In other words, people who view that others are granting requests become more likely to do so because they view granting requests as a normal thing.

A second technique is called the "Door-In-The-Face Technique." In this technique the requestor will first ask the requestee for a favor that is larger in scope than the desired request. The requestee will then likely deny this request. The requestor will then ask the requestee a smaller request. The requestee is then two times more likely to grant this request after being asked a larger request than if this request was asked initially.

As to why this technique is successful, first the details of this technique are important to consider. This technique is only successful when the second request is immediately made by the same person who requested the initial request. It is likely that the requestee feels guilty for having denied the initial request and so is willing to grant what he perceives to be a smaller request to assuage his guilt. This reason seems especially salient when the first request is viewed to be a socially beneficial request. In this condition a person is more likely to grant the second request than if the first request is not seen to be socially beneficial.

Table 1 Results of changes in sales techniques

Strategy	Sales effect
Show the customer a more expensive car first	Increase second car sales 12%
Point out the popularity a particular car model	Increase warranty sales 16%
Ask for a small fee to subscribe to a service before selling an expensive warranty	Increase warranty sales 12%
Training sales personnel to act naturally with customers	Increase car sales 14%

18. What strategy is an example of the Door-In-The-Face Technique?
    A) Showing the customer a more expensive car first
    B) Pointing out the popularity of a particular car model
    C) Asking for a small fee to subscribe to a service before selling an expensive warranty
    D) Training sales personnel to act naturally with customers

19. What could be done to improve the strategy of asking a small fee to subscribe to a service before selling a warranty?
    A) Making the service more expensive
    B) Making the service vastly more expensive
    C) Telling the customer the fee helps support public radio
    D) Telling the customer the fee is recurring

20. A salesperson not making a sale after expecting he would and then justifying that that person did not really want to buy a car is an example of a resolution of what type of phenomenon?
    A) Belief perseverance
    B) Cognitive dissonance
    C) Mental heuristic
    D) Fundamental attribution error

21. Which of the following is likely to result in a lost sale?
    A) The customer overhearing the salespeople talking about sales techniques
    B) The customer seeing the sales team putting up signs advertising sales
    C) The customer being asked to sign up for a free discount membership
    D) The customer hearing that the sale is ending soon

Passage 5

There have been findings that individuals who have experienced a traumatic event, resulting in the development of Post-Traumatic Stress Disorder (PTSD), often have difficulty accurately recounting the traumatic incident. One explanation for the difficulties with memory involves the dual representation theory. This theory states that memories are encoded and stored in different ways and that traumatic memories are stored in two different ways. One way that memories are stored is through Verbally Accessible Memory (VAM). Information that is consciously processed is stored in VAM. This autobiographical information can later be recalled verbally. Information that is not consciously processed is stored in sensory accessible memory (SAM). This information consists of visuospatial and sensory information.

One model explaining this dual processing of traumatic information is that during traumatic situations the limbic system overrides executive processes, as more basic functions are more imperative for physical survival. Thus the information is processed in more basic ways, through sensory and visuospatial means, and stored in SAM. This has been supported in research by findings that when recalling information about a trauma and being stopped while doing so and asked to perform a verbal or visuospatial task, people had more trouble performing the visuospatial task than the verbal compared to when they were not recalling traumatic information. This suggests that the presence of the intrusive traumatic memories is dependent on visuospatial resources, which are allocated to these memories and not available to devote to other activities requiring visuospatial skills.

22. Which of the following would suggest that trauma is, in fact, processed in the VAM?
    A) Individuals recalling a number of details about smells they experienced during the trauma
    B) Individuals having a harder time memorizing a list of coping strategies while they are recounting their trauma
    C) An individual seems to lack words for describing his traumatic experience
    D) The presence of persistent flashbacks to the trauma

23. What could be a beneficial effect of processing trauma through the VAM?
    A) An individual is then able to allocate executive processes to address traumatic symptoms
    B) Verbal traumatic experience is less threatening than sensory trauma
    C) Less cognitive resources need to be allocated
    D) Medication can then be prescribed

24. What is an evolutionary psychology explanation for why traumatic information comes to be encoded in the SAM?
    A) Information encoded in the VAM allows the individual to generate helpful strategies for avoiding future traumas.
    B) Information processed in the SAM is easier to ignore than if it is processed in the VAM.
    C) Information processed in the limbic system results in quicker reactions to threats.
    D) The SAM is less sensitive to traumatic incidents than the VAM.

25. Which of the following is not considered a symptom of trauma?
    A) Re-experiencing the trauma through flashbacks
    B) Avoiding triggers related to the trauma
    C) Dissociating when thinking about the trauma
    D) Lowered intellectual functioning

These questions are **NOT** related to a passage.

26. A five-year old subject enrolls in Vail Primary School for kindergarten. After arriving, she must acclimate to the new environment. This is an example of:

    A) primary socialization.
    B) secondary socialization.
    C) anticipatory socialization.
    D) re-socialization.

27. A trainer at the circus is attempting to train an elephant to stand up on its hind legs through the use of a food reward. When starting out, the trainer gives one food reward every time the elephant stands up in response to a hand signal. Later on, the trainer gives a food reward after going through the hand signal-stand up routine five times in a row. Which two schedules of reinforcement has the trainer shifted between?

    A) Fixed ratio schedule to fixed interval schedule
    B) Fixed interval schedule to variable interval schedule
    C) Fixed interval schedule to continuous reinforcement
    D) Continuous reinforcement to fixed ratio schedule

28. A college student visits a foreign country as part of an exchange program and finds the habits of the locals to be unnatural and somewhat offensive. After returning home, the student takes a series of sociology courses and reevaluates his experiences based on the different standards of normal found in the foreign country. The student now evaluates the foreign society as less appealing than his own, but still quite natural in its own right. The student judged the foreign culture with:

    A) ethnocentrism followed by cultural relativism.
    B) ethnocentrism followed by assimilation.
    C) cultural relativism followed by assimilation.
    D) cultural relativism followed by ethnocentrism.

29. Which of the following is an example of aversive prejudice?

    A) Believing that all members of an in-group are unique, while all members of an out-group are the same as each other
    B) Feeling nervous in the presence of an out-group, even though cognitive thoughts and beliefs about the out-group are neutral
    C) Experiencing negative thoughts, feelings and behaviors about members of an out-group
    D) Intentionally attempting not to get involved in a situation that might trigger a severe phobia

This page intentionally left blank.

Passage 6

The following represents a portion of a treatment plan of a psychologist who is treating a client, John, who has been diagnosed with Borderline Personality Disorder (BPD), a type of personality disorder characterized by symptoms described in the plan.

"John began treatment with me about 6 months ago. He came to me presenting with a history of failed relationships, having a history of trauma, and having substance use issues. John described having a series of relationships in which he would become extremely attached to a partner whom he had known for only a short time. John would begin to feel overwhelmed by this closeness and soon there would be a fight between John and his partner, typically over something trivial. This would result in John distancing himself from her. After some time, John would become despondent and perceived to be abandoned by his partner and attempt reconciliation, which would result in John again becoming extremely attached. This cycle of attachment and separation would continue repeatedly, invariably resulting in the partner becoming overwhelmed and terminating the relationship. Throughout this relationship cycle, John would frequently abuse drugs and alcohol, during times when he felt overwhelmed by the intimacy of the relationship and also when he felt abandoned.

As John processed his current romantic relationships, he also began to address his past familial relationships. John experienced physical abuse by one of his parents. He described a cycle with the abusing parent, whereby his parent would behave unpredictably, sometimes abusing John for no apparent reason. This would soon be followed by this parent trying to reconcile with John. This pattern of feeling distance and closeness led to John having a disorganized style of attachment and seemed to create a template for how John learned to interact in future relationships.

For many people who have been raised without a sense of security, these feelings are manageable if they are able to understand the relationship between their feelings, actions, and thoughts. This process of being able to think about the relationship of these personal processes is called mentalization.

Mentalization is a process that invokes the prefrontal cortex, the area of the brain that is responsible for executive processes. When mentalizing, humans use their prefrontal cortex to examine how they are thinking and feeling in a situation. However, individuals with a disorganized style of attachment learn to react with arousal. This may happen if frequent feelings of frustration are evoked and paired with needs, resulting in a style of processing information that relies less on mentalization and the prefrontal cortex and more on hyperarousal.

To address these deficits in mentalization, John and I have been meeting in individual psychotherapy, with one of the goals of therapy being to try to help John improve in his ability to mentalize.

To monitor John's progress in therapy I have charted John's monthly scores, over the past 6 months, on the BPD Rating scale. This scale is an inventory of 10 behaviors characteristic of BPD."

Table 1 Results of the BPD ratings for six months

Month	Jan.	Feb.	Mar.	April	May.	June
BPD Score	8	9	10	10	8	9

30. Which of the following is likely NOT a factor explaining why John's scores on the BPD initially increased?
    A) Attachment based disorders take a long time to treat.
    B) John may have felt distress initially in his relationship with his therapist.
    C) John missed a sensitive period in his life for learning to mentalize.
    D) Mentalizing is a complicated task.

31. Why would John not have been diagnosed with BPD or any other personality disorder when he was a youth?
    A) Relationship issues do not begin until adulthood.
    B) Personality disorders may only be diagnosed in adults.
    C) Personality disorders were not diagnoses when John was younger.
    D) Youth relationships typically do not impact adult relationships.

32. What could be a secondary gain for John from continued non-improvement in his BPD scores, as indicated in the data?
    A) He wants to improve but doesn't know how.
    B) He could learn to mentalize.
    C) He could continue his relationship with his therapist.
    D) He could continue his pattern of failed romantic relationships.

33. If a brain scan shows that John's prefrontal cortex becomes more activated in the months following June, what might this suggest about John's emotional reactions?
    A) John will likely have less extreme reactions.
    B) John will likely have more extreme reactions.
    C) John will likely feel more attachment to his caregivers.
    D) John will likely feel less attachment to his caregivers.

Passage 7

There is a relationship between child behavior and child maltreatment, with an increasing recognition of the bidirectional influences of each of these factors. Children with behavioral disorders were found to be the largest subtype of children with disabilities, who as a group were two to three and a half times as likely to be maltreated than children without disabilities. It is typically assumed that child maltreatment results in child behavior issues. However, there is also evidence that disruptive child behavior can lead to increased child maltreatment. In a study of parenting behavior of parents with children with disruptive behavior and children without disruptive behavior, the greatest negative parenting behaviors were displayed by parents towards children with disruptive behaviors. This was true of parents of children with both behavioral disorders and without behavioral disorders, but was most pronounced among parents with children with behavioral disorders, suggesting that a history of child behavioral disorders tends to elicit negative parenting behaviors. The acknowledgment of the role of disruptive child behaviors in child maltreatment is not an assignation of responsibility to the child, however, as ultimately adults must address child behavior in a healthy manner. The relationship between child maltreatment and disruptive child behavior can be understood in part through the "coercion hypothesis."

Related to behaviorism, the coercion hypothesis illustrates the effect contingencies have on child and parent interactions and behavior patterns. According to this model, during parent-child interactions children can be reinforced when they respond to parent requests in negative ways when such negative responses lead to a cessation of the parent request.

This pattern of behavior eventually coalesces into a behavioral script, in which both parent and child expect this pattern to perpetuate and therefore accommodate this pattern. This script may come to dictate the child's behavior in other situations as well, leading to a pattern of refusal and disruptive behavior in school and in other settings, further solidifying this behavioral strategy.

Therefore, treatments for parents who have maltreated children or for children with disruptive behaviors seek to eliminate this pattern of defiance. Therapists attempt to address this pattern by asking parents to state their requests in clear terms and then upon non-compliance presenting the child with a choice between acceding to the request or receiving a negative consequence. Parents are instructed to remove the emotional content from their statements so that they do not become frustrated or lose control and do not establish a condition in which communication escalates in volume and negativity. In addition, parents are instructed to follow through with consequences consistently, even if the child eventually complies with the task, as consistency is important.

Parent Child Interaction Therapy (PCIT) is a type of therapy that aims to teach these behaviors. A meta-analysis was conducted to review studies in which PCIT has been evaluated for its effect on disruptive child behaviors. Outcome variables were gathered from measures of child disruptive behaviors before and after treatment. The pre-treatment scores were subtracted from the post-treatment scores in each measure and divided by the standard deviation to obtain the measure's study effect size. The study effect sizes were aggregated across studies and the overall results are presented as follows:

Table 1 Study results

Measure	Child Compliance	Child Disruptive Behavior	Parent Effective Instruction	Parent Follow-Through
Effect Size	+.48	-.86	+1.02	+.96

34. According to the coercion hypothesis, in what direction do the behaviors addressed in the study move?
    A) Parent behavior influences child behavior.
    B) Child behavior influences parent behavior.
    C) Parent and child behavior influence each other.
    D) Parent and child behavior do not influence each other.

35. What would be necessary to change for the improvements seen in the study to generalize beyond the research setting?
    A) Parent-child defiance
    B) Parent-child scripts
    C) Parent-child contingencies
    D) Parent-child frequency of requests

36. What are NOT contingencies that might motivate a child in the study?
    A) Avoid positive punishment of receiving a consequence for a disruptive behavior
    B) Seek positive reinforcement of parental approval for compliance
    C) Avoid negative reinforcement of receiving a punishment for non-compliance
    D) Avoid negative punishment of not being able to play for disruptive behavior

37. Had results from the PCIT sessions been reported over time, what pattern might have been observed in the measures?
    A) Greater initial parent effective instruction compared to later
    B) Decreased initial child compliance compared to later
    C) Decreased later parent follow-through compared to initially
    D) Increased later child disruptive behavior compared to initially

Passage 8

Since some of the original work done by Galton over a hundred years ago in developing instruments that can effectively measure intelligence, there has been a pronounced focus on developing tests that correctly measure intelligence. This is evidenced by the variety of tests that have been developed which purport to measure intelligence and the extensive research that has been conducted in an attempt to assess intelligence. There is a great deal at stake in developing effective measures of intelligence due to the large number of people whose intelligence is tested and the money invested in research. One of the main recurring questions in the efforts to measure intelligence is, "What is intelligence, exactly?" One aspect of this question is to what extent is intelligence a broad construct versus a number of specific abilities.

Weighing in on the side that IQ is a broad construct, Spearman defined intelligence as being a general intelligence, which he referred to as a g factor. This g factor was responsible for an individual's intellectual functioning on a variety of tasks. Rather than a number of separate abilities influencing an individual's performance on a task, proponents of this view of intelligence viewed the g factor as being the underlying factor which allowed an individual to learn these abilities. An advantage to viewing intelligence as being composed of a single factor is that it can be summarized as one measure, such as an IQ score.

Other theorists have viewed intelligence as being comprised of a number of separate abilities. These abilities are not necessarily related to each other. For example, an individual might be poor at math, but be exceptional at artistic endeavors. Within this view, that individual would be said to have high art intelligence, but poor math intelligence. An advantage to viewing intelligence in this manner is that a person's broad abilities are able to be represented more fully than by representing them by a single ability. Support for this view is that an individual's IQ score tends to remain quite stable over time.

Most modern intellectual testing combines the two approaches. For example, the Wechsler Adult Intelligence Scale (WAIS) is one of the most widely used measures of cognitive abilities. This tests consists of a number of subtests from which 4 index scores are derived. These indices are Verbal Ability, a measure of an individual's knowledge of and ability to use language, Perceptual Reasoning, a measure of an individual's ability to perceive and manipulate primarily visual information, Processing Speed, a measure of an individual's ability to quickly process information both with and without a motor component, and Working Memory, a measure of an individual's ability to store, manipulate, and recall information within a short time. Additionally an overall score is also generated, which is called the Full Scale Intelligence Quotient (FSIQ) score. This is purported to be an overall measure of an individual's cognitive abilities. The test is standardized so that a score of 100 represents the 50th percentile. One standard deviation in either direction is 15 points.

A WAIS assessment was administered to an individual named Michael at his university, and his scores are presented as follows:

Table 1 Results of WAIS assessment

Measure	Score
FSIQ	92
Verbal	84
Perceptual Reasoning	104
Processing Speed	100
Working Memory	89

38. What would be a good question to have answered about Michael before recommending particular remediation based upon his scores?
- A) Is he right or left-handed?
- B) Is English his first language?
- C) Is he able to see the information presented to him?
- D) Is he able to work with a time constraint?

39. What is a drawback to viewing intelligence as Spearman conceived it?
- A) Intelligence can be represented more succinctly.
- B) Research can focus on identifying what the underlying g factor is.
- C) An individual's cognitive strengths cannot be emphasized.
- D) Defining intelligence is a difficult task.

40. What is an argument against inherent factors influencing IQ?
- A) Similar IQ scores in families
- B) Differences in IQ scores in different nations
- C) IQ scores tending to increase overall in subsequent generations
- D) Different ethnicities having different average IQ scores depending on their nationality

41. What might be a good recommendation to help Michael in school?
- A) Obtain printed copies of lecture notes
- B) Request oral exams
- C) Ask to have his allotted test time reduced
- D) Focus on his overall ability, rather than his separate abilities

42. Rather than focusing on an individual's IQ scores, considering how the individual makes use of his abilities, such as his current work and his ability to adapt to his weaknesses, represents what view of assessment?
- A) Structuralism
- B) Functionalism
- C) Multiculturalism
- D) Heuristic assessment

These questions are **NOT** related to a passage.

43. A person walks by an overturned armored truck with tens of thousands of dollars worth of money scattered all around it on the ground. He decides not to pick up any, and continues walking past. On his return trip, he sees that a large number of people have gathered near the truck, and are picking up and pocketing the money. He walks up to the money on the ground and pockets some for himself. What best describes the change in his attitude and actions?
    A) Erickson's theory of developmental stages
    B) The bystander effect
    C) Groupthink
    D) Deindividuation

44. All of the following illustrate characteristics of ethnocentrism EXCEPT:
    A) A Japanese tourist in the United States asks for squid as a pizza topping. The pizza shop proprietor expresses confusion and some disgust.
    B) A Northeastern university gives preferential treatment to children and grandchildren of alumni in deciding who to admit.
    C) A person of Greek heritage expresses constant pride that the ancient Greeks, by inventing civilization, accomplished what no other group could have.
    D) A university professor in Spain writes a book on the colonization of Mexico by the Spanish without including material from historical or contemporary Native American sources.

45. An immigrant family finds economic success and moves to a wealthy neighborhood in a new state. In this state, the population of people from the immigrant family's home country is much lower than the national average, and there are no other immigrant families in the wealthy neighborhood. As a consequence of this move, the family may likely experience:
    A) low socioeconomic status.
    B) an absence of social capital.
    C) social exclusion.
    D) environmental injustice.

This page intentionally left blank.

Passage 9

In the course of one year, in the U.S. 20% of children and adolescents have mental health problem symptoms or signs and approximately 5% have "extreme functional impairment." The ramifications of these mental health issues in school include a drop-out rate among youth with these issues twice that of those without mental health difficulties, lower grades and test scores among youth with behavioral difficulties and inattention, and more restricted settings and special-education accommodations among youth with untreated mental health needs.

However, less than 30% of children in need of mental health services receive these services. The cost of treating children's mental health needs is $15 billion dollars per year. While this number may seem daunting, total yearly social costs associated with mental health issues are estimated to be $247 billion. These social costs include long-term costs to productivity, contagion effects, crime, etc. While the entirety of this $247 billion may not be recoupable through intervention efforts, it is possible to reclaim a great deal of it through effective interventions.

A substantial amount of research has demonstrated the positive impact mental health practitioners have had in schools. A meta-analysis of recent mental health interventions at a number of schools throughout the United States found a 64% rate of improvement in student academic performance and mental health functioning and a 95% improvement in mental health alone as a result of the interventions. In research studies, school psychologists have been shown to effectively engage students, work with educators and families, and implement interventions. These services have been shown to be effective in reducing dropout rates, increasing academic performance and reducing behavior problems, and helping increase teacher effectiveness. School psychologists have also been effective in addressing student mental health issues, social, emotional, and behavioral health concerns, and problem-solving and self-regulating skills.

In terms of the financial benefits of school-based mental health services, there are clear benefits in investing in mental health services early in students' lives. Results from an analysis of early intervention programs for low-income children indicated that there were savings in criminal justice, special education, and welfare assistance costs. A district school based psycho-educational program found benefits of $9,837 per student in long-term social problems aversion. Finally, school-based drug programs have been shown to provide $840 in long-term benefit compared with costs of $150 per student.

The following data summarizes research comparing a number of indicators of health at high schools with dedicated mental health services and schools without those services.

Table 1 Effect of mental health services on high schools

School	Drop-out %	% of students with passing standardized test scores	% in special education
With Services	20	73	8
Without Services	42	61	12

46. Which of the following is NOT a benefit to providing mental health services for students at schools?
    A) Improved academic performance
    B) Reduced mental health issues
    C) Improved family functioning
    D) Reduced social costs

47. Which of the following could be a confounding factor in the research presented in the table?
    A) Special education is a type of mental health service
    B) Standardized testing test ceiling effects
    C) Schools with mental health services are likely different than schools without those services
    D) A higher dropout percent means fewer students are available for standardized testing

48. Which of the following may be a barrier to implementing mental health services at schools?
    A) Short-term costs
    B) Long-term costs
    C) Short-term benefits
    D) Long-term benefits

49. Why might it be beneficial to an individual without children in school to support mental health services in schools?
    A) Longer school hours for students
    B) Increased tax revenue from more productive graduates
    C) Improved student academics
    D) Increases in special education services

50. Students who witness their classmates benefitting from mental health services and become more willing to seek out these services themselves have benefitted from a reduction in what?
    A) Social facilitation
    B) Deindividuation
    C) Stigma
    D) Conformity

Passage 10

Neurons get information from other neurons via dendrites. Dendrites, which look similar to branches extending from a tree, get the information from other neurons via synaptic receptors. Some dendrites increase their capacity for information with the use of dendritic spines, short extensions which increase the available surface area for receiving information.

Information received in the dendrites is communicated to the main area of the neuron, the cell body, which contains the nucleus, ribosomes, mitochondria, and other structures. The neuron controls the flow of information from the cell body. The membrane of the neuron keeps an electrical gradient between the inside and outside of the cell. This gradient is typically in a state of polarization, in which there is a slightly negative electrical potential within the membrane versus outside the membrane, in a condition known as the resting potential.

A stimulus may act upon the neuron causing it to become depolarized. When the neuron reaches a certain threshold of depolarization, then an action potential may occur. The action potential is sent down the main efferent branch from the neuron, the axon, in a process called propagation of the action potential. This electrical message is aided in conduction via a coating surrounding the axon called the myelin sheath. The action potential is regenerated along the axon at the nodes of Ranvier, uncoated areas in which sodium ions again enter the axon and propagate an action potential at each node. This continues until the axon terminates at a pre-synaptic cleft. At this cleft the axon's electric transmission is converted to a chemical message that is transmitted across a synapse.

A synapse is the gap between two neurons at which point the neurons communicate. The message communicated across the synapse first begins in the cell body of the transmitting neuron, in which the chemicals are synthesized which serve as neurotransmitters. Some different types of neurotransmitters include amino acids, peptides, acetylcholoine, monoamines, and purines. These different neurotransmitters serve different functions. Other neurotransmitters are synthesized in the presynaptic terminal, closer to where they will be released. The process of producing these neurotransmitters is quite slow, so the body uses a number of alternative techniques, such as recycling to reduce the wait.

These neurotransmitters are carried down the axons with the action potentials as described above. When they reach the end of the axon to the presynaptic terminal, the action potential causes gates to open, through which calcium flows. This calcium causes the neuron to release neurotransmitters to release into the synaptic cleft, in a process known as exocytosis. The neurotransmitter then crosses the synaptic cleft to the postsynaptic membrane in the next neuron.

Some of the major neurotransmitters and their primary functions are presented in the following table:

Table 1 Examples of Neurotransmitters

Neurotransmitter	Function
Acetylcholine	Stimulating muscles; brain arousal
Dopamine	Voluntary movements; reward & pleasure
Serotonin	Mood & emotions; regulating basic functions
Glutamate	Learning & memory
Endorphins	Reduction of pain

51. What pair of neurotransmitters, at inappropriate levels, are implicated in the tremors exhibited in Parkinson's Disease?
    A) Serotonin and Glutamate
    B) Endorphins and Dopamine
    C) Dopamine and Acetylcholine
    D) Acetylcholine and Glutamate

52. What is the purpose of neurotransmitter reuptake?
    A) Reuse neurotransmitters
    B) Keep neurotransmitters in the synapse
    C) Block the uptake of neurotransmitters
    D) To increase resting potential

53. What might occur in a mirror neuron when observing an action in another person?
    A) Resting potential
    B) Action potential
    C) Neurotransmitter reuptake
    D) Polarization

54. What relationship do motor neurons have with the CNS?
    A) Efferent to the CNS
    B) Afferent to the CNS
    C) Proximal to the CNS
    D) Distal to the CNS

55. What may lead to the cognitive slowing observed in Alzheimer's Disease?
    A) Neurotransmitter confusion
    B) Decreased level of action potential
    C) Myelin sheath deterioration
    D) Exocytosis

These questions are **NOT** related to a passage.

56. Which of the following characteristics are associated with classical conditioning?
 I. Reward and punishment
 II. Reinforcement schedules
III. Conditioned and unconditioned responses
    A) I only
    B) III only
    C) I and II only
    D) I, II and III

57. A subject, when taking an opioid drug, experiences euphoric effects. After continuing to take the opioid for some time, he finds that the euphoric effects are no longer as strong, and he increases his dosage. Which of the following best describes what is taking place?
    A) The reward pathway in the subject's brain is becoming more tolerant of the increase in dopamine that the opioids cause.
    B) The reward pathway in the subject's brain is becoming less tolerant of the increase in dopamine that the opioids cause.
    C) Classical conditioning results in more tolerance of the opioid.
    D) Operant conditioning results in less tolerance of the opioid.

58. A subject, who feels he has not been sleeping well, experiences dream-like hallucinations before falling asleep at night. He finds it hard to move when waking up, or when about to fall asleep, and notices some loss of muscle control when he becomes emotional. Which of the following is the subject most likely experiencing?
    A) Circadian sleep cycles
    B) Insomnia
    C) Narcolepsy
    D) Sleep apnea

59. Which of the following are elements of the specific modality model of attention?
 I. Tasks that use the same modality being more likely to interfere with one another.
 II. Tasks becoming automatic and therefore requiring fewer attentional resources.
III. One single, undifferentiated pool of mental resources.
    A) I only
    B) II only
    C) III only
    D) I and III only

This page intentionally left blank.

Section 3 Answers and Explanations

Key					
1	C	21	A	41	A
2	B	22	B	42	B
3	C	23	A	43	D
4	B	24	C	44	B
5	A	25	D	45	C
6	B	26	B	46	C
7	D	27	D	47	C
8	A	28	A	48	A
9	A	29	B	49	B
10	D	30	C	50	C
11	A	31	B	51	C
12	A	32	C	52	A
13	C	33	A	53	B
14	B	34	C	54	A
15	D	35	B	55	C
16	D	36	C	56	B
17	D	37	B	57	A
18	A	38	B	58	C
19	C	39	C	59	A
20	B	40	D		

Passage 1 Explanation

Risk attitudes are generally assessed under one of two frameworks: **behavioral neuroscientists** who assess personality traits of harm avoidance and novelty seeking, and behavioral **economists** who measure financial risk-taking decisions. In a study designed to evaluate these two frameworks, a group of 23 participants were given four different assessments. The following **correlation matrix** was developed:

Key words: risk attitude, neuroscientists, economists

Contrast: Risk as personality trait vs. financial decisions

	Novelty-Seeking	Harm Avoidance	Extraversion	Economic Risk-Taking
Novelty-Seeking	1	-0.65	-0.33	+0.02
Harm Avoidance	-0.65	1	-0.27	+0.05
Extraversion	-0.33	-0.27	1	-0.11
Economic Risk-Taking	+0.02	+0.05	-0.11	1

Table 1 Correlation matrix between three different temperament categories and one assessment of economic behavior.

Table 1 shows us that there is a strong negative correlation between novelty-seeking and harm avoidance and a weak negative correlation between novelty-seeking and extraversion, as well as harm avoidance and extraversion. There is no real correlation (positive or negative) between economic risk-taking and the temperaments studied.

Higher **dopaminergic activity** is associated with increased novelty-seeking and risk-taking behaviors. This led researchers to investigate a **particular gene for a dopamine receptor**. Early studies suggested that a particular gene variant, the 7R allele, was correlated with increased risk-taking. However, a **meta-study** encompassing nearly 4,000 subjects found **no significant correlation** between variations in the dopamine receptor and either novelty-seeking or risk-taking behavior.

Cause-and-effect: increased dopaminergic activity is associated with novelty-seeking and risk-taking

Contrast: early on we thought this one dopamine receptor was involved, but a bigger study showed it wasn't

Given the lack of compelling results with the gene for this dopamine receptor, many researchers turned their attention to **serotonergic activity**. The **SLC6A4** gene is involved in regulation of serotonin. One allele variant in this gene is a **shorter version of the promoter region** for the gene. This shorter promoter region results in decreased transcriptional efficiency. In a study, researchers found that those who were **homozygous carriers** of this shortened allele variant took 28% **less risk** in an economic exercise with real-money payouts. Such homozygous individuals were also more likely to demonstrate **neuroticism** and **harm avoidance**.

Key terms: serotonergic, SLC6A4

Cause-and-effect: homozygous carriers of the short SLC6A4 took less risk, were more harm-avoidant and neurotic

1. The data in table 1 suggest that if a psychiatrist is treating a patient who has made a number of very risky financial investments in life, the result of which leaves the patient in dire financial straits, the psychiatrist will also likely find that:

    A) the patient will score very high on assessments of novelty-seeking.

    B) there will be a positive correlation with assessments of extraversion.

    C) **the patient may exhibit high or low scores in temperament inventories assessing novelty-seeking and extraversion.**

    D) there is at least a somewhat elevated chance that the person does have the shorter promoter region in his SLC6A4 gene.

The correlation matrix shows us that economic risk-taking behavior is not correlated with any of the other temperaments studied. Thus, choice C is correct and the patient may exhibit high or low scores.

D: The short promoter region is associated with less risk, not more.

2. In the first study described in the passage:

    A) there is a methodological flaw in comparing three temperament measures but only one behavioral economic measure.

    B) **the statistical power of the study is limited by the small number of study participants.**

    C) demonstrates that there are different genetic bases of risk-taking behaviors in different life domains.

    D) is flawed because it failed to find the accepted strong positive correlation between novelty-seeking and harm avoidance.

The first study presented only tested 23 participants. The smaller the pool of people studied, the less statistical power the data has. Thus choice B is correct.

A: This is not a flaw, as one could certainly design a research protocol to look for a correlation between three different factors and one kind of behavior.

C: The study only presents some weak correlations and gets nowhere near making a causal claim about the genetic bases of different kinds of risk behavior.

D: This is false as there is not an accepted positive correlation between novelty-seeking and harm avoidance.

3. Disorders related to the 7R allele that had been thought to be associated with increased risk-taking behavior could theoretically be associated with any of the following disorders EXCEPT:

    A) schizophrenia.

    B) Parkinson's disease.

    C) **Korsakoff's syndrome.**

    D) bipolar disorder.

The 7R allele discussed related to the brain's dopaminergic systems. Choice A, B, and D are all diseases associated with disorders of dopaminergic activity. The right answer, choice C is due to a thiamine (vitamin B1) deficiency in the brain.

4. A person who is homozygous for the shortened SLC6A4 promoter region gene variant would likely display which

of the following temperaments?

   A) Higher than average novelty-seeking
   B) **Slightly increased extraversion but lower than average novelty seeking**
   C) Both decreased harm avoidance and decreased extraversion
   D) Novelty-seeking behaviors that could be higher or lower than average

The passage tells us that individuals who are homozygous for the shortened SLC6A4 promoter region score higher in harm avoidance. We see from the correlation matrix that harm avoidance is negatively correlated with novelty-seeking. It's also (weakly) negatively correlated with extraversion, making choice B's "slightly increased" less likely, but choice B is still the best option.

A, D: Novelty-seeking is very unlikely to be higher than average given that harm avoidance and novelty-seeking are strongly negatively correlated.
C: The passage tells us that this gene variant is associated with harm-avoidance, so this answer choice contradicts the passage.

5. The early studies that found a correlation between a particular dopamine receptor variant which was later disproven by the large meta-study could have made any of the following errors EXCEPT:

   A) **an excess of effort placed on correctly establishing external validity.**
   B) systematic error that incorrectly flagged participants as having a particular gene variant when they did not.
   C) a sample size that was too small to generate meaningful data.
   D) a methodological bias that failed to adequately screen for confounders.

Choices B, C, and D all describe classic flaws that can encountered when constructing an experiment. Biases, confounders, systematic errors, and too-small sample sizes all reduce the validity of an experiment. Choice A, the correct answer, is not a problem – external validity is a good thing and effort to establish it would only make an experiment more sound.

Passage 2 Explanation

During **sleep**, the brain passes through 5 distinct phases. These phases are characterized by the type of **EEG wave pattern** that occurs during each of them. The first phase of sleep is the **pre-sleep**, when the body and mind is relaxed and the brain is producing regular **alpha** waves. Next, comes **phase I sleep**, or sleep onset, when a person may experience imagery primarily drawn from information from that day, or **hypnogogic** imagery. The next phase is **phase II sleep**, which is a **transition** from the alpha waves to the **larger and slower delta** waves. Phase II sleep lasts about **10 to 30 minutes**. **Phase III and IV are known as slow-wave** sleep, when delta wave patterns are observed. The body then begins **REM** sleep, the phase in which humans **dream**, about 15 to 30 minutes after beginning phase III and IV. In REM sleep, **brain waves are short and rapid**, similar to brain waves when awake. REM cycles occur about **every 90 minutes**, with the REM phases lasting longer and the delta wave phases being shorter as the night progresses.

Key terms: sleep, alpha waves, delta waves, pre-sleep, phases of sleep, REM sleep

The source of **dream material** is somewhat **mysterious**. Researchers have **tried multiple methods to influence the content of dreams**. Researchers have tried to provoke a sleeping subject with stimuli, such as water, a particular sound, or a particular image before or during sleep. These presentations of stimuli have been **only moderately incorporated** into dreams and not in any significant manner to affect thematic issues of the dream. In terms of the type of dream material, **almost all involves visual** material, about **half contains some auditory** material, and about 15 percent contains **other sensory information**.

Opinion: Where people get their dream ideas from is mysterious. Researchers haven't been able to influence dream content much.
Contrast: visual vs. auditory dream content, nearly all dreams have visual material but only half have auditory

It is clear, however, that **REM sleep is essential**. In a type of **hereditary disease** the afflicted persons' **thalamus becomes damaged**, leading them to become **unable to enter REM sleep**. The effects of the disease typically begin around middle age, causing extreme physical problems for the individuals and eventually leading to a coma and then **death after several months** without proper sleep. As to the purpose the REM sleep serves, an experiment was conducted in which the part of a cat's brain which causes its body to not move during sleep was altered, allowing the animal to move. When it began REM sleep the cat **behaved** in a manner **as if it were stalking prey**. The researchers theorized that REM sleep is a time that **animals rehearse strategies** for it to function well.

Opinion: REM sleep is essential. For animals it is when they rehearse behaviors.
Cause and effect: A disease that damages the thalamus and leads to no REM sleep is fatal after several months without REM sleep.

For humans it appears that **REM sleep** serves to **consolidate autobiographical memories** and to attempt to **make sense** of them. The information stored in **short-term memory in the hippocampus** is reviewed and integrated to the prefrontal cortex. The neural circuits that connect this information are reinforced as the memories are rehearsed during REM sleep. This process was investigated in a study in which researchers examined the effect REM sleep had on **visuospatial learning**. Researchers showed participants a number of faces. Participants then went to sleep. The researchers allowed half of the participants to have REM sleep and prevented half from having REM sleep. The researchers then queried the participants on their ability to recall the faces the next day. The average number of faces recalled by the two groups is presented as follows:

Figure 1 Effect of REM sleep on recall

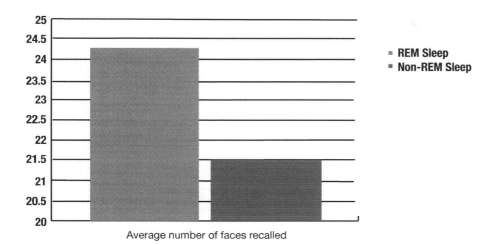

Average number of faces recalled

Figure 1 shows us that those participants who entered REM sleep were able to recall several more faces than those who did not have REM sleep.

6. What could be a confounding factor in the study?
    A) Those without REM sleep moved less during the night.
    B) **Those without REM sleep were more tired.**
    C) Those without REM sleep weren't able to rehearse the faces.
    D) Those without REM sleep did not have hypnogogic imagery.

    Answer: B – Those without REM sleep may have simply been more tired than those with REM. Thus, their lowered performance may reflect fatigue rather than less memory.

7. Which of the following does NOT support REM sleep functioning to help the brain rehearse important information?
    A) REM brain waves are similar to awake brain waves.
    B) Cats were observed performing in ways that are functional for them during REM.
    C) Those without REM performed less well on tasks than those with REM.
    D) **A disordered thalamus impacts REM sleep negatively.**

    Answer: D – The thalamus does not have the function of rehearsing information. It regulates bodily functions. All the other reasons were given as evidence of what happens during REM.

8. What could be a reason why infants spend many more hours in REM sleep than adults?
    A) **Infants are learning much more new material and require REM to consolidate it.**
    B) Infants are beginning to perceive color, which requires more REM.
    C) Infants don't actually enter REM sleep.
    D) If infants don't get REM sleep it can prove fatal.

    Answer: A – Answer D is also true, but is true also for adults, so it does not explain why it is relevant for infants more so.

9. What sleep pattern could be expected of study participants the first night after the study?

    A) **<u>Non-REM participants would begin REM sleep sooner than REM participants.</u>**

    B) Non-REM participants would remain in phase I sleep longer than REM participants.

    C) Non-REM participants would delay onset of REM as they did the previous night.

    D) Non-REM participants would demonstrate more delta waves than typical for them.

Answer: A – Non-REM participants would demonstrate sleep rebound, in which because they lacked proper REM sleep they would begin it more immediately and have more of it than typical or the REM participants would have.

Passage 3 Explanation

As adolescents look to distinguish themselves from their parents, some of their behaviors may go against the values of their parents. They often **don't think about future** consequences. For these reasons, many adolescents use drugs and alcohol during their adolescent years with their usage decreasing as they get older.

Cause and effect: lack of frontal cortex development makes adolescents focus on the present; identity formation leads to experimentation with different behaviors

However, in some adolescents, drug and alcohol **use can lead to abuse** and then dependence. In these adolescents, drugs and alcohol become a problem and can have **far-reaching consequences** such as legal, health, psychological, and financial problems. The adolescents that come to abuse drugs or be dependent on drugs may have differences from their peers, who only use these substances recreationally, in that among adolescent heavy drug users there are the **presence of risk factors, lack of protective factors, a biological predisposition, and psychological contributions.**

Cause and effect: drug use can lead to abuse depending on a variety of factors

Some risk factors that are associated with drug abuse include **low parental involvement, peer pressure, and having problem-behaving friends**. Some **protective factors** that adolescent problem users might be lacking include individual factors, such as appropriate **intellectual** functioning, family factors, such as close relationships with a **parent figure**, and extrafamilial context, such as connections to **positive organizations**.

Cause and effect: drug abuse is increased by a number of factors and there are protective factors that can decrease drug abuse

Some adolescents may have some **biological contributing factors** such as having a **genetic disposition** to becoming substance users, **lacking cognitive resources**, or being more disposed to **thrill seeking** and less concerned with consequences. Just having these traits alone is not enough to become addicted to drugs or alcohol. However, these biological factors may contribute when in the presence of other factors.

Cause and effect: biological factors can increase the likelihood of drug dependence

To assess the contribution of each of these factors to adolescent drug abuse, a **retrospective survey** was taken of **adolescents who were in treatment for substance use** problems and a control group of adolescents. These adolescents were queried about having the presence of the factors addressed above. The percent of adolescents having these issues are presented as follows:

Contrast: presence of various factors in a control group vs. drug abusers

Figure 1 Effects of various factors on drug abuse

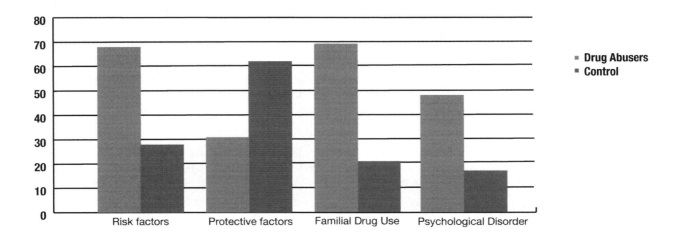

Figure 1 shows us that drug abusers are more likely to have risk factors, lack protective factors and are much more likely to have a family member who abuses drugs.

10. Which of the following is NOT a protective factor against adolescent drug abuse?
    A) High school achievement
    B) High Socio-economic status
    C) Involvement in school sports
    D) **Parental substance use**

    Answer: D – Parental substance use is a risk factor, not a protective factor.

11. Why do adolescents have difficulty making fully-informed decisions?
    A) **Their frontal cortex has not fully developed.**
    B) They are becoming more independent as adolescents.
    C) Their brainstem lacks certain neurotransmitters.
    D) There are psychological factors.

    Answer: A – The frontal cortex is not fully developed until after adolescence. The frontal cortex handles many important executive processes, such as making decisions.

12. Which of the following is a factor that the control group had a higher level of than the drug abusing adolescents?
    A) **Extra-familial support**
    B) Peer groups with substance use issues
    C) Disorders, such as depression
    D) Substance use within the family

    Answer: A – According to the chart, the only category in which the control adolescents were higher was preventative factors, an example of which is family support.

13. Why would an intervention like encouraging adolescents to "just say no to drugs" NOT be effective?

    A) It was not repeated enough.

    B) It was not shameful enough.

    C) **It did not address the biopsychosocial factors involved with drug use.**

    D) It did not account for adolescent cognitive immaturity.

Answer: C – As was seen in the passage, there are many reasons why adolescents use drugs. This intervention was too limited in its scope.

These questions are **NOT** related to a passage.

14. Attribution of humanitarian efforts, democracy, and altruism to capitalist designs aimed at controlling the masses is an element of:
    A) functionalism.
    B) **conflict theory.**
    C) symbolic interactionism.
    D) the cross-cultural perspective.

> Conflict theory is an analysis of social structures, institutions, and interactions from the viewpoint that emphasizes the different goals of each group, and how that can result in conflict. Karl Marx is the thinker typically associated with laying out the conflicts that underlie capitalist society. Thus seeing components of a capitalist society simply as tools used to control the masses would a conflict-theory viewpoint.

> A: Functionalism focuses on how different structures in society interact with each other to create a cohesive whole, and stresses interdependence, not conflict.
> C: Symbolic interactionism focuses on the small-scale interactions between individuals in a society rather than the large-scale societal forces asked about in the question.
> D: Cross-cultural studies look at how different cultures intersect - an idea not present in the question.

15. After western societies abolished slavery, political leaders hoped that freed slaves moving to new cities and communities would experience:
    A) racism.
    B) discrimination.
    C) segregation.
    D) **assimilation.**

> In the late 19th and early 20th century, much of the focus was on assimilating minority groups into the majority culture, rather than respecting their cultures as distinct and worthwhile in their own right. The classic "melting pot" idea indicated this attitude. In extreme cases, governments attempted to force assimilation (e.g. of American Indians or Australian aboriginals). At the time, this was a well-meant effort meant for "their own good". Clearly the goal was not hoping that such groups would experience racism, discrimination, or segregation.

16. In George Orwell's novel, 1984, the protagonist Winston Smith works as a historical revisionist for the totalitarian government. Such a government is characterized by:
I. a single political party.
II. propaganda and indoctrination of people.
III. a centrally planned economy.
    A) I only
    B) I and II only
    C) II and III only
    D) **I, II and III**

> Authoritarian and totalitarian governments are characterized by the monlithic power of a single political party which attempts to control all aspects of public life, including the economy.

17. Ed earns $150k annually from salary and investments, is 56 years old, leads the local chapter of Toastmasters (a social group devoted to improvement of public speaking), and works as a policy-maker at the state government level. The primary characteristic defining Ed's social status is his:

    A) $150k annual salary.

    B) 56 years of age.

    C) verbal and oratory proficiency.

    D) **<u>government policy-making work.</u>**

In most societies, one's occupation is the most important factor determining one's status.

Passage 4 Explanation

A **manager** of a car dealership would like to **increase his dealership's sales**. In order to do so, he has created a training program for his employees, which is presented as follows:

Opinion: manager wants to increase sales

Dear employees,

First of all, there are some techniques that can be helpful in increasing sales. The first is called the **"Foot-In-The-Door Technique."** In this technique, one person asks another person for a **small favor**. After that favor is granted, the requestor then asks the requestee for a **larger favor**. Asking for that initial favor first **increases** a person's **compliance** in granting the second request.

Key terms: "Foot In The Door Technique"
Cause and effect: agreeing to a small favor increases likelihood of granting large favor

Related to granting a first request, people that are told that **other people have granted a first request** will be more likely to grant a second request. In other words, people who view that others are granting requests become more likely to do so because they view granting requests as a **normal thing**.

Cause and effect: people will comply if they think compliance is normal because others have complied

A second technique is called the **"Door-In-The-Face Technique."** In this technique the requestor will first ask the requestee for a favor that is **larger in scope** than the desired request. The requestee will then likely **deny** this request. The requestor will then ask the requestee a **smaller request**. The requestee is then two times **more likely to grant this request** after being asked a larger request than if this request was asked initially.

Key terms: "Door In The Face Technique"
Cause and effect: rejecting an initial request that is very large increases the chance that someone will grant a second, smaller request.

As to why this technique is successful, first the details of this technique are important to consider. This technique is **only successful** when the second request is **immediately** made by the **same person** who requested the initial request. It is likely that the requestee **feels guilty** for having denied the initial request and so is willing to grant what he perceives to be a smaller request to assuage his guilt. This reason seems **especially** salient when the first request is viewed to be a **socially beneficial** request. In this condition a person is more likely to grant the second request than if the first request is not seen to be socially beneficial.

Cause and effect: a sense of guilt over rejecting a request increases compliance with a second request

Table 1 Results of changes in sales techniques

Strategy	Sales effect
Show the customer a more expensive car first	Increase second car sales 12%
Point out the popularity a particular car model	Increase warranty sales 16%
Ask for a small fee to subscribe to a service before selling an expensive warranty	Increase warranty sales 12%
Training sales personnel to act naturally with customers	Increase car sales 14%

Table 1: We see that all of the strategies employed were able to increase sales (either of cars or warranties) by roughly similar amounts

18. What strategy is an example of the Door-In-The-Face Technique?
    A) **Showing the customer a more expensive car first**
    B) Pointing out the popularity of a particular car model
    C) Asking for a small fee to subscribe to a service before selling an expensive warranty
    D) Training sales personnel to act naturally with customers

    Answer: A – Showing the customer a more expensive car first is an example of asking for a large favor, with the result of increased second car sales.

19. What could be done to improve the strategy of asking a small fee to subscribe to a service before selling a warranty?
    A) Making the service more expensive
    B) Making the service vastly more expensive
    C) **Telling the customer the fee helps support public radio**
    D) Telling the customer the fee is recurring

    Answer: C – It is helpful if a first request is socially beneficial, which supporting public radio would likely be considered to be.

20. A salesperson not making a sale after expecting he would and then justifying that that person did not really want to buy a car is an example of a resolution of what type of phenomenon?
    A) Belief perseverance
    B) **Cognitive dissonance**
    C) Mental heuristic
    D) Fundamental attribution error

    Answer: B – A discrepancy between a belief, the salesperson believing the customer wanted to buy the car, and a behavior, the customer not buying the car, creates cognitive dissonance. The justification that the customer didn't really want the car is a way for the salesperson to resolve this dissonance.

21. Which of the following is likely to result in a lost sale?

  A) **<u>The customer overhearing the salespeople talking about sales techniques</u>**
  B) The customer seeing the sales team putting up signs advertising sales
  C) The customer being asked to sign up for a free discount membership
  D) The customer hearing that the sale is ending soon

  Answer: A – The customer may feel that he is being tricked if he hears the salespeople talking about sales techniques, which would lead to him being less likely to buy.

Passage 5 Explanation

There have been findings that individuals who have experienced a **traumatic event**, resulting in the development of **Post-Traumatic Stress Disorder** (PTSD), often have **difficulty accurately recounting** the traumatic incident. One explanation for the difficulties with memory involves the **dual representation theory**. This theory states that memories are encoded and stored in different ways and that traumatic memories are stored in two different ways. One way that memories are stored is through **Verbally Accessible Memory** (VAM). Information that is consciously processed is stored in VAM. This autobiographical information can later be recalled verbally. Information that is not consciously processed is stored in **sensory accessible memory** (SAM). This information consists of visuospatial and sensory information.

Key terms: PTSD, dual representation theory, VAM, SAM
Cause and effect: the difficulty recalling traumatic events is associated with the two types of memory storage

One model explaining this dual processing of traumatic information is that during traumatic situations the **limbic system overrides executive** processes, as **more basic** functions are more imperative for physical survival. Thus the **information is processed** in more basic ways, through **sensory and visuospatial means**, and stored in SAM. This has been supported in research by findings that when recalling information about a trauma and being stopped while doing so and asked to perform a verbal or visuospatial task, people had **more trouble performing the visuospatial task** than the verbal compared to when they were not recalling traumatic information. This suggests that the presence of the intrusive traumatic memories is dependent on visuospatial resources, which are allocated to these memories and not available to devote to other activities requiring visuospatial skills.

Key terms: limbic, executive
Contrast: trauma makes people store memories in more basic ways (limbic vs. executive)

22. Which of the following would suggest that trauma is, in fact, processed in the VAM?
    A) Individuals recalling a number of details about smells they experienced during the trauma
    B) **Individuals having a harder time memorizing a list of coping strategies while they are recounting their trauma**
    C) An individual seems to lack words for describing his traumatic experience
    D) The presence of persistent flashbacks to the trauma

    Answer: B – As was specified in the passage, an indication of trauma being stored in SAM is that individuals had a harder time performing a visuospatial task while recalling their trauma. Thus, an indication of VAM processing would be having a harder time with a verbal task while processing trauma. In addition, this answer can be derived by eliminating other answers, which are actual indications of trauma, which is processed in the SAM.

23. What could be a beneficial effect of processing trauma through the VAM?
    A) **An individual is then able to allocate executive processes to address traumatic symptoms**
    B) Verbal traumatic experience is less threatening than sensory trauma
    C) Less cognitive resources need to be allocated
    D) Medication can then be prescribed

    Answer: A – As stated in the passage, executive processes are overridden during times of trauma, resulting in the trauma being encoded in SAM. When the trauma is processed in VAM, executive processes are able to be marshaled to generate coping strategies.

24. Which of the following is an evolutionary psychology explanation for why traumatic information comes to be encoded in the SAM?
    A) Information encoded in the VAM allows the individual to generate helpful strategies for avoiding future traumas.
    B) Information processed in the SAM is easier to ignore than if it is processed in the VAM.
    C) **Information processed in the limbic system results in quicker reactions to threats.**
    D) The SAM is less sensitive to traumatic incidents than the VAM.

    Answer: C – As stated in the passage, traumatic information which is processed in the limbic system leads to its being stored in the SAM. By being processed in the limbic system an individual is able to react quicker to threats, thus ensuring survival. These traits are likely to be passed to future generations, thus providing an evolutionary psychology explanation.

25. Which of the following is not considered a symptom of trauma?
    A) Re-experiencing the trauma through flashbacks
    B) Avoiding triggers related to the trauma
    C) Dissociating when thinking about the trauma
    D) **Lowered intellectual functioning**

    Answer: D – Answers A-C are symptoms of trauma.

These questions are **NOT** related to a passage.

26. A five-year old subject enrolls in Vail Primary School for kindergarten. After arriving, she must acclimate to the new environment. This is an example of:
    A) primary socialization.
    B) **secondary socialization.**
    C) anticipatory socialization.
    D) re-socialization.

Secondary socialization refers to the process of learning norms and behaviors which are appropriate to a smaller group within a larger society. A school setting is one such example of a sub-group within a larger society. Here, the five-year-old subject must adjust not only to a new school, but to the new rules and norms of a kindergarten learning environment. This makes (B) the best answer.

A: Primary socialization involves individuals learning the basic rules and norms of their culture. It typically takes place in the home rather than in school. Here the prompt does not refer specifically to the basic rules of behavior, but instead entering a school environment; this relates more closely to secondary socialization.
C: Anticipatory socialization is when individuals attempt to predict or rehearse appropriate behavior for future situations. This is not taking place in the prompt.
D: Re-socialization is when previous behaviors and reflexes are replaced with new behaviors and reflexes. It is unclear from the prompt whether it will be necessary for the subject to discontinue old behaviors in the new school environment. All we know is that the subject is entering a sub-group within a larger society. As such, (B) is the better choice.

27. A trainer at the circus is attempting to train an elephant to stand up on its hind legs through the use of a food reward. When starting out, the trainer gives one food reward every time the elephant stands up in response to a hand signal. Later on, the trainer gives a food reward after going through the hand signal-stand up routine five times in a row. Which two schedules of reinforcement has the trainer shifted between?
    A) Fixed ratio schedule to fixed interval schedule
    B) Fixed interval schedule to variable interval schedule
    C) Fixed interval schedule to continuous reinforcement
    D) **Continuous reinforcement to fixed ratio schedule**

Giving one reward per response qualifies as a continuous reinforcement schedule, the first half of answer (D). Giving one reward per fixed number of responses qualifies as a fixed ratio schedule, the second half of answer (D). This makes (D) the right answer.

A: The first part of training counts as continuous reinforcement, not a fixed ratio schedule. In the second part of training, there is no indication from the prompt that the intervals between reinforcement and the previous reinforcement are designed to be the same length every time, which is required for a fixed interval schedule.
B: The prompt does not indicate that the trainer is intentionally using reinforcement either based on a fixed length of time since the previous reinforcement, or based on a variable amount of time since the previous reinforcement.
C: The first part of training does not involve each reinforcement being scheduled at fixed amounts of time later than the previous reinforcement; this eliminates a fixed interval schedule from consideration. Additionally, continuous reinforcement would require a reward after each response, which is not happening in the second half of training – instead, five responses are required for a reward.

28. A college student visits a foreign country as part of an exchange program and finds the habits of the locals to be unnatural and somewhat offensive. After returning home, the student takes a series of sociology courses and reevaluates his experiences based on the different standards of normal found in the foreign country. The student now evaluates the foreign society as less appealing than his own, but still quite natural in its own right. The student judged the foreign culture with:
    A) **ethnocentrism followed by cultural relativism.**
    B) ethnocentrism followed by assimilation.
    C) cultural relativism followed by assimilation.
    D) cultural relativism followed by ethnocentrism.

    Ethnocentrism involves judging another culture by the values and beliefs of one's own culture, and concluding that the other culture is inferior. Here, the student finding the other culture "unnatural" or offensive is an example of the student's ethnocentrism. Moving to a view in which a culture is viewed through its own values and understood as worthwhile it its own right is cultural relativism. By coming to better understand the other culture, the student moved towards a perspective of cultural relativism.

29. Which of the following is an example of aversive prejudice?
    A) Believing that all members of an in-group are unique, while all members of an out-group are the same as each other.
    B) **Feeling nervous in the presence of an out-group, even though cognitive thoughts and beliefs about the out-group are neutral.**
    C) Experiencing negative thoughts, feelings and behaviors about members of an out-group.
    D) Intentionally attempting not to get involved a situation that might trigger a severe phobia.

    For something to qualify as aversive prejudice, thoughts and beliefs about the out-group will be either neutral, or a mix of positive and negative; feelings and emotions about the out-group, though, will be negative. (B) is therefore the correct answer.

    A: This is an example of out-group homogeneity.
    C: This is an example of dominative prejudice.
    D: This is an example of avoidance behavior.

Passage 6 Explanation

The following represents a portion of a treatment plan of a psychologist who is treating a client, John, who has been diagnosed with **Borderline Personality Disorder (BPD)**, a type of personality disorder characterized by symptoms described in the plan.

Key terms: Borderline Personality Disorder

"John began treatment with me about 6 months ago. He came to me presenting with a history of **failed relationships**, having a history of **trauma**, and having **substance use** issues. John described having a series of relationships in which he would become **extremely attached** to a partner whom he had known for only a short time. John would begin to feel **overwhelmed** by this closeness and soon there would be a fight between John and his partner, typically over something trivial. This would result in John **distancing** himself from her. After some time, John would become despondent and perceived to be abandoned by his partner and attempt reconciliation, which would result in John again becoming extremely attached. This cycle of **attachment and separation** would continue repeatedly, invariably resulting in the partner becoming overwhelmed and terminating the relationship. Throughout this relationship cycle, John would **frequently abuse drugs and alcohol**, during times when he felt overwhelmed by the intimacy of the relationship and also when he felt abandoned.

Opinion: The patient engaged in cycles of attachment and withdrawal in relationships and abused drugs and alcohol.

As John processed his current romantic relationships, he also began to **address his past familial relationships**. John experienced **physical abuse** by one of his parents. He described a cycle with the abusing parent, whereby his parent would behave unpredictably, sometimes **abusing John for no apparent reason**. This would soon be followed by this parent trying to **reconcile** with John. This pattern of feeling distance and closeness led to John having a **disorganized style of attachment** and seemed to create a template for how John learned to interact in future relationships.

Key terms: disorganized attachment style
Cause and effect: The abuse and reconciliation pattern that John experienced in childhood created a disorganized attachment style that carried into adulthood.

For many people who have been raised **without a sense of security** these **feelings are manageable if they are able to understand** the relationship between their feelings, actions, and thoughts. This process of being able to think about the relationship of these personal processes is called **mentalization**.

Key terms: mentalization
Cause and effect: A lack of safety and an inability to properly express needs creates frustration; this frustration can be managed by understanding it through mentalization.

Mentalization is a process that invokes the **prefrontal cortex**, the area of the brain that is responsible for **executive processes.** When mentalizing, humans use their prefrontal cortex to **examine how they are thinking and feeling** in a situation. However, individuals with a **disorganized style** of attachment learn to react with arousal. This may happen if frequent feelings of frustration are evoked and paired with needs, resulting in a style of processing information that relies less on mentalization and the prefrontal cortex and more on **hyperarousal**.

Key terms: mentalization, prefrontal cortex, hyperarousal

Cause and effect: People with disorganized attachment are unable to engage their prefrontal cortex and become overwhelmed by their feelings.

To address these deficits in **mentalization**, John and I have been meeting in **individual psychotherapy**, with one of the goals of therapy being to try to help John improve in his ability to mentalize.

Opinion: Therapy is helpful for the patient by teaching him to mentalize about his experiences in a safe environment, which he can then transfer outside of the therapy sessions.

To monitor John's progress in therapy I have charted John's monthly scores, over the past 6 months, on the BPD Rating scale. This scale is an inventory of 10 behaviors characteristic of BPD."

Table 1 Results of the BPD ratings for six months

Month	Jan.	Feb.	Mar.	April	May.	June
BPD Score	8	9	10	10	8	9

Table 1 shows us that John's progress has remained relatively steady over the past six months.

30. Which of the following is likely NOT a factor explaining why John's scores on the BPD initially increased?
    A) Attachment based disorders take a long time to treat.
    B) John may have felt distress initially in his relationship with his therapist.
    C) **John missed a sensitive period in his life for learning to mentalize.**
    D) Mentalizing is a complicated task.

    Answer: C – As discussed in the passage during therapy clients can develop the capacity to mentalize.

31. Why would John not have been diagnosed with BPD or any other personality disorder when he was a youth?
    A) Relationship issues do not begin until adulthood.
    B) **Personality disorders may only be diagnosed in adults.**
    C) Personality disorders were not diagnoses when John was younger.
    D) Youth relationships typically do not impact adult relationships.

    Answer: B – As youths' personalities are assumed to still be developing until adulthood and personality disorders are seen to be relatively stable disorders, these disorders are not diagnosable until adulthood.

32. What could be a secondary gain for John from continued non-improvement in his BPD scores, as indicated in the data?
    A) He wants to improve but doesn't know how.
    B) He could learn to mentalize.
    C) **He could continue his relationship with his therapist.**
    D) He could continue his pattern of failed romantic relationships.

    Answer: C – A secondary gain is a benefit a client incurs from continuing to present with his issues. For John, who may avoid recreating feelings of abandonment, this may allow him to have a continued relationship with the psychologist.

33. If a brain scan shows that John's prefrontal cortex becomes more activated in the months following June, what might this suggest about John's emotional reactions?

A) **John will likely have less extreme reactions.**
B) John will likely have more extreme reactions.
C) John will likely feel more attachment to his caregivers.
D) John will likely feel less attachment to his caregivers.

Answer: A — Preceding June, John's BPD Rating scale scores were high, suggesting he is still experiencing symptoms of BPD, which include extreme emotional reactions. If John's prefrontal cortex is more activated, this suggests he is reacting with less hyperarousal and is better able to use mentalization to reflect on his experiences, making him have less extreme reactions.

Passage 7 Explanation

There is a relationship between **child behavior and child maltreatment**, with an increasing recognition of the **bidirectional** influences of each of these factors. Children with behavioral disorders were found to be the largest subtype of children with disabilities, who as a group were two to three and a half times as likely to be maltreated than children without disabilities. It is typically assumed that **child maltreatment results in child behavior issues**. However, there is also evidence that **disruptive child behavior can lead to increased child maltreatment**. In a study of parenting behavior of parents with children with disruptive behavior and children without disruptive behavior, the greatest negative parenting behaviors were displayed by parents towards children with disruptive behaviors. This was true of parents of children with both behavioral disorders and without behavioral disorders, but was most pronounced among parents with children with behavioral disorders, suggesting that a **history of child behavioral disorders** tends to **elicit negative parenting behaviors**.

Key terms: maltreatment, behavioral disorders
Cause and effect: bad parenting makes kids misbehave, and bad child behavior causes parents to treat their children badly

Related to **behaviorism**, the **coercion hypothesis** illustrates the effect contingencies have on child and parent interactions and behavior patterns. According to this model, during parent-child interactions children can be reinforced when they **respond** to parent requests in **negative ways** when such negative responses **lead to a cessation of the parent request**.

Cause and effect: A child will act defiant towards the parent because he learns that misbehaving will lead to the parent withdrawing an unwanted request.

This pattern of behavior eventually **coalesces into a behavioral script**, in which both parent and child **expect this pattern** to perpetuate and therefore accommodate this pattern. This script may come to dictate the child's behavior in other situations as well, **leading to a pattern of refusal** and disruptive behavior in school and in other settings, further solidifying this behavioral strategy.

Key terms: behavioral script, pattern of refusal
Cause and effect: Defiant behavior with a parent can then lead to defiant behavior generally; patterns of defiant behavior can harm the child

Therefore, treatments for parents who have maltreated children or for children with disruptive behaviors seek to eliminate this pattern of defiance. Therapists attempt to address this pattern by asking parents to **state their requests in clear terms** and then upon non-compliance **presenting the child with a choice** between acceding to the request or receiving a negative consequence. Parents are instructed to **remove the emotional content** from their statements so that they do not become frustrated or lose control and do not establish a condition in which communication escalates in volume and negativity. In addition, parents are instructed to **follow through with consequences consistently**, even if the child eventually complies with the task, as consistency is important.

Cause and effect: To break down the defiant pattern parents are taught to consistently apply consequences and avoid getting emotional.

Parent Child Interaction Therapy (PCIT) is a type of therapy that aims to teach these behaviors. A meta-analysis was conducted to review studies in which PCIT has been evaluated for its effect on disruptive child behaviors. Outcome variables were gathered from measures of child disruptive behaviors before and after treatment. The pre-treatment scores were subtracted from the post-treatment scores in each measure and divided by the standard deviation to obtain the measure's study effect size. The study effect sizes were aggregated across studies and the overall results are presented as follows:

Key terms: Parent-Child Interaction Therapy

Cause and effect: PCIT can affect parent and child behavior.

Table 1 Study results

Measure	Child Compliance	Child Disruptive Behavior	Parent Effective Instruction	Parent Follow-Through
Effect Size	+.48	-.86	+1.02	+.96

Table 1 shows a beneficial effect of PCIT on the behavior of both parents and children.

34. According to the coercion hypothesis, in what direction do the behaviors addressed in the study move?
    A) Parent behavior influences child behavior.
    B) Child behavior influences parent behavior.
    C) **Parent and child behavior influence each other.**
    D) Parent and child behavior do not influence each other.

    Answer: C – According to the coercion hypothesis, parent and child behavior influence each other, with child defiance or compliance leading to the type of command and follow through given from the parent and vice-versa.

35. What would be necessary to change for the improvements seen in the study to generalize beyond the research setting?
    A) Parent-child defiance
    B) **Parent-child scripts**
    C) Parent-child contingencies
    D) Parent-child frequency of requests

    Answer: B – According to the passage, scripts refer to the expectation of a pattern of behavior. If the behavior is to generalize outside of the research setting both parents and children must expect that their new strategies will be effective there.

36. What are NOT contingencies that might motivate a child in the study?
    A) Avoid positive punishment of receiving a consequence for a disruptive behavior
    B) Seek positive reinforcement of parental approval for compliance
    C) **Avoid negative reinforcement of receiving a punishment for non-compliance**
    D) Avoid negative punishment of not being able to play for disruptive behavior

    Answer: C – This is not negative reinforcement; this is punishment. Negative reinforcement is when something is removed in order to increase a behavior. An example would be having less chores for completing previous chores.

37. Had results from the PCIT sessions been reported over time, what pattern might have been observed in the measures?
    A) Greater initial parent effective instruction compared to later
    B) **<u>Decreased initial child compliance compared to later</u>**
    C) Decreased later parent follow-through compared to initially
    D) Increased later child disruptive behavior compared to initially

Answer: B – It is likely that as parents increased the commands they gave the child, rather than avoiding giving them, the child would initially be non-compliant, as is typical in these parent-child scripts. Eventually compliance would increase.

Passage 8 Explanation

Since some of the original work done by **Galton** over a hundred years ago in developing instruments that can effectively measure intelligence, there has been a pronounced focus on developing tests that **correctly measure intelligence**. This is evidenced by the **variety** of tests that have been developed which purport to measure intelligence and the extensive research that has been conducted in an attempt to assess intelligence. There is a great deal at stake in developing effective measures of intelligence due to the large number of people whose intelligence is tested and the money invested in research. One of the main recurring questions in the efforts to measure intelligence is, **"What is intelligence, exactly?"** One aspect of this question is to what extent is intelligence a **broad construct versus a number of specific abilities**.

Key terms: Galton, measure intelligence
Opinion: The key question is what exactly intelligence is and the broad vs. specific view of intelligence

Weighing in on the side that IQ is a **broad** construct, **Spearman** defined intelligence as being a **general** intelligence, which he referred to as a **g factor**. This g factor was responsible for an individual's intellectual functioning on a variety of tasks.

Key terms: Spearman, g factor
Opinion: Spearman believes intelligence is a single general trait

Other theorists have viewed intelligence as being comprised of a **number of separate abilities**. These abilities are **not necessarily related** to each other. For example, an individual might be poor at math, but be exceptional at artistic endeavors.

Opinion: Some think that intelligence is multiple unrelated skills and that a multiple skill approach gives a better representation of a person's intelligence.

Most modern intellectual testing **combines the two** approaches. For example, the **Wechsler Adult Intelligence Scale (WAIS)** is one of the most **widely used** measures of cognitive abilities. This tests consists of a number of subtests from which **4 index scores** are derived. These indices are Verbal Ability, a measure of an individual's knowledge of and ability to use language, Perceptual Reasoning, a measure of an individual's ability to perceive and manipulate primarily visual information, Processing Speed, a measure of an individual's ability to quickly process information both with and without a motor component, and Working Memory, a measure of an individual's ability to store, manipulate, and recall information within a short time. Additionally an overall score is also generated, which is called the Full Scale Intelligence Quotient (FSIQ) score. This is **purported to be an overall measure of an individual's cognitive abilities**. The test is standardized so that a score of 100 represents the 50th percentile. One standard deviation in either direction is 15 points.

Key terms: Wechsler Adult Intelligence Scale
Opinion: Modern IQ tests try to strike a balance

A WAIS assessment was administered to an individual named Michael at his university, and his scores are presented as follows:

Table 1 Results of WAIS assessment

Measure	Score
FSIQ	92
Verbal	84
Perceptual Reasoning	104
Processing Speed	100
Working Memory	89

Table 1 shows us the results of the IQ test for one individual. We can see that his verbal skill was the lowest and his perceptual reasoning and processing speed were his best. His overall IQ was a bit below average.

38. What would be a good question to have answered about Michael before recommending particular remediation based upon his scores?
    A) Is he right or left-handed?
    B) **Is English his first language?**
    C) Is he able to see the information presented to him?
    D) Is he able to work with a time constraint?

    Answer: B – Based on his scores Michael is more than one standard deviation away from average in his Verbal abilities. Knowing if English is his first language might explain some of his difficulties and would change how Michael's remediation is approached.

39. What is a drawback to viewing intelligence as Spearman conceived it?
    A) Intelligence can be represented more succinctly.
    B) Research can focus on identifying what the underlying g factor is.
    C) **An individual's cognitive strengths cannot be emphasized.**
    D) Defining intelligence is a difficult task.

    Answer: C – Spearman viewed intelligence as consisting of a g factor, which represented an individual's overall abilities. He did not focus on emphasizing individual abilities.

40. What is an argument against inherent factors influencing IQ?
    A) Similar IQ scores in families
    B) Differences in IQ scores in different nations
    C) IQ scores tending to increase overall in subsequent generations
    D) **Different ethnicities having different average IQ scores depending on their nationality**

    Answer: D – This finding would support there being differences in IQ scores based on cultural factors, rather than based on inherent abilities.

41. What might be a good recommendation to help Michael in school?
   A) **<u>Obtain printed copies of lecture notes</u>**
   B) Request oral exams
   C) Ask to have his allotted test time reduced
   D) Focus on his overall ability, rather than his separate abilities

   Answer: A – Michael seems to be weakest in his Verbal abilities. Thus, obtaining printed notes would help him utilize his strengths, his visual processing.

42. Rather than focusing on an individual's IQ scores, considering how the individual makes use of his abilities, such as his current work and his ability to adapt to his weaknesses, represents what view of assessment?
   A) Structuralism
   B) **<u>Functionalism</u>**
   C) Multiculturalism
   D) Heuristic assessment

   Answer: B – Functionalism emphasizes how abilities manifest in an individual's life.

These questions are **NOT** related to a passage.

43. A person walks by an overturned armored truck with tens of thousands of dollars worth of money scattered all around it on the ground. He decides not to pick any up, and continues walking past. On his return trip, he sees that a large number of people have gathered near the truck, and are picking up and pocketing the money. He walks up to the money on the ground and pockets some for himself. What best describes the change in his attitude and actions?

   A) Erickson's theory of developmental stages.
   B) The bystander effect.
   C) Groupthink.
   D) **<u>Deindividuation.</u>**

Characteristics of deindividuation include loss of capacity for self-awareness and self-evaluation, and a diminished sense of personal responsibility. All of these appear to happen when the person decides to take the money once he is part of a crowd, even though he would not take the money when by himself. This makes (D) the best answer.

A: Erickson's stages of development relate to the development of self, identity, trust and social independence at different ages. It does not explain why the person in the prompt behaves differently during the initial trip than during the return trip.
B: The bystander effect takes place when the presence of others makes someone less likely to provide help than if that person were alone. Here, the person is equally unlikely to help regardless of whether or not others are present. Although a diminished sense of personal responsibility occurs with the bystander effect, there is no other connection with the events in the prompt, making (D) the superior answer.
C: Groupthink occurs when members of an in-group want to minimize intra-group conflict, and feel compelled to avoid unpleasant debate and make consensus decisions. Here, it seems unlikely that the strangers gathered to pick up money constitute an in-group, or that the person in the prompt is motivated by a desire to avoid unpleasant debate with them.

44. All of the following illustrate characteristics of ethnocentrism EXCEPT:

   A) A Japanese tourist in the United States asks for squid as a pizza topping. The pizza shop proprietor expresses confusion and some disgust.
   B) **<u>A Northeastern university gives preferential treatment to children and grandchildren of alumni in deciding who to admit.</u>**
   C) A person of Greek heritage expresses constant pride that the ancient Greeks, by inventing civilization, accomplished what no other group could have.
   D) A university professor in Spain writes a book on the colonization of Mexico by the Spanish without including material from historical or contemporary Native American sources.

Characteristics of ethnocentrism include: people seeing things primarily from the perspective of their own culture, the belief that one's culture or ethnic group is the most important, and the belief that one's own culture is the most natural way of seeing the world. (A), (C) and (D) each include an example of one of these; (B) does not, however, and this makes it the correct answer.

A: Here, the tourist and the shop proprietor are each seeing things from the perspective of their own culture. What's normal to the one is strange and confusing to the other.
B: Correct. Rather than an example of ethnocentrism, which relates only to cultural or ethnic differences, this is an example of perpetuating social stratification through institutional discrimination.
C: The person here believes in the superiority of his own ethnic group, which is one of the qualities of

ethnocentrism.

D: Here, the university professor believes it is natural to include the Spanish perspective in the book, but also that it is unimportant to include a perspective from a different culture. The belief that one's own cultural perspective is the most natural way to view the world is characteristic of ethnocentrism.

45. An immigrant family finds economic success and moves to a wealthy neighborhood in a new state. In this state, the population of people from the immigrant family's home country is much lower than the national average, and there are no other immigrant families in the wealthy neighborhood. As a consequence of this move, the family may likely experience:

    A) low socioeconomic status.

    B) an absence of social capital.

    C) <u>social exclusion.</u>

    D) environmental injustice.

Social exclusion may result from this immigrant family moving to a neighborhood where they stand out as the only family that is different from their neighbors.

A: The question tells us that the family has found economic success, allowing them to move to a wealthy neighborhood. So they do not have a low socioeconomic status.

B: While they may have lower social capital than other well-established members of the community, we've no reason to suspect that this family doesn't have some social connections (through other immigrant families in their old state, etc.) to provide social capital.

D: Environmental injustice is typically suffered by those of low socioeconomic status (e.g. having a toxic waste dump placed near a poor neighborhood), rather than by those in the wealthy neighborhood described in the question

Passage 9 Explanation

In the course of one year in the U.S. 20% of **children and adolescents have mental health problem symptoms** or signs and approximately 5% have "extreme functional impairment." The ramifications of these mental health issues in school include a **drop-out rate** among youth with these issues **twice** that of those without mental health difficulties, **lower grades and test scores** among youth with behavioral difficulties and inattention, and **more** restricted settings and **special-education** accommodations among youth with untreated mental health needs.

Cause and effect: Failing to address the mental health needs of children leads to a series of problems

However, **less than 30% of children in need** of mental health services **receive** these services. The cost of treating children's mental health needs is $15 billion dollars per year. While this number may seem daunting, total yearly social costs associated with mental health issues are estimated to be $247 billion. These social costs include long-term costs to productivity, contagion effects, crime, etc. While the entirety of this $247 billion may not be recoupable through intervention efforts, **it is possible to reclaim a great deal of it through effective interventions**.

Opinion: Because so few children get the mental health services they need, a lot of money is wasted and could be reclaimed through earlier intervention

A substantial amount of research has demonstrated the **positive impact mental health practitioners** have had in schools. A meta-analysis of recent mental health interventions at a number of schools throughout the United States found a **64% rate of improvement in student academic performance** and mental health functioning and a 95% improvement in mental health alone as a result of the interventions. In research studies, school psychologists have been shown to **effectively engage students**, work with educators and families, and implement interventions. These services have been shown to be effective in **reducing dropout rates, increasing academic performance and reducing behavior problems, and helping increase teacher effectiveness**. School psychologists have also been effective in addressing student mental health issues, social, emotional, and behavioral health concerns, and problem-solving and self-regulating skills.

Opinion: School psychologists benefit schools in a number of ways

In terms of the financial benefits of school-based mental health services, there are **clear benefits in investing in mental health services** early in students' lives. Results from an analysis of early intervention programs for low-income children indicated that there were savings in criminal justice, special education, and welfare assistance costs. A district school based psycho-educational program found benefits of **$9,837 per student in long-term social problems aversion**. Finally, school-based **drug programs** have been shown to provide **$840 in long-term benefit compared with costs of $150** per student.

Cause and effect: Because early intervention mental health services can reduce future problems, they end up saving school systems and society a lot of money in the long run.

The following data summarizes research comparing a number of indicators of health at high schools with dedicated mental health services and schools without those services.

Table 1 Effect of mental health services on high schools

School	Drop-out %	% of students with passing standardized test scores	% in special education
With Services	20	73	8
Without Services	42	61	12

Table 1 shows us the various benefits that school districts get from having mental health services, including lower dropout rate, better test scores, and fewer kids in special education.

46. Which of the following is NOT a benefit to providing mental health services for students at schools?
    A) Improved academic performance
    B) Reduced mental health issues
    C) **Improved family functioning**
    D) Reduced social costs

    Answer: C – The passage does not cite findings of improved family functioning as a result of mental health services at school.

47. Which of the following could be a confounding factor in the research presented in the table?
    A) Special education is a type of mental health service
    B) Standardized testing test ceiling effects
    C) **Schools with mental health services are likely different than schools without those services**
    D) A higher dropout percent means fewer students are available for standardized testing

    Answer: C – It is likely that schools with mental health services have other resources available which can help students or likely have students with more resources themselves. Thus, better student outcomes may be attributable to these factors, rather than the mental health services.

48. Which of the following may be a barrier to implementing mental health services at schools?
    A) **Short-term costs**
    B) Long-term costs
    C) Short-term benefits
    D) Long-term benefits

    Answer: A – According to the passage, there is a substantial immediate cost for providing mental health services. However, there is a long-term savings from providing these services.

49. Why might it be beneficial to an individual without children in school to support mental health services in schools?
    A) Longer school hours for students
    B) **Increased tax revenue from more productive graduates**
    C) Improved student academics
    D) Increases in special education services

Answer: B – A social benefit is that students receiving mental health services tend to become more productive workers, which would lead to increased tax revenue.

50. Students who witness their classmates benefitting from mental health services and become more willing to seek out these services themselves have benefitted from a reduction in what?
    A) Social facilitation
    B) Deindividuation
    C) **Stigma**
    D) Conformity

Answer: C – Witnessing other people doing something that may have previously seemed taboo can lead to the stigma being reduced. This can encourage people to do things like seek mental health services.

Passage 10 Explanation

Neurons get information from other neurons via **dendrites**. Dendrites, which look similar to branches extending from a tree, get the information from other neurons via **synaptic receptors**. Some dendrites increase their capacity for information with the use of **dendritic spines**, short extensions which **increase the available surface area** for receiving information.

Key terms: neurons, dendrites, synaptic receptors
Cause and effect: dendritic spines increase available surface area

Information received in the dendrites is communicated to the main area of the neuron, the **cell body**, which contains the nucleus, ribosomes, mitochondria, and other structures. The neuron controls the flow of information from the cell body. The membrane of the neuron keeps an electrical gradient between the inside and outside of the cell. This gradient is typically in a **state of polarization**, in which there is a **slightly negative electrical potential within the membrane** versus outside the membrane, in a condition known as the **resting potential**.

Key terms: cell body, polarization, resting potential

A stimulus may act upon the neuron causing it to become **depolarized**. When the neuron reaches a certain threshold of depolarization, then an action potential may occur. The action potential is sent down the **main efferent branch from the neuron**, the axon, in a process called propagation of the action potential. This electrical message is aided in conduction via a coating surrounding the axon called the **myelin sheath**. The action potential is regenerated along the axon at the **nodes of Ranvier**, uncoated areas in which **sodium ions again enter** the axon and propagate an action potential at each node. This continues until the axon terminates at a pre-synaptic cleft. At this cleft the axon's electric transmission is converted to a chemical message that is transmitted across a synapse.

Key terms: axon, nodes of Ranvier, myelin sheath
Cause and effect: sodium entering the cell propagates the signal

A **synapse** is the gap between two neurons at which point the neurons communicate. The message communicated across the synapse first begins in the cell body of the transmitting neuron, in which the chemicals are synthesized which serve as **neurotransmitters**. Some different types of neurotransmitters include amino acids, peptides, acetylcholoine, monoamines, and purines. These different neurotransmitters serve different functions. Other neurotransmitters are **synthesized** in the presynaptic terminal, closer to where they will be released. The process of producing these neurotransmitters is quite slow, so the body uses a number of alternative techniques, such as **recycling to reduce the wait**.

Key terms: synapse, neurotransmitters
Cause and effect: recycling the neurotransmitters speeds up the process

These neurotransmitters are carried down the axons with the action potentials as described above. When they reach the end of the axon to the presynaptic terminal, the action potential causes gates to open, **through which calcium flows**. This **calcium** causes the neuron to release neurotransmitters into the synaptic cleft, in a process known as **exocytosis**. The neurotransmitter then crosses the synaptic cleft to the postsynaptic membrane in the next neuron.

Cause and effect: the calcium flowing into the axon causes it to release the neurotransmitters into the synapse.

Some of the major neurotransmitters and their primary functions are presented in the following table:

Table 1 Examples of Neurotransmitters

Neurotransmitter	Function
Acetylcholine	Stimulating muscles; brain arousal
Dopamine	Voluntary movements; reward & pleasure
Serotonin	Mood & emotions; regulating basic functions
Glutamate	Learning & memory
Endorphins	Reduction of pain

Table 1 lists a number of neurotransmitters. Skim it quickly and move on. If you need any of the information in it, you'll just come back and look it up.

51. What pair of neurotransmitters, at inappropriate levels, are implicated in the tremors exhibited in Parkinson's Disease?
    A) Serotonin and Glutamate
    B) Endorphins and Dopamine
    C) **Dopamine and Acetylcholine**
    D) Acetylcholine and Glutamate

    Answer: C – Dopamine and acetylcholine are both involved in muscle functions. Therefore, irregular muscle movements are the result of inappropriate levels of those neurotransmitters.

52. What is the purpose of neurotransmitter reuptake?
    A) **Reuse neurotransmitters**
    B) Keep neurotransmitters in the synapse
    C) Block the uptake of neurotransmitters
    D) To increase resting potential

    Answer: A – As stated in the passage, the production of neurotransmitters is a slow process. Therefore, neurons reuse neurotransmitters.

53. What might occur in a mirror neuron when observing an action in another person?
    A) Resting potential
    B) **Action potential**
    C) Neurotransmitter reuptake
    D) Polarization

    Answer: B – Mirror neurons may fire when an individual observes another person engaging in some action. They are postulated to be involved in empathy and mirroring.

54. What relationship do motor neurons have with the CNS?
    A) **Efferent to the CNS**
    B) Afferent to the CNS
    C) Proximal to the CNS
    D) Distal to the CNS

    Answer: A – Motor neurons bring information away from the CNS, or are efferent. Sensory neurons bring information to the CNS and are afferent.

55. What may lead to the cognitive slowing observed in Alzheimer's Disease?
    A) Neurotransmitter confusion
    B) Decreased level of action potential
    C) **Myelin sheath deterioration**
    D) Exocytosis

    Answer: C – As stated in the passage, the myelin sheath aids in conduction of the action potential along the axon. Deterioration of the sheath would thus lead to cognitive slowing.

These questions are **NOT** related to a passage.

56. Which of the following characteristics are associated with classical conditioning?
 I. Reward and punishment
 II. Reinforcement schedules
III. **Conditioned and unconditioned responses**
   A) I only
   B) **III only**
   C) I and II only
   D) I, II and III

Choice I, reward and punishment (or, positive and negative reinforcement), is a characteristic of operant conditioning, not classical conditioning. Choice II, reinforcement schedules, is also a characteristic of operant conditioning. Only choice III is a characteristic of classical conditioning, in which a specific response begins as an unconditioned response to an unconditioned stimulus, and eventually becomes a conditioned response to a conditioned stimulus. This makes (B) the correct answer.

57. A subject, when taking an opioid drug, experiences euphoric effects. After continuing to take the opioid for some time, he finds that the euphoric effects are no longer as strong, and he increases his dosage. Which of the following best describes what is taking place?
   A) **The reward pathway in the subject's brain is becoming more tolerant of the increase in dopamine that the opioids cause.**
   B) The reward pathway in the subject's brain is becoming less tolerant of the increase in dopamine that the opioids cause.
   C) Classical conditioning results in more tolerance of the opioid.
   D) Operant conditioning results in less tolerance of the opioid.

The answer is (A). The brain's reward pathway can produce sensations of pleasure or euphoria when stimulated; opioids can stimulate this pathway extrinsically by increasing dopamine levels. With continued use of such drugs over time, the user's sensitivity changes, and larger doses of the drug are needed in order to achieve the same effect; this is known as increased tolerance of a drug.

B: Less tolerance would mean that less of a drug is needed to produce the same effect, not more.
C: Classical conditioning, which results in a subject developing a conditioned response to a previously neutral stimulus, is not related to the scenario in the prompt.
D: Operant conditioning, which results in learning taking place through a system of positive and negative reinforcement, may affect behavior in some cases. However, even if it were to affect behavior here, it would not cause the brain's reward pathway to be less tolerant of drug use.

58. A subject, who feels he has not been sleeping well, experiences dream-like hallucinations before falling asleep at night. He finds it hard to move when waking up, or when about to fall asleep, and notices some loss of muscle control when he becomes emotional. Which of the following is the subject most likely experiencing?
  A) Circadian sleep cycles
  B) Insomnia
  C) **Narcolepsy**
  D) Sleep apnea

The answer here is (C). Narcolepsy is characterized by hallucinations before falling asleep and during naps. It is also characterized by sleep paralysis (inability to move when waking up or falling asleep) and by cataplexy (loss of muscle control).

A: Circadian sleep cycles describe the schedule of normal sleep, not a sleep disorder.
B: Insomnia is the inability to sleep at night. The several specific symptoms in the prompt, though, call for a more specific diagnosis.
D: Sleep apnea is related to abnormalities in the breathing pattern while sleeping, such as pauses in breathing or shallower breathing. Although it can cause sleep problems, there is no evidence here that the subject's problems are specifically caused by apnea while sleeping.

59. Which of the following are elements of the specific modality model of attention?
  I. **Tasks that use the same modality being more likely to interfere with one another.**
 II. Tasks becoming automatic and therefore requiring fewer attentional resources.
III. One single, undifferentiated pool of mental resources.
  A) **I only**
  B) II only
  C) III only
  D) I and III only

Here, choice (I) describes the specific modality model of attention. An example would be verbal modality being used to simultaneously write a letter and listen to the radio; the fact that both of these draw on the same modality means they are likelier to interfere with each other if done at the same time. Choice (II) describes the resource theory of attention, and choice (III) describes Kahneman's theory of attention. Answer choice (A), which includes (I) but not (II) or (III), is correct.

Section 4: 59 Questions, 95 Minutes

Passage 1

A certain freshwater fish species that lives in the Amazon river and its tributaries demonstrates three different mating strategies by the males. Reproduction begins with the females selecting a small, safe area under an overhang. Males then compete for permission to enter the female's selected nesting site. The females are significantly larger than the males and can easily injure or kill a male that has not been given permission to enter the nest. Once a male has entered the nest, the female lays the eggs, after which the male will fertilize them.

Males will adopt one of three strategies when attempting to mate: conflict, avoidance, or stealth. Males that elect conflict will engage in direct combat with other males, often inflicting and receiving injuries. The victorious male will mate with the female after the competitor has been driven off. Males that elect avoidance will simply patrol the area looking for available females, and will back down immediately when confronted by another male. Thus they avoid conflict, but also lose out on potential mating opportunities. Finally, males that elect stealth will attempt to enter the nesting site without being detected by other males or even the female. Interestingly, the females' mating behavior does not vary once the male is in the nest. They will lay their eggs upon finding a male in the nest, whether the male was given permission to enter or simply entered by stealth.

	Conflict	Avoidance	Stealth
Conflict	1/2 - I	0	1/3
Avoidance	1	0	2/3
Stealth	2/3	1/3	1/2

Table 1 Encounters between male fish 1 (top row) and male fish 2 (left column) and the payoff for fish 1 as a result of the encounter. Payoff of successful mating = 1 and I = injury chance.

The success of a given strategy depends on the types of strategies adopted by the other males and the encounters between them. Early in the season, sneaking fish will tend to be much more successful as their strategies allow them to move quickly from nest to nest looking for potential mates. The table demonstrates the results of encounters between males of different strategies, with the payoff given as the average result of the encounter over the course of the mating season for a particular population.

1. Based on the description in the passage, the most successful reproduction strategy is likely to be:
    A) stealth.
    B) avoidance.
    C) conflict, so long as the value for I is less than 2/3.
    D) indeterminate, as successful mating will depend on additional factors.

2. In a sub-species of the fish, males have also demonstrated a fourth strategy involving conflict unless the other male begins fighting back vigorously. The male will quickly back down and mimic the behavior of a defeated male but then attempt to use stealth to enter the nest. The advantage of this strategy is that it provides which of the following?
    A) Flexibility to change behavior in response to the strategies adopted by the other fish
    B) The ability to avoid any injures due to confrontation
    C) An overall higher level of reproductive success
    D) A meta-stable strategy that will be present in any equilibrium

3. In addition to the behaviors described in the passage, a small percentage of males are born physiologically fertile but behaviorally sterile. They will not even attempt to reproduce, but will instead defend nests from a certain common predator species. These fish:
    A) are demonstrating intra-specific commensalism with the females whose nests they defend.
    B) have an allele that must decrease over time due to their lack of reproduction.
    C) are behaving altruistically, increasing the inclusive fitness of their local population.
    D) have some sort of neurological damage to their central nervous system that causes them to misinterpret the females as not being potential mates.

4. Some evidence suggests that these strategies are genetically determined but may also be shaped by operant learning. Which of the following would most strengthen the theory that the males' strategy choice is a result of operant conditioning rather than purely genetic?
    A) Those males that grow to be larger than average will almost always adopt a conflict strategy.
    B) Males taking an avoidance strategy will often flee from other objects that are not even fish, if those objects have certain features (coloration, patterns, etc) that look like other male fish of the species.
    C) Males who adopt a stealth strategy may sire offspring who will adopt either the stealth or the avoidance strategy, not exclusively the stealth strategy.
    D) Males will typically adopt a conflict strategy and, after being injured, switch to a stealth strategy and will only switch to avoidance upon several unsuccessful attempts at stealth.

5. Upon entering the nest, males induce females to lay eggs by flashing a patch of bright orange scales on their ventral side. These scales weigh the male fish down and make movement metabolically expensive. Yet there is a strong correlation between the mass of these scales and male reproductive success. This feature is likely a result of:
    A) divergent selection.
    B) stabilizing selection.
    C) sexual selection.
    D) allopatric speciation.

Passage 2

A program to reduce bullying will ideally have many components. It is helpful to consider Bronfenbrenner's Systems Model, in which the individual is conceptualized in terms of increasingly broader systems within his environment, to address bullying from different levels of analysis.

Figure 1 Bronfenbrenner's model to reduce bullying

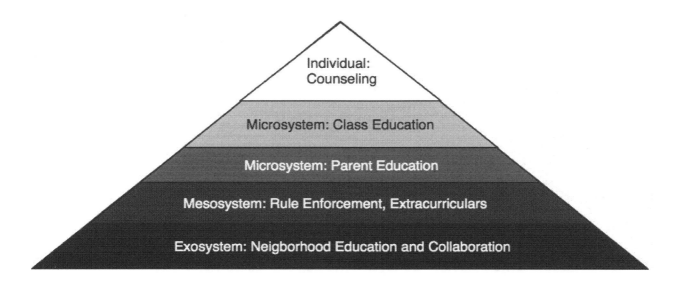

First, at the community level, there should be efforts to reach out to people in the neighborhood to help look out for bullying. A lot of bullying happens outside of school, on the way home from school, or at gathering places for youths. At the family level, parents should be brought in to assist in the efforts. Parents should be made aware of any behavior their children might be exhibiting that would indicate the children were either being bullied or bullying. Some of these behaviors would be having a lack of friends, becoming more withdrawn, strongly disliking school, and being involved in any online bullying.

At a school level, students should be made aware of the rules around bullying. There should be policies spelled out explicitly that address the issue. The consequences will not involve suspension or sitting in a detention room, but will instead focus on restitution to the bullied individual and community and demonstrating knowledge of the policies.

At the class level, students should be educated on the dynamics involved in bullying. A peer-involved restorative justice program should be implemented. By involving the parties involved with bullying, those bullying and those being bullied, both parties can get a message from their social group that bullying is unacceptable. Oftentimes, bullies may not realize their behavior is off-putting. They may instead see themselves as cool.

Finally, at the individual level both bullies and victims should be addressed in a counseling format. Victims can focus on the effects that bullying has had on them and also work on developing social skills. Bullies also can work on more effective social skills. In addition, it is important to remember that having been a victim is also strongly correlated with being a bully. Bullies should address any earlier trauma they experienced that may have introduced this unequal power dynamic to them.

6. What would be an example of a microsystem level intervention to address substance use?
   A) Teaching refusal skills to an individual
   B) Family counseling to support the individual
   C) National policies to toughen penalties for drug suppliers
   D) National policies to mandate insurers treat substance use disorders as they would any other medical condition

7. Why might a community have a problem with bullying, an individual issue?
   A) Lack of community resources for programs
   B) Lack of integration of Bronfenbrenner's systems
   C) Individual issues
   D) Inherent community flaws

8. What could be a possible macrosystem level intervention towards bullying?
   A) De-emphasizing aggression as a valued trait at a cultural level
   B) Having community forums to address bullying
   C) Encouraging bullied individuals to stand up for themselves
   D) Having bullying awareness days at a school

9. What could be a criticism of the bullying program from Bronfenbrenner's model?
   A) Communities may not agree with the model
   B) Individuals may not realize their impact on communities
   C) In different cultures, individuals are influenced by their environment differently
   D) The model does not consider the impact broad policies can have on the individual

10. Which of the following is NOT an explanation why a person who has been bullied come to bully others?
   A) Through social learning this individual has come to learn that bullying can get a person what they want
   B) Through socialization this individual has come to learn that aggression is not an inappropriate way to interact with others
   C) Through neurobiological theory this individual has come to have a higher threshold for tolerating stress and aggression
   D) Through cognitive behavioral theory this individual has experienced mistrust in his caregivers and has come to repeat these dynamics of mistrust in his relationships

Passage 3

Gate control theory is a comprehensive way to understand an individual's perception of pain. This model considers that pain is both psychogenic and somatic, that is, originating both in an individual's perceptions and his body. Before this model was developed, psychological factors were only considered to be reactions to pain. However, since the development of this model, psychological factors are understood to influence the perception of pain.

In terms of affective factors, a number of disorders can impact how a person is able to perceive pain and generate strategies for tolerating it. Depression is a prominent disorder involved with chronic pain, impacting as many as 40-50% of individuals experiencing pain. There is a cyclic relationship between experiencing pain and depression, where chronic pain can cause depression, but depression also impacts the perception of pain. For individuals experiencing depression and chronic pain, it can be hard to generate strategies for addressing the pain, leading to a sense of helplessness about how to address the issues. As a result, many individuals may utilize passive coping strategies for managing pain, such as using medication, being inactive, or using drugs or alcohol.

A number of cognitive factors are also associated with experiencing pain. Research has shown that patients who view their pain as signifying a progressive degenerative disease, rather than as a stable condition that will improve, experience more severe pain. In addition, patients who had experienced pain previously when involved in physical activity have a learned expectation that future activity will result in pain, resulting in less helpful physical activity on their part.

Catastrophic thinking has been found to be associated with more severe perception of pain. On the other hand, patients who employ coping strategies, or ways of managing pain, tend to experience less severe pain. There are two types of coping strategies that patients can employ, overt and covert coping strategies. Overt coping strategies are active strategies to manage pain, such as engaging in healthy behavior. Covert strategies involve distracting oneself from the pain, such as through meditation or obtaining information about the chronic condition.

A way that pain is typically assessed in treatment is by using a "pain thermometer" in which patients are asked to rate the severity of their pain from 1 to 10. In a study which examined the implementation of a treatment program for patients with chronic pain, which emphasized using coping strategies, developing a sense of self-efficacy, and being active, patients in a control group and in the treatment group were asked to rate their level of pain before and after the program. The average results of the two groups are presented on the pain thermometers as follows:

Table 1 Effect of treatment on pain perception

Group	Before Treatment	After Treatment
Treatment	1=Less Severe ← More Severe=10 → 7.9	1=Less Severe ← More Severe=10 → 5.3
Control	1=Less Severe ← More Severe=10 → 6.1	1=Less Severe ← More Severe=10 → 5.1

Differences between the two groups from pre − to post-treatment is significant $p < .0001$

11. A patient assumes his pain will not get better. In his treatment he is asked to find research about his condition each day for a week. This is an example of what type of strategy?
    A) Humanistic
    B) Psychodynamic
    C) Cognitive Behavioral
    D) Neurobiological

12. How can the results of the study be summarized?
    A) The treatment group had a greater decrease in pain than the control group
    B) The control group had a greater decrease in pain than the treatment group
    C) The treatment group had a greater increase in pain than the control group
    D) The control group had a greater increase in pain than the treatment group

13. What might account for a significant decrease in pain in the control group, who are told that they receiving treatment in the study but are not actually receiving the treatment?
    A) Avoidance learning
    B) Expectancy theory
    C) Placebo effect
    D) Conditioned learning

14. This passage suggests that what else should be assessed in addition to assessing a patient's level of pain?
    A) Somatic issues
    B) Psychogenic issues
    C) The area of the body in which the pain is occurring
    D) The neurobiological factors involved with pain

These questions are **NOT** related to a passage.

15. Which of the following characterize sympathetic nervous system activation?
 I. Redirection of glucose and other resources from the digestive organs to the brain and heart.
 II. Reduced sensitivity to pain.
III. Synthesis of glycogen.
   A) I only
   B) I and II only
   C) II and III only
   D) I, II and III

16. Over the course of a decade, approximately 45,000 native Africans emigrate from their home countries to a major Western city. Once there, most attempt to find housing. However, due to discriminatory treatment from the native-born residents of the city, many of these immigrants end up living in particular neighborhoods where the local majority of residents are also recent African immigrants. What best describes this situation?
   A) Formation of ethnocentrism in response to institutional barriers to assimilation.
   B) Formation of ethnic enclaves in response to institutional barriers to assimilation.
   C) Formation of cultural relativism in response to institutional barriers to assimilation.
   D) Formation of cultural relativism in response to ethnocentrism.

17. In City A, residents are observed to allow elevator passengers to exit before boarding the elevator themselves. In City B, residents are observed to attempt to board the elevator before the previous passengers have exited. What best describes the difference between these two situations?
   A) One norm is caused by a formal institution and the other is caused by an informal institution.
   B) One norm is caused by institutionalization, and the other norm is caused by social function.
   C) Institutionalization of structures of social order has occurred differently in each city.
   D) One city has developed a material culture and the other has developed a non-material culture.

18. Which of the following characterize urbanization?
 I. Migration from urban areas to rural areas
 II. Breakdown of social bonds between an individual and the surrounding community
III. Increased industrialization
   A) I only
   B) II only
   C) I and III only
   D) II and III only

Passage 4

Traditionally, organizational approaches to stress management in the workplace have been focused on addressing employee stress at the secondary-level of intervention and fostering secondary-level interventions for managing stress. An example of a secondary-level intervention in managing stress is an employee training program for learning skills for handling customer complaints at a retail store. The goals of the program are for the employees to be able to manage the complaints effectively, which will ideally reduce the stress they experience from this activity. Benefits typically subside over time, though this may also be an artifact of the extinction of the learned skills, indicating the need for booster sessions.

Another issue with this view of stress reduction is that it is a reactive approach. As in the example, employees are taught how to effectively manage stress in reaction to stress that is initiated from the customer. The source of the stress is not addressed and there is no focus on how to proactively reduce it.

An alternative level of intervention besides for secondary-level interventions is primary-level interventions. The goal in primary-level interventions is to try to proactively address the source of the stress to attempt to eliminate it before it arises. Primary-level facet of stress to consider is the employee perception of control. Employees not feeling in control of their work output has been identified as a salient source of stress. Employees should be encouraged to feel empowered in their contribution to the organization and should also feel creative control over their work. Policies to encourage employee contributions and eliciting feedback from employees can be done to foster a sense of employee control.

A final primary-level strategy for addressing workplace stress is to manage employee stress from work demand. Employees feeling overloaded with work is a significant source of stress. Organizations should first consider the reality of the expectations imposed on employees and consider the impact that staff reduction and increased expectations might have on employee stress and concomitant employee performance.

To evaluate the impact of primary and secondary-level interventions on employee satisfaction – a broad measure encompassing employee retention, productivity, and other measures identified as salient to employee satisfaction, rated from 0 to 100, a study was conducted at an organization. At this organization, employees were randomly assigned to participate in either a primary or secondary-level intervention. Measures of employee satisfaction were reported over time. January was an initial reading of employee satisfaction, before the interventions were implemented. The results are presented as follows:

Figure 1 Employee satisfaction following stress reduction intervention

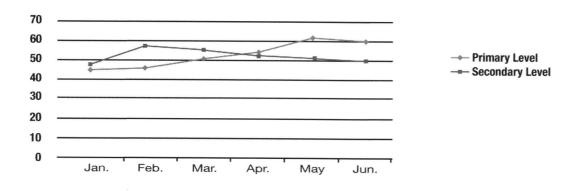

19. What could account for the initial increase in employee satisfaction followed by the gradual decrease in the secondary-level intervention group?

    A) Skill knowledge and use is decreasing over time
    B) Reduced initial work expectations
    C) Increased initial healthcare, followed by gradual reductions
    D) Reductions in noise level, lessening in impact as time passes

20. What could be done to increase the effects of a secondary level intervention in the later months?

    A) A refresher class in the skills that were taught
    B) Focusing on optimizing employee time
    C) Have a training session after an employee problem
    D) Have a stress needs assessment

21. What term indicates a beneficial type of stress which can motivate employees?

    A) Distress
    B) Constress
    C) Cathartic stress
    D) Eustress

22. What could be an effective primary-level intervention against in-group bias at the workplace?

    A) Teaching employees social skills so they can enter work cliques
    B) Providing workplace-wide education about the impact of excluding co-workers
    C) Teaching employees health strategies they can use to reduce stress
    D) Educating the workforce on the proper procedures for reporting discrimination

Passage 5

When humans are first born, it does not appear that there are differences in their ability to discern differences in facial characteristics among different ethnicities. However, by 3 months of age, they begin to be able to discern differences between faces of the ethnic identity to which they are primarily exposed. This finding was observed by showing newborn infants and infants at 3 months of age pictures of faces of people of different ethnicities, in a type of research design called a visual preference paradigm. The length of time the infants gazed at a face was considered a reflection of how novel this face appeared to them. Infants will gaze longer at faces they view to be novel. It was found that infants looked at different faces of the ethnicity to which they were primarily exposed more frequently at 3 months, but not at birth, suggesting that they were able to perceive differences among the faces of the race with which they were familiar.

However, another study demonstrated that 3 month old infants are capable of becoming familiar with faces of people of different ethnicities after a short time of exposure. In this study, the infants were shown pictures of faces of people of ethnicities of which they initially didn't recognize differences. After exposure to these faces for a short time, the infants were able to better discriminate among these faces with which they had previously been unfamiliar. This study seemed to show that through exposure to people of different ethnicities, infants can become more familiar with those people.

However, this ability to recognize faces of a different ethnicity seems to lessen throughout the infant's development through a process called perceptual narrowing. Infants begin to show lack of recognition of faces of other ethnicities from 6 months onwards, even after exposure to these faces. This effect is also shown to occur across different ethnicities, with babies of different ethnicities shown to be able to discriminate among faces of their own ethnicity better than faces of other ethnicities.

These findings would seem to indicate that infants are born neutral in their ability to discern differences among ethnicities and develop a familiarity with a certain ethnicity over time. However, what determines for what ethnicity infants will develop an ability to discern? Studies seem to point to infants developing this ability among the ethnicity to which they are primarily exposed. In a study that took place in Israel, researchers assessed African infants who had been raised by Israeli caretakers. It was found that the African infants were able to recognize differences in Israeli faces and not the faces of their own ethnicity. This would seem to indicate that infants develop recognition for characteristics of faces to which they are exposed from an early period onwards.

23. What is another example of perceptual narrowing?
    A) Gaining an ability to discern faces more clearly
    B) Losing the ability to distinguish sounds not used in a certain language
    C) Having more entrenched views on race as a person ages
    D) Demonstrating gender norms with age

24. What argument against having a pronounced ability for infants to be able to discern facial characteristics of their own ethnicity is given in this passage?
    A) Infants tend to look at faces of their own ethnicity longer because they can discern differences
    B) Across ethnicities infants are able to recognize faces from their own ethnicity more easily
    C) Infants raised by people from different ethnicities demonstrate an ability to discern differences in faces from their caretaker's ethnicity
    D) An infant becomes less able to learn differences in other ethnicities' faces as he ages

25. This passage suggests that a way to enhance an individual's ability to discern facial characteristics of ethnicities different than his own is which of the following?
    A) Encouraging a child to avoid perceiving racial characteristics
    B) Exposing an infant to ethnicities different than his own
    C) Having an infant raised solely by a caretaker of a different ethnicity
    D) Using a visual preference paradigm

26. In a visual preference paradigm, it can be expected that an infant would gaze longer at:
    A) a stimulus to which he is exposed for a lengthy period of time.
    B) a pattern that is familiar to him.
    C) an unusual shape.
    D) no inferenes can be made.

These questions are **NOT** related to a passage.

27. Which of the following characterize parasympathetic nervous system activation?
  I. Decreased heart rate
 II. Decreased digestive activity
III. Conversion of glucose into glycogen
    A) I only
    B) I and II only
    C) I and III only
    D) II and III only

28. A number of urban commuters, when surveyed individually regarding their opinion of a new rail line in their city, express nuanced views which include both pluses and minuses. Later, these commuters participate in a focus group and are again asked to give their opinion. After discussing the issue amongst themselves for 45 minutes, they report their opinions to the focus group director, except now they report more extreme and less nuanced positions than they previously expressed, with roughly half the group taking strong "approve" positions and the remainder taking strong "disapprove" positions. What best describes this result?
    A) Socialization
    B) Peer pressure
    C) Groupthink
    D) Group polarization

29. Which of the following characterize Albert Bandura's conception of the social cognitive perspective of personality?
  I. A belief in one's own abilities
 II. Observational learning
III. Neuroticism
    A) I and II
    B) I and III
    C) II and III
    D) I, II and III

30. Members of a gymnastics team are observed to perform simple maneuvers better when watched by a small audience than when alone. However, when learning complicated triple flips, the presence of an audience causes their performance to worsen and they tend to make more mistakes. What best accounts for this?
    A) The bystander effect
    B) Peer pressure
    C) Socialization
    D) Social facilitation

Passage 6

It is important to consider the impact of culture on psychotherapeutic medication. There are multiple biopsycho-social factors that impact the effect of medicine on people of different cultures. Ethnicity has, for some time, been observed to impact the biological response to medication, especially medications which impact genes that vary by ethnicities. However, culture has been less researched in terms of its impact on biological response to medication. One way culture has impacted medication response is through diet, which typically varies by culture. For example, drug researchers have observed the pharmokinetic effects, or impact of drugs on the body, of immigrants. They found that when immigrants' diets change from the diet of their native country to that of their new country their pharmokinetic response also changes to become more similar to that of the individuals in their new culture.

Cultural differences among doctors also influences medication efficacy. First of all, doctors may be influenced by their culture in how they prescribe medication. There may be a number of systems, such as insurance companies, health organizations, or the patient's own expectations, which impact the way the doctor prescribes medication. The way that doctors perceive and diagnose patient issues is affected by culture. Research has shown that in the U.S. Caucasian doctors tend to over-pathologize African-American and Hispanic patients.

Culture may also impact the way in which the illness is viewed. Asians especially, and more recently Westerners, use alternative remedies, such as natural medication, physical healing techniques, and alternative health care providers. These practices are typically viewed as being more safe and non-invasive than taking pharmaceuticals. However, these practices can impact other treatment regimens. As a result, a patient should be assessed for engagement in alternative treatments, when considering new treatment plans and their level of willingness to engage in prescribed medication.

The presentation of the medication may have cultural significance and affect efficacy. The form, color, and amount of the medication may all impact the way people from different cultures view it. For example, Caucasians were found to regard white capsules as analgesics. The contents of the medicine may preclude some cultures from taking them due to their beliefs, an example of which is Muslims being averse to taking medications containing alcohol due to religious beliefs. Patients may not disclose their aversion to taking a certain medicine and may assume that there are no alternatives; therefore querying a patient's willingness to comply with treatment is advised.

When developing a new drug, pharmaceutical companies must show the drug to be more efficacious than a placebo drug in research. In a study in which a pharmaceutical company was examining the efficacy of a new drug for depression, the company evaluated how much improvement study participants had compared to a placebo drug. To further assess for the effects of culture, the company conducted the study on three different continents. The average percent improvement of participants taking the drug compared to those taking placebo in each continent are shown as follows:

Table 1 Effectiveness of a drug over placebo

North America	Africa	Asia
25%	38%	33%

The difference in improvements between continents was significant ($p < .0001$).

31. Which of the following could *least* likely account for the difference in drug efficacy seen in the study?
    A) Different cultural expectations of the efficacy of the drug
    B) Cultural differences affecting drug pharmokinetics
    C) Cultural differences in the relationship between study researcher and participant
    D) Immigrant participants' diets may have changed

32. Doctors diagnosing some ethnic groups with more severe disorders is an example of what kind of discrimination?
    A) Individual
    B) Institutional
    C) Both Individual and Institutional
    D) Neither Individual nor Institutional

33. Which of the following is NOT a question that would be helpful for a prescribing doctor to ask his patient?
    A) How do you feel about this prescription?
    B) Are you using any other treatments for your condition?
    C) What do you think of the shape of this medicine?
    D) What might prevent you from taking the medicine as directed?

34. What would NOT be an effective public health strategy to help consider cultural factors in medicine?
    A) Encouraging immigrant patients to retain the diets of their native country
    B) Informing doctors about cultural factors for which to assess
    C) Providing patients with information about drugs and natural healing
    D) Requiring pharmaceutical companies to disclose with what cultures drugs have been evaluated

35. Which of the following is NOT a way that researchers could remove some of the location effects from the study?
    A) Consider the expectations of the participants and the pill administration method
    B) Distinguish the placebo pill from the trial medication
    C) Measure the pharmacokinetic effects of the drug
    D) Consider the impact of cultural factors on diagnosis

Passage 7

In an experiment, researchers told participants that they could potentially receive either 1) a guaranteed $15 or 2) have a 50% chance of receiving either $10 or $20 respectively. When given this choice most people choose option 1, to receive the guaranteed money. However, the expected gain from this offer is the same. In option 1 there is a 100% likelihood of receiving $15, for an expected gain of $15, and in option 2 there is a 50% chance of receiving $10 and a 50% chance of receiving $20 for an expected gain of also $15.

If this experiment were phrased another way, and now a person were given $20 and told he could either 1) give back a guaranteed $5 or 2) have a 50% chance of giving back either $0 or $10 respectively most people would choose option 2. However, this experiment is the same as the previous experiment in terms of expected gain, that of $15 with either option. The difference between the two experiments is in the way in which the offers are framed.

As an explanation as to why the framing of the offers should affect the choice people tend to make, prospect theory explains that people often see expected gains or losses in terms of their departure from an assumed expected amount. So, first of all, people tend to consider a departure from an amount in terms of its relative departure, rather than absolute departure. For example, an individual making $100,000 will value a $10,000 raise more than a person making $1,000,000.

Within this principle, whether a person is gaining or losing money is the important factor, with those gaining money tending to be more aversive to risk and those losing money tending to be more favorable to risk. For individuals who start with $0, any gain is a substantial increase, making them more aversive to risk and happy to take the guaranteed amount. For individuals who start with $20, a greater loss may not seem as drastic, as they are starting with an amount of money, leaving them more inclined to court risk.

Prospect theory can be applied to public health promotion. An example of a loss-framed public health announcement is that if you don't stop smoking you might get lung cancer and a gain framed announcement is that if you stop smoking you will be healthier.

Also, health procedures can be framed in terms of detection of a physical disease, such as through an examination, or prevention of a disease, such as through exercise. Detection of a disease is generally seen as riskier by the consumer. Prevention is seen as less risky, on the other hand, as its purpose is to maintain health.

An experiment was conducted to determine how well participants responded to messages that were either gain framed or loss framed and applied to health behaviors that either involved detection or prevention. The average rate of participant compliance with the message is presented as follows:

Table 1 Experiment results

	Loss Framed Message	Gain Framed Message
Detection Behavior	67%	48%
Prevention Behavior	51%	68%

36. Based on the results of the study, which message would likely lead to the greatest rate of compliance of encouraging people to eat healthily every day?

    A) Not eating healthy can lead to a number of diseases

    B) Eating healthy can help you feel your best

    C) Eating junk food leaves you feeling like junk

    D) Obesity is at an all time high in the United States

37. In what desired behavior would the message, "Heart disease is the number one killer in the U.S.," be least likely to induce compliance?

    A) Encouraging people to get their cholesterol checked yearly

    B) Encouraging people to eat low-fat foods

    C) Encouraging people to exercise daily

    D) Encouraging people to reduce stress

38. When considering choices, an individual might rank homicide as a greater threat than heart disease because it is on the news more prominently. What type of biased thinking did this person use in committing this error?

    A) Fundamental attribution error

    B) Stereotyped threat

    C) Availability heuristic

    D) Belief perseverance

39. If a man receives a $1,000 bonus, how might comparing his bonus to his co-workers make his mood more negative?

    A) If his co-workers received the same amount as he did

    B) If his co-workers received less than he did

    C) If his co-workers received more than he did

    D) If he is not able to compare his bonus to his co-workers' bonuses.

Passage 8

Ethnic identity is dynamic and changes at different points in an individual's life. Marcia's general model of identity development is useful for describing an individual's identity in a number of respects. It is also fluid, in that an individual may be at different points in the model at different times with respect to different aspects of identity. The model characterizes an individual as being at one of 4 points in his identity development. Throughout this model, the term "identity crisis" is used to describe an event which would precipitate an individual to begin exploring his identity.

First, an individual may be in identity diffusion. This individual may or may not have experienced an identity crisis that would lead him to begin seeking out an identity. He is currently uncommitted to a particular identity.

An individual may also be in a foreclosed identity. This individual has agreed to an identity that was imposed externally. The individual did not arrive at this identity through exploration or through his own efforts. An individual may also be in moratorium. An individual in this stage is actively seeking out an identity. He is aware that different identities are available and is seeking to choose one for himself.

Finally, an individual may be in identity achievement. This individual has explored the range of options of identity available. He has considered several identities and has arrived at one that is consonant with his own values.

To assess the impact an individual's status has on his ability to complete tasks, researchers first rated participants' answers to a variety of statements about their views of their identity. Researchers classified participants into one of the identity categories in the Marcia model, then measured the time it took to complete a task. Researchers then compared the average task completion times. The results are presented as follows:

Table 1 Task completion based on identity status

Identity Status	Completion Time
Identity Achievement	15.6
Foreclosure	19.2
Moratorium	29.6
Identity Diffusion	27.4

An identity model for classifying African-Americans' ethnic identity has been proposed by Cross. An individual proceeds through this model in sequential order. The first stage is the Pre-encounter stage. Individuals in this stage have assimilated to American values. For these individuals, ethnicity is not a very salient part of their identity. Next is the Encounter stage, which occurs after the individual has had some experience which leads to an ethnic identity crisis. Ethnic identity begins to take on importance. The individual can become confused or alarmed that this previously unnoticed aspect has become salient.

The next stage is Immersion. During this stage, individuals have become fully immersed in their ethnic identity. They identify with their ethnic identity, to the point these aspects are unrealistically inflated, and they may feel a resentment of the dominant ethnicity.

The final stage is Internalization. In this stage, the individual has accepted that there are some aspects of his ethnic identity which may be imperfect. The individual has also balanced his ethnic identification with other aspects of himself, yet advocates for his ethnic community.

40. What stages are most similar in the Cross African-American ethnic identity model and the Marcia identity model?
    A) Internalization and moratorium
    B) Immersion and diffusion
    C) Internalization and identity achievement
    D) Encounter and foreclosure

41. In what identity status would an individual be who has agreed to study what his parents want him to study in college without any input from him?
    A) Identity achievement
    B) Moratorium
    C) Diffusion
    D) Foreclosure

42. Which of the following would likely NOT be a variable which would moderate the relationship between identity status and task completion time in the study?
    A) Type A personality status
    B) Cognitive skills
    C) Reference group
    D) Manual dexterity

43. According to Erikson's psychosocial stages of development, an individual who does not successfully resolve his issue of identity likely experiences what state?
    A) Inferiority
    B) Mistrust
    C) Guilt
    D) Role Confusion

These questions are **NOT** related to a passage.

44. A bar exam preparation company begins an advertising campaign intended to describe the strengths of its bar preparation course, mentioning such facts as the company's competitive pricing and the high bar passage rate of previous students. Later, the company attempts to gain students for its course by redesigning its books and other materials to be more visually enticing, and by hiring more attractive campus representatives. The two campaigns are characterized by, respectively:

   A) Attempting to change attitudes through peripheral-route processing, and then by central-route processing.
   B) Attempting to change attitudes through central-route processing, and then by peripheral-route processing.
   C) Attempting to change attitudes through central-route processing, and then by choice-of-route processing.
   D) Attempting to change attitudes through choice-of-route processing, and then by central-route processing.

45. Which of the following characterize(s) Kohlberg's theory of morality development?
   I. A first stage where individuals focus on the direct consequences of actions.
  II. A second stage where individuals believe society, or other outside forces, to be the principal determinants of morally appropriate actions.
 III. A third stage where individuals focus on the importance of using morality to form closer-knit societies

   A) I only
   B) I and II only
   C) I and III only
   D) I, II and III

46. A student spending a semester abroad in Japan decides to spend a week's vacation visiting China. While wandering around the streets of Beijing's outskirts he sees a Chinese grandmother encouraging her four-year-old son to take his pants down and defecate off the sidewalk onto the street. The student reacts with an overwhelming sense of disgust. This reaction is an example of:

   A) ethnocentrism.
   B) material culture.
   C) operant conditioning.
   D) culture shock.

This page intentionally left blank.

Passage 9

Having other people present typically leads an individual to experience physiological arousal. The impact this arousal has on performance depends on the type of task the individual is performing. It has been found that in the presence of groups individuals tend to demonstrate dominant responses, or responses which are well-rehearsed and familiar to the individual. When the task is complicated performance will be impaired.

Social facilitation is seen when researchers watch individuals performing tasks and then introduce confederates who observe the individuals performing. The percentage of success of those individuals is recorded before the confederates are introduced and after they are introduced. The participants are classified according to their proficiency in the task as being either high performers or low performers. A study in which researchers observed basketball players and recorded their percentage of shots made before and after introducing confederates was conducted with the results presented as follows:

Table 1 Performance in the presence of others

Performance Level	Before Confederates	After Confederates
High performers	68%	74%
Low performers	42%	36%

Groups also impact individual behavior through deindividuation. This refers to people feeling that they are less personally responsible for their behavior in a group and as a result behaving in ways they normally wouldn't while alone. Deindividuation changes individual behavior through anonymity and diverts the individual's attention away from his own values. An example of the deindividuation that can occur in a group was provided by researchers who observed children Trick-or-Treating for Halloween. The researchers put out candy and instructed children to only take one piece. Conditions that fostered children only taking one piece included having the children asked their name, being alone, and having a mirror present in front of the candy.

Finally, the opinions of a group tend to become more extreme after group discussion. This effect is known as polarization. A reason for this is that the group is likely to hear more arguments of the opinion the group is favoring. Group members will hear these arguments and become more persuaded and also continue to further the argument in more extreme directions.

47. According to the data, what group might be most likely to perform well in front of a group?
    A) Good students performing novel calculations
    B) Poor singers performing a song
    C) Novice mechanics changing a tire
    D) An experienced factory worker performing a duty on an assembly line

48. Which of the following would NOT be a way to avoid groupthink?
    A) Have group members with a variety of views on the topic
    B) Record individual views before topics are discussed
    C) Include individuals in positions of authority in the group
    D) Present all sides on the issue

49. What could be done to avoid inflammatory rhetoric in online commentary?
    A) Allow individuals to gravitate towards topics they feel passionate about
    B) Allow the online group to rebuke the commentators
    C) Require users to use their actual names
    D) Ask difficult questions, requiring non-dominant answers

50. A group member presenting a more extreme opinion than another group member who he views as high status in order to appear favorable to the group is known as what process?
    A) Upward social comparison
    B) Downward social comparison
    C) Lateral social comparison
    D) Inverse social comparison

51. Each of the following factors would help the low performing group in the study to perform better EXCEPT:
  I. Become more familiar with the task
 II. Perform in front of observers
III. Place observers behind one-way mirrors such that the subjects do not know they are being observed
    A) I only
    B) II only
    C) III only
    D) I and III only

Passage 10

Alzheimer's Disease (AD) is a form of dementia with a prevalence of 2 to 3% in people over the age of 65, with this rate doubling every 5 years. AD is irreversible and its effects can be debilitating, necessitating long-term care at a high cost. The biggest risk factor for AD is aging. However, a hereditary link has been established, with a two to four-fold increase in the incidence of AD among those with a first-degree relative with AD.

Severe cholinergic deficits in the cerebral cortex, specifically in the basal forebrain from the hippocampus to neocortex, have been found in those with AD. Thus it is hypothesized that a cause of AD is the reduced ability of the brain to synthesize acetylcholine. These findings have led to attempts to treat AD with cholinergic agonists, a strategy that has proven to be quite effective in treating some forms of dementia. However, attempts to increase acetylcholine in those with AD has been less effective, perhaps due to permanent changes in brain structure of those with AD. These changes can be seen in post-mortem examinations of the brain, in which amyloid plaques and neurofibrillary tangles can be seen, both considered the hallmark signs of AD.

Frequently concordant with the development of AD are other behavioral and emotional issues, such as depression, anxiety, aggression, and paranoia, among other issues. Disorders such as these may be the primary presenting issue for many families of individuals with AD. Thus, treatment of these issues is indicated. These issues may be treated as they are typically treated in individuals without AD. However, preventative strategies for avoiding the development of these issues is indicated in those who have developed AD. Preventative strategies include encouraging and maintaining wellness behaviors, such as exercise and active behavior, support groups, and other psychoeducation, among other efforts.

The following is a small case study of a 75 year-old individual who presented at a medical center for complaints about forgetting things, such as where he places things at his home, sometimes getting lost on the way home from the store, and feeling sad often. However, he is still able to remember incidents from his past and the names of his family members. Tests were conducted to assess his intelligence, memory, and difficulties with daily living skills, with the test given and the results in terms of age-normed percentile given:

Table 1 Patient Assessment results

Intelligence Test	Memory Test	Daily Living Skills Functioning Test
30%	32%	39%

52. What type of memory appears intact in the man?
   A) Anterograde, but not retrograde
   B) Retrograde, but not anterograde
   C) Both retrograde and anterograde
   D) Neither retrograde nor anterograde

53. The relative ineffectiveness of cholinergic agonists in treatment of AD suggests what type of neural process is NOT possible in AD?
   A) Neural pruning
   B) Neural conditioning
   C) Neuroplasticity
   D) Neural networking

54. What is the expected prevalence of AD for a man as old as the man in the case study?
   A) 2-3%
   B) 4-6%
   C) 8-12%
   D) 16-24%

55. Which of the following topics would NOT be helpful to know more about when attempting to diagnose the man with AD?
   A) His IQ when he was younger
   B) If someone in his family has AD
   C) His mental health status now
   D) If amyloid plaques are present in his brain

These questions are **NOT** related to a passage.

56. What best describes the relationship between symbols and language?
    A) Symbols can result in group socialization; language allows for both group socialization and individual socialization.
    B) Symbols help sustain continuity of a culture; language can be interpreted and reinterpreted over time.
    C) Symbols carry shared meaning in a culture; language constitutes a subcategory of symbols which is a set of representations that conveys meaning about the world.
    D) Symbols are a subcategory of language which, unlike language, are only understood by certain members of a culture.

57. Which of the following are examples of demographic transitions in Thompson's demographic transitions model?
    I. Immigrants from a poorer country enter a richer country in large numbers.
    II. Lower birthrates and lower mortality in a country over time result in the percentage of elderly citizens increasing, and the percentage of young citizens decreasing.
    III. Members of a minority ethnic group flee their homeland on a large scale to avoid persecution by the ethnic majority.
    A) I only
    B) II only
    C) I and II
    D) I, II and III.

58. A person with a very visible bruise on his hand worries that it will lead to worse blood circulation, and possibly loss of hand function. After some time passes and the bruise remains, he finds that he is unable to move his hand more than a little, even though tests show his blood circulation in his hand and arm is normal and no other medical causes are detected explaining the person's loss of hand function. What best characterizes this person's condition?
    A) Body dysmorphic disorder
    B) Generalized anxiety disorder
    C) Conversion disorder
    D) Hypochondriasis

59. A patient experiencing memory loss symptoms consults with two medical professionals in an attempt to find the cause of his condition. The first person he sees focuses on possible past head injuries, and runs several medical tests on the patient. The second person he sees asks about the patient's environment, his social life, and his stress levels; he also conducts a personality evaluation of the patient. What best characterizes the differing approaches of the two medical professionals?
    A) The first is using a biomedical approach, while the second is using a biopsychosocial approach.
    B) The first is using a biopsychosocial approach, while the second is using a biomedical approach.
    C) The first is using a biological approach, while the second is using a psychological approach.
    D) The first is using a biological approach, while the second is using a sociological approach.

This page intentionally left blank.

Section 4 Answers and Explanations

Key					
1	D	21	D	41	D
2	A	22	B	42	C
3	C	23	B	43	D
4	D	24	C	44	B
5	C	25	B	45	B
6	B	26	C	46	D
7	A	27	C	47	D
8	A	28	D	48	C
9	C	29	A	49	C
10	D	30	D	50	A
11	C	31	D	51	B
12	A	32	C	52	B
13	C	33	C	53	C
14	B	34	A	54	C
15	B	35	B	55	D
16	B	36	B	56	C
17	C	37	A	57	B
18	D	38	C	58	C
19	A	39	C	59	A
20	A	40	C		

Passage 1 Explanation

A certain freshwater fish species that lives in the Amazon river and its tributaries demonstrates **three different mating strategies** by the males. Reproduction begins with the females selecting a small, safe area under an overhang. Males then compete for **permission to enter** the female's selected nesting site. The **females** are **significantly larger** than the males and can easily injure or kill a male that has not been given permission to enter the nest. Once a male has entered the nest, the female lays the eggs, after which the male will fertilize them.

Key terms: different mating strategies

Cause-and-effect: the females' larger size means she can kill any male that attempts to enter the nest without permission

Males will adopt one of three strategies when attempting to mate: conflict, avoidance, or stealth. Males that elect **conflict** will engage in **direct combat** with other males, often inflicting and receiving injuries. The **victorious male will mate** with the female after the competitor has been driven off. Males that elect **avoidance** will simply patrol the area looking for available females, and will **back down** immediately when confronted by another male. Thus they avoid conflict, but also lose out on potential mating opportunities. Finally, males that elect **stealth** will attempt to **enter the nesting site without being detected** by other males or even the female. Interestingly, the females' mating behavior does not vary once the male is in the nest. They will lay their eggs upon finding a male in the nest, whether the male was given permission to enter or simply entered by stealth.

Key terms: conflict, avoidance stealth

Contrast: the variations in the various mating strategies

	Conflict	Avoidance	Stealth
Conflict	1/2 - I	0	1/3
Avoidance	1	0	2/3
Stealth	2/3	1/3	1/2

Table 1 Encounters between male fish 1 (top row) and male fish 2 (left column) and the payoff for fish 1 as a result of the encounter. Payoff of successful mating = 1 and I = injury chance.
Table 1 shows us that during an encounter between two males, the conflict strategy trumps avoidance, that conflict v. conflict brings a cost of potential injury, and that stealth is more successful sneaking by an avoidance male rather than a conflict male.

The **success** of a given strategy **depends on the types of strategies** adopted by the other males and the encounters between them. **Early in the season**, sneaking fish will tend to be much more successful as their strategies allow them to move quickly from nest to nest looking for potential mates. The table demonstrates the results of encounters between males of different strategies, with the payoff given as the average result of the encounter over the course of the mating season for a particular population.

Key term: success, season

Cause-and-effect: whether a strategy is successful depends on the strategies being adopted by other males, and on other factors such as time of year (how far into mating season it is)

1. Based on the description in the passage, the most successful reproduction strategy is likely to be:
   A) stealth.
   B) avoidance.
   C) conflict, so long as the value for I is less than 2/3.
   D) indeterminate, as successful mating will depend on additional factors.

The passage tells us that the success of a strategy is not determined simply by the outcome of an individual male-male conflict, but rather by different factors, including the strategies of the other males in the area and the time of year.

2. In a sub-species of the fish, males have also demonstrated a fourth strategy involving conflict unless the other male begins fighting back vigorously. The male will quickly back down and mimic the behavior of a defeated male but then attempt to use stealth to enter the nest. The advantage of this strategy is that it provides which of the following?
   A) Flexibility to change behavior in response to the strategies adopted by the other fish
   B) The ability to avoid any injures due to confrontation
   C) An overall higher level of reproductive success
   D) A meta-stable strategy that will be present in any equilibrium

Given that the passage tells us that success depends on the strategies being adopted by the other males, an ability to adjust one's strategy in response to that factor is likely to be a significant advantage.

B: This new strategy may not help avoid "any" injury, since the fish will only back down after the other male has started fighting vigorously.
C: We're told nothing about overall level of success among fish who adopt this strategy. There may be some deleterious side-effect for these fish.
D: The word "any" is too strong as we can't know if this strategy would be present in any equilibrium.

3. In addition to the behaviors described in the passage, a small percentage of males are born physiologically fertile but behaviorally sterile. They will not even attempt to reproduce, but will instead defend nests from a certain common predator species. These fish:
   A) are demonstrating intra-specific commensalism with the females whose nests they defend.
   B) have an allele that must decrease over time due to their lack of reproduction.
   C) are behaving altruistically, increasing the inclusive fitness of their local population.
   D) have some sort of neurological damage to their central nervous system that causes them to misinterpret the females as not being potential mates.

Altruism is behavior that benefits another at a cost to oneself. Here, the male fish is giving up the opportunity to mate even though it is physiologically capable of doing so. It then places itself in danger by defending the nest from predators. This altruistic behavior increases the overall fitness of the local population of these fish, thus increasing inclusive fitness.

A: Commensalism is a benefit to one organism and neither a benefit nor a harm to another.
B: The allele doesn't have to decrease over time, as there may be some advantage conferred by it though kin selection, creating a stable frequency in the population.
D: Nothing in the question or passage suggests that these fish have neurological damage.

4. Some evidence suggests that these strategies are genetically determined but may also be shaped by operant

learning. Which of the following would most strengthen the theory that the males' strategy choice is a result of operant conditioning rather than purely genetic?

A) Those males that grow to be larger than average will almost always adopt a conflict strategy.

B) Males taking an avoidance strategy will often flee from other objects that are not even fish, if those objects have certain features (coloration, patterns, etc) that look like other male fish of the species.

C) Males who adopt a stealth strategy may sire offspring who will adopt either the stealth or the avoidance strategy, not exclusively the stealth strategy.

D) Males will typically adopt a conflict strategy and, after being injured, switch to a stealth strategy and will only switch to avoidance upon several unsuccessful attempts at stealth.

Operant conditioning is a form of learning in which the individual learns based on the outcomes or responses to behaviors. Here, only choice D describes the individual observing the response to his behaviors and then adjusting. For example, being injured for taking a conflict strategy is a classic operant positive punishment that will decrease the conflict behavior.

5. Upon entering the nest, males induce females to lay eggs by flashing a patch of bright orange scales on their ventral side. These scales weigh the male fish down and make movement metabolically expensive. Yet there is a strong correlation between the mass of these scales and male reproductive success. This feature is likely a result of:

A) divergent selection.

B) stabilizing selection.

C) sexual selection.

D) allopatric speciation.

Sexual selection is a form of directional selection pressure in which certain phenotypic features are preferentially selected for during the mating process even if such features (e.g. a peacock's feathers) have no direct correlation with fitness. Here, the bright orange scales are like a peacock's feathers.

Passage 2 Explanation

A program to **reduce bullying** will ideally have many components. It is helpful to consider **Bronfenbrenner's Systems Model**, in which the individual is conceptualized in terms of **increasingly broader systems** within his environment, to address bullying from different levels of analysis.

Key terms: Bronfenbrenner's Systems Model
Opinion: Programs to reduce bullying should begin early, have many components, and may follow Bronfenbrenner's model.

Figure 1 Bronfenbrenner's model to reduce bullying

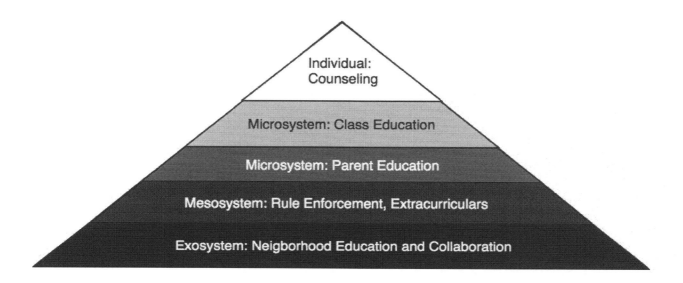

Figure 1 shows us the levels of Bronfenbrenner's model

First, at the **community level**, there should be efforts to reach out to people in the neighborhood to help **look out for bullying**. A lot of bullying **happens outside of school**, on the way home from school, or at gathering places for youths. At the **family level**, parents should be brought in to assist in the efforts. **Parents should be made aware** of any behavior their children might be exhibiting that would indicate the children were either being bullied or bullying. Some of these behaviors would be having a **lack of friends**, becoming more **withdrawn**, **strongly disliking school**, and being involved in any online bullying.

Opinion: Parents need to be attentive to their child's behavior to determine if the child is being bullied.

At a **school level**, students should be made aware of the rules around bullying. There should be policies spelled out explicitly that address the issue. The consequences will not involve suspension or sitting in a detention room, but will instead focus on **restitution to the bullied individual** and community and demonstrating knowledge of the policies.

Opinion: At the school level, bullying prevention means that teasing and other bullying behaviors will require intervention.

At the **class level**, students should be educated on the dynamics involved in bullying. A **peer-involved restorative justice** program should be implemented. By involving the parties involved with bullying, those bullying and those being bullied, both parties can get a message from their social group that **bullying is unacceptable**. Oftentimes, bullies may not realize their behavior is off-putting. They may instead see themselves as cool.

Opinion: Peers should intervene to stop bullying and make it clear that it's unacceptable.

Finally, at the individual level both **bullies and victims** should be addressed in a **counseling** format. Victims can focus on the effects that bullying has had on them and also work on developing social skills. Bullies also can work on more effective **social skills**. In addition, it is important to remember that having been a victim is also strongly correlated with being a bully. Bullies should address any **earlier trauma** they experienced that may have introduced this unequal power dynamic to them.

Opinion: Both bullies and victims should get counseling to address their issues.

6. What would be an example of a microsystem level intervention to address substance use?
  A) Teaching refusal skills to an individual
  B) **Family counseling to support the individual**
  C) National policies to toughen penalties for drug suppliers
  D) National policies to mandate insurers treat substance use disorders as they would any other medical condition

  Answer: B – The family is at the microsystem level in Bronfenbrenner's model.

7. Why might a community have a problem with bullying, an individual issue?
  A) **Lack of community resources for programs**
  B) Lack of integration of Bronfenbrenner's systems
  C) Individual issues
  D) Inherent community flaws

  Answer: A – According to Bronfenbrenner's model, systems are related and an issue at a community level can impact individuals.

8. What could be a possible macrosystem level intervention towards bullying?
  A) **De-emphasizing aggression as a valued trait at a cultural level**
  B) Having community forums to address bullying
  C) Encouraging bullied individuals to stand up for themselves
  D) Having bullying awareness days at a school

  Answer: A – The macrosystem involves cultural traits, so macrosystem level interventions would impact at a cultural level.

9. What could be a criticism of the bullying program from Bronfenbrenner's model?
  A) Communities may not agree with the model
  B) Individuals may not realize their impact on communities
  C) **In different cultures, individuals are influenced by their environment differently**
  D) The model does not consider the impact broad policies can have on the individual

Answer: C – Bronfenbrenner's model may have differing validity in different cultures as in some cultures the individual may be relatively unaffected by the community, in which case community interventions would not be indicated.

10. Which of the following is NOT an explanation why a person who has been bullied come to bully others?
    A) Through social learning this individual has come to learn that bullying can get a person what they want.
    B) Through socialization this individual has come to learn that aggression is not an inappropriate way to interact with others.
    C) Through neurobiological theory this individual has come to have a higher threshold for tolerating stress and aggression.
    D) **Through cognitive behavioral theory this individual has experienced mistrust in his caregivers and has come to repeat these dynamics of mistrust in his relationships.**

Answer: D – This answer states that the theory is cognitive behavioral, but the explanation is a psychoanalytic explanation.

Passage 3 Explanation

Gate control theory is a comprehensive way to understand an individual's perception of pain. This model considers that pain is both **psychogenic** and **somatic**, that is, originating both in an individual's perceptions and his body. **Before** this model was developed, **psychological** factors were **only considered to be reactions** to pain. However, since the development of this model, psychological factors are understood to influence the perception of pain.

Key terms: Gate control theory, psychogenic, somatic
Contrast: psychological factors used to be considered only reactions to pain, now we know they contribute to pain perception.

In terms of affective factors, a number of **disorders** can impact how a person is able to perceive pain and generate strategies for tolerating it. **Depression** is a prominent disorder involved with chronic pain, impacting as many as **40-50% of individuals experiencing pain**. There is a cyclic relationship between experiencing pain and depression, where chronic pain can cause depression, but depression also impacts the perception of pain. For individuals experiencing depression and chronic pain, it can be hard to generate **strategies for addressing the pain**, leading to a sense of **helplessness** about how to address the issues. As a result, many individuals may utilize **passive** coping strategies for managing pain, such as using **medication, being inactive, or using drugs or alcohol**.

Key terms: depression
Cause and effect: depression leads to helplessness and passive approaches to pain management

A number of **cognitive factors** are also associated with experiencing pain. Research has shown that patients who view their pain as signifying a **progressive degenerative disease**, rather than as a stable condition that will improve, experience **more severe pain**. In addition, patients who had experienced pain previously when involved in physical activity have a **learned** expectation that **future activity will result in pain**, resulting in **less helpful physical activity** on their part.

Key terms: cognitive factors
Cause and effect: people who view their disease as progressive and getting worse will experience greater pain; those who associate pain with physical activity will engage in less activity.

Catastrophic thinking has been found to be associated with more severe perception of pain. On the other hand, patients who employ coping strategies, or ways of managing pain, tend to experience less severe pain. There are two types of coping strategies that patients can employ, overt and covert coping strategies. **Overt coping** strategies are active strategies to manage pain, such as **engaging in healthy behavior**. **Covert** strategies involve **distracting** oneself from the pain, such as through meditation or obtaining information about the chronic condition.

Key terms: catastrophic thinking
Contrast: overt vs. covert coping strategies
Cause and effect: pain can be addressed by teaching coping skills

A way that pain is typically assessed in treatment is by using a **"pain thermometer"** in which patients are asked to rate the severity of their pain from 1 to 10. In a study which examined the implementation of a **treatment program** for patients with chronic pain, which **emphasized using coping strategies**, developing a sense of self-efficacy, and being active, patients in a control group and in the treatment group were asked to rate their level of pain before and after the program. The average results of the two groups are presented on the pain thermometers as follows:

Key terms: pain thermometer, treatment program, coping strategies

Table 1 Effect of treatment on pain perception

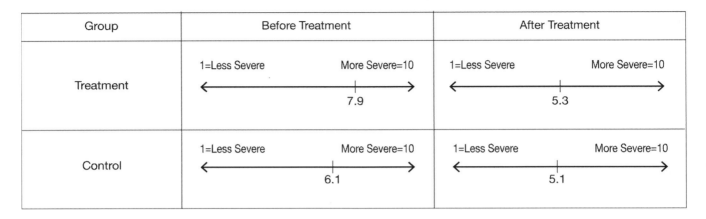

Differences between the two groups from pre − to post-treatment is significant p<.0001

Table 1 shows us that both the treatment and control group experienced a decrease in pain, but that the treatment group had a larger overall decrease.

11. A patient assumes his pain will not get better. In his treatment he is asked to find research about his condition each day for a week. This is an example of what type of strategy?
    A) Humanistic
    B) Psychodynamic
    C) **Cognitive Behavioral**
    D) Neurobiological

    Answer: C − In this strategy the patient is asked to address his catastrophic thoughts by engaging in a behavior that is designed to change his thinking, which is a Cognitive Behavioral strategy.

12. How can the results of the study be summarized?
    A) **The treatment group had a greater decrease in pain than the control group**
    B) The control group had a greater decrease in pain than the treatment group
    C) The treatment group had a greater increase in pain than the control group
    D) The control group had a greater increase in pain than the treatment group

    Answer: A − Both groups decreased in their pain level, but the treatment group decreased in pain more than the control group.

13. What might account for a significant decrease in pain in the control group, who are told that they receiving treatment in the study but are not actually receiving the treatment?
    A) Avoidance learning
    B) Expectancy theory
    C) **Placebo effect**
    D) Conditioned learning

Answer: C – The placebo effect occurs when participants in an experiment demonstrate a certain benefit after expecting to benefit, even though they are not receiving the treatment.

14. This passage suggests that what else should be assessed in addition to assessing a patient's level of pain?
    A) Somatic issues
    B) **Psychogenic issues**
    C) The area of the body in which the pain is occurring
    D) The neurobiological factors involved with pain

Answer: B – This passage illustrated that pain involves psychological factors as well as physical ones. In addition, psychological factors can have a causative influence on pain, not just be reactions to pain.

These questions are **NOT** related to a passage.

15. Which of the following characterize sympathetic nervous system activation?
 I. **Redirection of glucose and other resources from the digestive organs to the brain and heart.**
 II. **Reduced sensitivity to pain.**
 III. Synthesis of glycogen.
   A) I only
   B) **I and II only**
   C) II and III only
   D) I, II and III

   Choice (I) describes a component of the "fight-or-flight" response, which the sympathetic nervous system helps to cause when it becomes activated. Choice (II) is a consequence of sympathetic nervous system activation as well. Choice (III), however, relates to the digestive system combining glucose molecules into stored glycogen, which is accomplished through use of the parasympathetic – not the sympathetic – nervous system. Choice (B), which includes choices (I) and (II), is correct.

16. Over the course of a decade, approximately 45,000 native Africans emigrate from their home countries to a major Western city. Once there, most attempt to find housing. However, due to discriminatory treatment from the native-born residents of the city, many of these immigrants end up living in particular neighborhoods where the local majority of residents are also recent African immigrants. What best describes this situation?
   A) Formation of ethnocentrism in response to institutional barriers to assimilation.
   B) **Formation of ethnic enclaves in response to institutional barriers to assimilation.**
   C) Formation of cultural relativism in response to institutional barriers to assimilation.
   D) Formation of cultural relativism in response to ethnocentrism.

   The answer is (B). The term "ethnic enclaves" refers to culturally distinct areas with large percentages of a particular ethnicity. The term "assimilation" means a group – here, a group of immigrants – becoming more similar to those already present in a society. Here, the African immigrants are attempting to do something, namely finding housing, which could help the assimilation process. Inability to find housing outside of ethnic enclaves, however, often presents an obstacle to opportunities that could help immigrants assimilate into mainstream society.

   A: Ethnocentrism means using the standards of one's own culture to judge other cultures. Here, the prompt does not mention that any such judgment is taking place. Even if one assumes that the discriminatory treatment is due to ethnocentrism on the part of the native Westerners, (A) is still incorrect because it lists ethnocentrism as a result rather than a cause.
   C: Cultural relativism refers to the view that every culture's characteristics and practices should be judged using only the standards of that culture, not the standards of outside cultures. Here, no participants in the prompt are making such judgments.
   D: As noted in the explanation to choice (C), cultural relativism is not involved with the prompt's fact pattern.

17. In City A, residents are observed to allow elevator passengers to exit before boarding the elevator themselves. In City B, residents are observed to attempt to board the elevator before the previous passengers have exited. What best describes the difference between these two situations?
   A) One norm is caused by a formal institution and the other is caused by an informal institution.
   B) One norm is caused by institutionalization, and the other norm is caused by social function.
   C) **Institutionalization of structures of social order has occurred differently in each city.**

D) One city has developed a material culture and the other has developed a non-material culture.

The answer is (C). The standard practice of what to do when boarding an elevator, which is a structure or form of social order, is different in each city. This is because in each city, different norms and customs have been "institutionalized," meaning have become embedded in a society.

A: A formal institution is one (such as a government or a religious church) which sets forth rules that are intended to shape behavior. An informal institution is one which, even though it might affect conduct, is not designed to regulate conduct. Here, the elevator-boarding norms have no connection to formal institutions, and may not be a response to informal institutions either.
B: Both norms are caused by institutionalization, not just one. Additionally, social function relates to the effect or intended effect of an institution on society, and also affects the norms in both cities, not just one.
D: Material culture refers to the physical objects used by a society, and the ways in which people define their culture through use of these objects. Non-material culture refers to non-physical ideas that every culture has about itself – for instance, organizations, institutions, norms and rules. Here, each city possesses both material and non-material cultures; this does not account for the difference in elevator-boarding customs.

18. Which of the following characterize urbanization?
 I. Migration from urban areas to rural areas
 II. **Breakdown of social bonds between an individual and the surrounding community**
 III. **Increased industrialization**
  A) I only
  B) II only
  C) I and III only
  D) **II and III only**

Choice (I) is the reverse of what happens during urbanization. Choice (II) describes anomie, which frequently characterizes what occurs when a population migrates to cities. Choice (III), increased industrialization, also often accompanies population shifts to urban areas. For these reasons, choice (D) is correct.

Passage 4 Explanation

Traditionally, organizational approaches to **stress management** in the workplace have been focused on addressing employee stress at the **secondary-level** of intervention and fostering secondary-level interventions for managing stress. An example of a secondary-level intervention in managing stress is an employee training program for learning skills for handling customer complaints at a retail store. The goals of the program are for the employees to be able to manage the complaints effectively, which will ideally reduce the stress they experience from this activity. Benefits typically **subside over time**, though this may also be an artifact of the extinction of the learned skills, indicating the need for booster sessions.

Key terms: stress management, secondary-level
Cause and effect: A secondary-level approach makes stress reduction the employee's job
Opinion: These types of efforts do some good, but the effect fades over time

Another issue with this view of stress reduction is that it is a **reactive approach**. As in the example, employees are taught how to effectively manage stress in reaction to stress that is initiated from the customer. The **source of the stress is not addressed** and there is no focus on how to proactively reduce it.

Opinion: Secondary-level approaches aren't as good because they require that there's already a problem and the source of the stress isn't dealt with.

An alternative level of intervention besides for secondary-level interventions is **primary-level interventions**. The goal in primary-level interventions is to try to proactively address the source of the stress to attempt to **eliminate it before it arises**.

Key terms: primary-level intervention, culture, management style

A primary-level facet of stress to consider is the **employee perception of control**. Employees not feeling in control of their work output has been identified as a salient source of stress. Employees should be **encouraged to feel empowered** in their contribution to the organization and should also feel creative control over their work. Policies to encourage employee contributions and eliciting feedback from employees can be done to foster a sense of employee control.

Cause and effect: Employee stress can be reduced by increasing employee's sense of control over their work.

A final primary-level strategy for addressing workplace stress is to manage employee stress from **work demand**. Employees feeling **overloaded with work is a significant source of stress**. Organizations should first consider the reality of the expectations imposed on employees and consider the impact that staff reduction and increased expectations might have on employee stress and concomitant employee performance.

Cause and effect: Overloading work demands increases stress and can ultimately harm profits when employees start to drop in performance.

To evaluate the impact of primary and secondary-level interventions on **employee satisfaction** – a broad measure encompassing employee retention, productivity, and other measures identified as salient to employee satisfaction, rated from 0 to 100, a study was conducted at an organization. At this organization, employees were randomly assigned to participate in either a primary or secondary-level intervention. Measures of employee satisfaction were reported over time. **January** was an initial reading of employee satisfaction, **before the interventions were implemented**. The results are presented as follows:

Figure 1 Employee satisfaction following stress reduction intervention

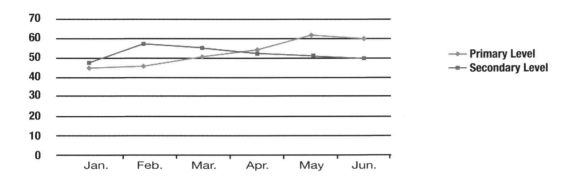

Figure 1 shows us that the secondary level interventions lead to a quick increase in employee satisfaction but then lead to a gradual decrease, whereas the primary-level interventions had little effect at first but created bigger overall gains.

19. What could account for the initial increase in employee satisfaction followed by the gradual decrease in the secondary-level intervention group?
    A) **Skill knowledge and use is decreasing over time**
    B) Reduced initial work expectations
    C) Increased initial healthcare, followed by gradual reductions
    D) Reductions in noise level, lessening in impact as time passes

    Answer: A – This is an example of a secondary-level intervention and how its effect can lessen over time, leading to a tapering off effect.

20. What could be done to increase the effects of a secondary level intervention in the later months?
    A) **A refresher class in the skills that were taught**
    B) Focusing on optimizing employee time
    C) Have a training session after an employee problem
    D) Have a stress needs assessment

    Answer: A – This is an example of a booster class, in which skills are refreshed via another training.

21. What term indicates a beneficial type of stress which can motivate employees?
    A) Distress
    B) Constress
    C) Cathartic stress
    D) **Eustress**

    Answer: D – Eustress is a term which is used to refer to stress, which can be motivational. Distress is stress that is in excess and harmful.

22. What could be an effective primary-level intervention against in-group bias at the workplace?
   A) Teaching employees social skills so they can enter work cliques
   B) **Providing workplace-wide education about the impact of excluding co-workers**
   C) Teaching employees health strategies they can use to reduce stress
   D) Educating the workforce on the proper procedures for reporting discrimination

   Answer: B – This is a primary-level intervention. The other answers are secondary-level or irrelevant (C).

Passage 5 Explanation

When humans are **first born**, it does **not** appear that there are **differences** in their ability to discern differences in facial characteristics among different ethnicities. However, **by 3 months** of age, they begin to be able to discern differences between faces of the ethnic identity to which they are primarily exposed. This finding was observed by showing newborn infants and infants at 3 months of age pictures of faces of people of different ethnicities, in a type of research design called a **visual preference paradigm**. The length of **time** the infants gazed at a face was considered a reflection of how **novel** this face appeared to them. Infants will gaze longer at faces they view to be novel. It was found that infants looked at **different faces** of the ethnicity to which they were primarily exposed **more frequently** at 3 months, but not at birth, suggesting that they were able to perceive differences among the faces of the race with which they were familiar.

Key terms: visual preference paradigm
Contrast: first born vs. 3 months, it's not until babies are three months old that they can tell differences between faces of their ethnicity

However, another study demonstrated that **3 month** old infants are capable of **becoming familiar** with faces of people of different ethnicities after a short time of exposure. In this study, the infants were shown pictures of faces of people of ethnicities of which they initially didn't recognize differences. **After exposure** to these faces for a short time, the infants were able to better **discriminate among these faces** with which they had previously been unfamiliar. This study seemed to show that through exposure to people of different ethnicities, infants can become more familiar with those people.

Cause and effect: exposure to faces of different ethnicities lets babies detect differences between faces of people of that ethnicity

However, this ability to recognize faces of a different ethnicity seems to **lessen** throughout the infant's development through a process called **perceptual narrowing**. Infants begin to show lack of recognition of faces of other ethnicities from **6 months onwards**, **even after exposure** to these faces. This effect is also shown to occur across different ethnicities, with babies of different ethnicities shown to be able to discriminate among faces of their own ethnicity better than faces of other ethnicities.

Key terms: perceptual narrowing
Cause and effect: aging causes babies to lose the ability to recognize faces of other ethnicities from six months onwards

These findings would seem to indicate that infants are born neutral in their ability to discern differences among ethnicities and develop a familiarity with a certain ethnicity over time. However, what determines for what ethnicity infants will develop an **ability to discern**? Studies seem to point to infants developing this ability among the ethnicity to which they are **primarily exposed**. In a study that took place in Israel, researchers assessed **African infants** who had been raised by **Israeli caretakers**. It was found that the African infants were able to **recognize differences in Israeli faces** and not the faces of their own ethnicity. This would seem to indicate that infants develop recognition for characteristics of faces to which they are exposed from an early period onwards.

Key terms: Israeli/African study
Cause and effect: ability to distinguish between different faces is caused by early exposure to faces of a particular ethnicity.

23. What is another example of perceptual narrowing?
    A) Gaining an ability to discern faces more clearly
    B) **Losing the ability to distinguish sounds not used in a certain language**
    C) Having more entrenched views on race as a person ages
    D) Demonstrating gender norms with age

    Answer: B – Perceptual narrowing is losing the ability to discern certain stimuli from disuse. An example of this is losing the ability to hear or pronounce certain sounds if these sounds are not used in an individual's language.

24. What argument against having a pronounced ability for infants to be able to discern facial characteristics of their own ethnicity is given in this passage?
    A) Infants tend to look at faces of their own ethnicity longer because they can discern differences
    B) Across ethnicities infants are able to recognize faces from their own ethnicity more easily
    C) **Infants raised by people from different ethnicities demonstrate an ability to discern differences in faces from their caretaker's ethnicity**
    D) An infant becomes less able to learn differences in other ethnicities' faces as he ages

    Answer: C – Infants raised by caretakers of ethnicities different than their own show an ability to discern differences in faces of the caretakers' ethnicity, similar to infants with ethnicities the same as their caretakers.

25. This passage suggests that a way to enhance an individual's ability to discern facial characteristics of ethnicities different than his own is:
    A) Encouraging a child to avoid perceiving racial characteristics
    B) **Exposing an infant to ethnicities different than his own**
    C) Having an infant raised solely by a caretaker of a different ethnicity
    D) Using a visual preference paradigm

    Answer: B – According to the passage, infants begin to be able to perceive facial characteristics of ethnicities to which they are exposed at a young age. It is also stated that infants can be exposed to other ethnicities and develop the ability to perceive characteristics of that ethnicity. Answer C would likely enhance an infant's ability to perceive the caretaker's ethnicity, but not more than one ethnicity as the question indicated.

26. In a visual preference paradigm, it can be expected that an infant would gaze longer at:
    A) a stimulus to which he is exposed for a lengthy period of time.
    B) a pattern that is familiar to him.
    C) **an unusual shape.**
    D) no inferences can be made .

    Answer: C – In the visual preference paradigm infants gaze longer at stimuli that are novel to them. An example of this is an unusual shape.

These questions are **NOT** related to a passage.

27. Which of the following characterize parasympathetic nervous system activation?
  I. **Decreased heart rate.**
 II. Decreased digestive activity.
III. **Conversion of glucose into glycogen.**
    A) I only
    B) I and II only
    C) **I and III only**
    D) II and III only

Choices (I) and (III) are results of parasympathetic nervous system activation; however, choice (II) is a result of sympathetic nervous system activation, and is the reverse of what happens when the parasympathetic nervous system is activated. Therefore, the correct response will include choices (I) and (III) but not choice (II), making (C) the correct answer.

28. A number of urban commuters, when surveyed individually regarding their opinion of a new rail line in their city, express nuanced views which include both pluses and minuses. Later, these commuters participate in a focus group and are again asked to give their opinion. After discussing the issue amongst themselves for 45 minutes, they report their opinions to the focus group director, except now they report more extreme and less nuanced positions than they previously expressed, with roughly half the group taking strong "approve" positions and the remainder taking strong "disapprove" positions. What best describes this result?
    A) Socialization
    B) Peer pressure
    C) Groupthink
    D) **Group polarization**

Group polarization is defined as the tendency of group members to express more extreme views when part of a group than they were initially inclined to express when acting individually. This describes the dynamic described in the prompt, and hence the answer is (D).

A: Socialization relates to the adoption of norms. There are no identifiable group norms being adopted by individuals here.
B: Peer pressure relates to pressure on a group member to adopt the norms of a group. Again, here this is not taking place.
C: Groupthink is when members of a group excessively strive for consensus. Here, the group members divide between two different viewpoints, so groupthink is not the best explanation.

29. Which of the following characterize Albert Bandura's conception of the social cognitive perspective of personality?
  I. **A belief in one's own abilities**
 II. **Observational learning**
III. Neuroticism
    A) **I and II**
    B) I and III
    C) II and III
    D) I, II and III

Self-efficacy, or a belief in one's own abilities, is a characteristic of personality in Bandura's social cognitive theory, so choice (I) is correct. Additionally, observational learning – also known as social learning – is a characteristic of social cognitive personality theory, so choice (II) is also correct. Neuroticism, while a component of theories relating to the trait perspective of personality, is not a component of the social cognitive perspective. Choice (A), which includes choices (I) and (II), is the answer.

30. Members of a gymnastics team are observed to perform simple maneuvers better when watched by a small audience than when alone. However, when learning complicated triple flips, the presence of an audience causes their performance to worsen and they tend to make more mistakes. What best accounts for this?
    A) The bystander effect
    B) Peer pressure
    C) Socialization
    D) **Social facilitation**

Social facilitation is the phenomenon wherein people do better on simple, familiar tasks when others are present, but worse on less familiar or less well-practiced tasks when others are present. This makes (D) the correct answer.

A: The bystander effect refers to the phenomenon wherein observers are less likely to assist someone else if others are also present.
B: Peer pressure takes place when members of a group put pressure on an individual to conform to their group norms.
C: Socialization is when an individual acquires norms and values of a society, as well as an identity which forms a connection between that individual and society.

Passage 6 Explanation

It is important to consider the **impact of culture on psychotherapeutic medication**. There are multiple biopsychosocial factors that impact the effect of medicine on people of different cultures. **Ethnicity** has, for some time, been observed to **impact the biological response to medication**, especially medications which impact **genes** that vary by ethnicities. However, culture has been less researched in terms of its impact on biological response to medication. One way culture has impacted medication response is through **diet**, which typically varies by culture. For example, drug researchers have observed the pharmokinetic effects, or impact of drugs on the body, of immigrants. They found that **when immigrants' diets change** from the diet of their native country to that of their new country **their pharmokinetic response also changes** to become more similar to that of the individuals in their new culture.

Key terms: culture, ethnicity, psychotherapeutic, pharmokinetic
Cause and effect: ethnicity can change how people respond to drugs, though genes and diet.

Cultural differences among doctors also influences medication efficacy. First of all, doctors may be influenced by their culture in how they prescribe medication. There may be a number of systems, such as insurance companies, health organizations, or the patient's own expectations, which impact **the way the doctor prescribes** medication. The way that doctors perceive and diagnose patient issues is affected by culture. Research has shown that in the U.S. **Caucasian doctors tend to over-pathologize African-American and Hispanic** patients.

Cause and effect: the culture of the doctor also affects how drugs are used, with white doctors over-treating black and hispanic patients.

Culture may also impact the way in which the **illness is viewed**. **Asians** especially, and more recently **Westerners**, use **alternative remedies**, such as natural medication, physical healing techniques, and alternative health care providers. These practices are typically **viewed as being more safe** and non-invasive than taking pharmaceuticals. However, these practices can impact other treatment regimens. As a result, a patient should be **assessed for engagement in alternative treatments**, when considering new treatment plans and their level of willingness to engage in prescribed medication.

Opinion: White and Asian patients are more likely to engage in alternative remedies which can change their compliance with prescribed treatment

The **presentation** of the medication may have cultural significance and affect efficacy. The **form, color, and amount of the medication** may all impact the way people from different cultures view it. For example, **Caucasians** were found to regard **white capsules as analgesics**. The contents of the medicine may preclude some cultures from taking them due to their beliefs, an example of which is **Muslims** being **averse** to taking medications containing **alcohol** due to religious beliefs. Patients may not disclose their aversion to taking a certain medicine and may assume that there are no alternatives; therefore querying a patient's **willingness to comply** with treatment is advised.

Cause and effect: the medium the medicine comes in can affect patient reaction to it
Contrast: White patients view white pills as pain-killers

When developing a new drug, pharmaceutical companies **must show the drug to be more efficacious than a placebo drug in research**. In a study in which a pharmaceutical company was examining the efficacy of a new drug for depression, the company evaluated how much improvement study participants had compared to a placebo drug. To further assess for the effects of culture, the company conducted the study on **three different continents**.

The average percent improvement of participants taking the drug compared to those taking placebo in each continent are shown as follows:

Table 1 Effectiveness of a drug over placebo

North America	Africa	Asia
25%	38%	33%

The difference in improvements between continents was significant (p<.0001).

Table 1 shows us that the depression drug had the biggest effect over placebo in Africa and the least in North America.

31. Which of the following would *least* likely account for the difference in drug efficacy seen in the study?
    A) Different cultural expectations of the efficacy of the drug
    B) Cultural differences affecting drug pharmokinetics
    C) Cultural differences in the relationship between study researcher and participant
    D) **Immigrant participants' diets may have changed**

    Answer: D – While a change in diet due to immigration may affect the pharmokinetics of the individual, the result is that the drug would then behave similarly to the place to which he migrated. This answer does not account for the cultural differences.

32. Doctors diagnosing some ethnic groups with more severe disorders is an example of what kind of discrimination?
    A) Individual
    B) Institutional
    C) **Both Individual and Institutional**
    D) Neither Individual nor Institutional

    Answer: C – Doctors likely have their own cultural biases and in addition are trained at institutions that may not promote multicultural competency.

33. Which of the following is NOT a question that would helpful for a prescribing doctor to ask his patient?
    A) How do you feel about this prescription?
    B) Are you using any other treatments for your condition?
    C) **What do you think of the shape of this medicine?**
    D) What might prevent you from taking the medicine as directed?

    Answer: C – The appearance of the medicine, for example shape or color, and how it affects a patient's view of it is largely an unconscious process. Therefore asking a patient about it would likely not yield helpful information.

34. What would NOT be an effective public health strategy to help consider cultural factors in medicine?
    A) **Encouraging immigrant patients to retain the diets of their native country**
    B) Informing doctors about cultural factors for which to assess
    C) Providing patients with information about drugs and natural healing
    D) Requiring pharmaceutical companies to disclose with what cultures drugs have been evaluated

Answer: A – The change in diet can affect the pharmokinetics of a drug. However, this can be accounted for so patients do not necessarily need to change their diet.

35. Which of the following is NOT a way that researchers could remove some of the location effects from the study?
    A) Consider the expectations of the participants and the pill administration method
    B) **<u>Distinguish the placebo pill from the trial medication</u>**
    C) Measure the pharmacokinetic effects of the drug
    D) Consider the impact of cultural factors on diagnosis

Answer: B – Distinguishing the medication to the participants would eliminate the usefulness of having a placebo pill. Answer A is helpful because if participants expect that the pill will work the placebo effect may mask actual effects. Answer C is good because then researchers have a more unbiased measure of the effects of the drug. D is helpful because culture can impact diagnosis, resulting in participants with different severities of pathologies across sites.

Passage 7 Explanation

In an **experiment**, researchers told participants that they could potentially **receive** either 1) a guaranteed $15 or 2) have a 50% chance of receiving either $10 or $20 respectively. When given this choice **most people choose** option 1, to receive the **guaranteed money**. However, the expected gain from this offer is the same. In option 1 there is a 100% likelihood of receiving $15, for an expected gain of $15, and in option 2 there is a 50% chance of receiving $10 and a 50% chance of receiving $20 for an expected gain of also $15.

Opinion: When given a choice of getting money, most people choose the less-risky option

If this experiment were phrased another way, and now a person were **given $20** and told he could either 1) give back a guaranteed $5 or 2) have a 50% chance of giving back either $0 or $10 respectively **most people would choose option 2**. However, this experiment is the same as the previous experiment in terms of expected gain, that of $15 with either option. **The difference** between the two experiments is in the **way in which the offers are framed**.

Opinion: When given money and then given a chance of losing it, most people choose the more-risky option

As an explanation as to why the framing of the offers should affect the choice people tend to make, **prospect theory** explains that people often **see expected gains or losses** in terms of their **departure from an assumed expected amount**. So, first of all, people tend to consider a departure from an amount in terms of its relative departure, rather than absolute departure. For example, an individual making $100,000 will value a $10,000 raise more than a person making $1,000,000.

Key terms: Prospect theory, says that people view gains and losses relative to some expectation

Within this principle, whether a person is gaining or losing money is the important factor, with those **gaining money tending to be more aversive to risk** and those losing money tending to be more favorable to risk. For individuals who start with $0, any gain is a substantial increase, making them more aversive to risk and happy to take the guaranteed amount. For individuals who start with $20, a greater loss may not seem as drastic, as they are starting with an amount of money, leaving them more inclined to court risk.

Cause and effect: a person seeking gain is more risk-averse but a person seeking to avoid losses will be willing to take risk

Prospect theory can be applied to public health promotion. An example of a **loss-framed public health announcement** is that if you don't stop smoking you **might get lung cancer** and a **gain framed** announcement is that if you stop smoking **you will be healthier**.

Contrast: loss-framed message (smoking causes cancer) vs. gain-framed message (quitting smoking will make you feel better)

Also, **health procedures** can be framed in terms of **detection** of a physical disease, such as through an examination, **or prevention** of a disease, such as through exercise. **Detection of a disease is generally seen as riskier**. Prevention is seen as less risky, on the other hand, as its purpose is to maintain health.

Contrast: detection (a risky process) vs. prevention (a less-risky process)

An experiment was conducted to determine **how well participants responded to messages** that were either gain framed or loss framed and applied to health behaviors that either involved detection or prevention. The **average rate of participant compliance** with the message is presented as follows:

Table 1 Experiment results

	Loss Framed Message	Gain Framed Message
Detection Behavior	67%	48%
Prevention Behavior	51%	68%

Table 1 shows us that when a message is phrased as a potential loss, you get more compliance with detection behavior and when a message is phrased as a potential gain, you get more compliance with prevention behavior.

36. Based on the results of the study, which message would likely lead to the greatest rate of compliance of encouraging people to eat healthily every day?
    A) Not eating healthy can lead to a number of diseases
    B) **Eating healthy can help you feel your best**
    C) Eating junk food, leaves you feeling like junk
    D) Obesity is at an all time high in the United States

    Answer: B – Encouraging people to eat healthily is a prevention behavior; thus people should be most receptive to a gain framed message.

37. In what desired behavior would the message, "Heart disease is the number one killer in the U.S.," be least likely to induce compliance?
    A) **Encouraging people to get their cholesterol checked yearly**
    B) Encouraging people to eat low-fat foods
    C) Encouraging people to exercise daily
    D) Encouraging people to reduce stress

    Answer: A – This message is a loss-framed message, for which a detection behavior is the best match.

38. When considering choices, an individual might rank homicide as a greater threat than heart disease because it is on the news more prominently. What type of biased thinking did this person use in committing this error?
    A) Fundamental attribution error
    B) Stereotyped threat
    C) **Availability heuristic**
    D) Belief perseverance

    Answer: C – The availability heuristic describes an individual using information that is more readily available than other information to form his opinions.

39. If a man receives a $1,000 bonus, how might comparing his bonus to his co-workers make his mood more negative?
    A) If his co-workers received the same amount as he did
    B) If his co-workers received less than he did
    C) **<u>If his co-workers received more than he did</u>**
    D) If he cannot compare his bonus to his co-workers' bonuses.

    Answer: C – By framing the bonus as being less than what his co-workers received the man is now less happy about his bonus.

Passage 8 Explanation

Ethnic identity is **dynamic** and changes at different points in an individual's life. **Marcia's general model** of identity development is useful for describing an individual's identity in a number of respects. It is also fluid, in that an individual may be at different points in the model at different times with respect to different aspects of identity. The model characterizes an individual as being at one of 4 points in his identity development. Throughout this model, the term **"identity crisis"** is used to describe an event which would **precipitate an individual to begin exploring his identity**.

Key terms: ethnic identity, Marcia's model of identity, identity crisis

First, an individual may be in **identity diffusion**. This individual may or may not have experienced an identity crisis that would lead him to begin seeking out an identity. He is currently **uncommitted** to a particular identity. An individual may also be in a **foreclosed identity**. This individual has agreed to an identity that was **imposed externally**. The individual did not arrive at this identity through exploration or through his own efforts.

Key terms: identity diffusion, foreclosed identity

An individual may also be in **moratorium**. An individual in this stage is **actively seeking out an identity**. He is aware that different identities are available and is seeking to choose one for himself. Finally, an individual may be in **identity achievement**. This individual has explored the range of options of identity available. He has considered several identities and has **arrived at one** that is consonant with his own **values**.

Key terms: moratorium, identity achievement

To assess the impact an individual's status has on his **ability to complete tasks**, researchers first rated participants' answers to a variety of statements about their views of their identity. Researchers classified participants into one of the identity categories in the Marcia model, then **measured the time** it took to complete a task. Researchers then compared the average task completion times. The results are presented as follows:

Table 1 Task completion based on identity status

Identity Status	Completion Time
Identity Achievement	15.6
Foreclosure	19.2
Moratorium	29.6
Identity Diffusion	27.4

Table 1 shows us that a person who has a set identity, either through identity achievement or through foreclosure, is able to complete a task more quickly than one who has not.

An identity model for classifying **African-Americans' ethnic identity** has been proposed by **Cross**. An individual proceeds through this **model in sequential order**. The first stage is the **Pre-encounter** stage. Individuals in this stage have assimilated to American values. For these individuals, **ethnicity is not a very salient** part of their identity.

Key terms: Cross, African-American identity, pre-encounter stage
Contrast: In the Marcia model, people can be at various stages of identity at various times for various parts of their identity but in the Cross model, the stages are sequential.

Next is the **Encounter** stage, which occurs after the individual has had some experience which leads to an **ethnic identity crisis**. Ethnic identity begins to take on importance. The individual can become **confused** or alarmed that this previously unnoticed aspect has become salient.

Key terms: encounter stage
Cause and effect: Some experience creates an ethnic identity crisis that makes them confront their identity as a black person.

The next stage is **Immersion**. During this stage, individuals have become fully immersed in their ethnic identity. They **identify with their ethnic identity**, to the point that these aspects are **unrealistically inflated**, and they may feel a **resentment of the dominant ethnicity**.

Key terms: immersion stage
Cause and effect: A person in this stage has so strongly identified with their ethnic identity that it becomes an inflated part of their identity and they feel resentment of the majority culture.

The final stage is **Internalization**. In this stage, the individual has accepted that there are some aspects of his **ethnic identity which may be imperfect**. The individual has also **balanced** his ethnic identification with other aspects of himself, yet **advocates for his ethnic community**.

Key terms: internalization stage
Cause and effect: Advancing to the internalization stage means a person has developed a balanced view of his ethnic identity.

40. What stages are most similar in the Cross African-American ethnic identity model and the Marcia identity model?

A) Internalization and moratorium
B) Immersion and diffusion
C) **Internalization and identity achievement**
D) Encounter and foreclosure

Answer: C – These both represent the final stage in their respective identity processes.

41. In what identity status would an individual be who has agreed to study what his parents want him to study in college without any input from him?

A) Identity achievement
B) Moratorium
C) Diffusion
D) **Foreclosure**

Answer: D – Foreclosure is agreeing to an identity without purposely exploring it or other identities.

42. Which of the following would likely not be a variable which would moderate the relationship between identity status and task completion time in the study?

A) Type A personality status
B) Cognitive skills
C) **Reference group**
D) Manual dexterity

Answer: C – This variable refers to a factor that is outside the individual, whereas the other variables refer to variables that could affect an individual's completion time.

43. According to Erikson's psychosocial stages of development, an individual who does not successfully resolve his issue of identity likely experiences what state?

A) Inferiority
B) Mistrust
C) Guilt
D) **Role Confusion**

Answer: D – According to Erikson an individual addresses issues of identity in the stage Identity v. Role Confusion. Thus, an individual who does not successfully resolve the issue of identity experiences role confusion.

These questions are **NOT** related to a passage.

44. A bar exam preparation company begins an advertising campaign intended to describe the strengths of its bar preparation course, mentioning such facts as the company's competitive pricing and the high bar passage rate of previous students. Later, the company attempts to gain students for its course by redesigning its books and other materials to be more visually enticing, and by hiring more attractive campus representatives. The two campaigns are characterized by, respectively:

   A) Attempting to change attitudes through peripheral-route processing, and then by central-route processing.
   B) **Attempting to change attitudes through central-route processing, and then by peripheral-route processing.**
   C) Attempting to change attitudes through central-route processing, and then by choice-of-route processing.
   D) Attempting to change attitudes through choice-of-route processing, and then by central-route processing.

In the elaboration likelihood model of persuasion, central-route processing refers to an individual deciding issues on the merits by analyzing arguments and deciding if they are convincing. By contrast, peripheral-route processing refers to an individual forming an attitude about a message based not on the message itself, but on the characteristics surrounding the message – the credibility or attractiveness of the messenger, for example, or the quality of the message's presentation. Here, the first advertising campaign depends on the target audience using central processing to evaluate the merits of their sales pitch, while the second campaign depends on the target audience being influenced by cues which are external to the message itself. Choice (B) lists both of these in the correct order, and is therefore the right answer.

A: This contains the appropriate content, but lists it in the reverse order.
C: Choice-of-route refers to factors such as motivation and ability which determine whether a person uses a central route or a peripheral route to process an attempt at persuasion. It does not describe either of the two advertising campaigns.
D: Choice-of-route does not describe either of the two advertising campaigns, and central-route processing does not describe the second advertising campaign.

45. Which of the following characterize Kohlberg's theory of morality development?
 I. **A first stage where individuals focus on the direct consequences of actions.**
 II. **A second stage where individuals believe society, or other outside forces, to be the principal determinants of morally appropriate actions.**
III. A third stage where individuals focus on the importance of using morality to form closer-knit societies
   A) I only
   B) **I and II only**
   C) I and III only
   D) I, II and III

Kohlberg postulated a first, "Pre-Conventional" stage in which individuals focus on the direct consequences of actions, a second, "Conventional" stage where individuals believe society to be the main factor in determining whether an action is right or wrong, and a third, "Post-Conventional" stage where individuals focus on personal morality and universal ethical principles rather than on whether society would approve of their behavior. Choices (I) and (II) accurately describe the first two stages; choice (B), which includes both of these, is the answer.

46. A student spending a semester abroad in Japan decides to spend a week's vacation visiting China. While wandering around the streets of Beijing's outskirts he sees a Chinese grandmother encouraging her four-year-old son to take his pants down and defecate off the sidewalk onto the street. The student reacts with an overwhelming sense of disgust. This reaction is an example of:

    A) ethnocentrism.
    B) material culture.
    C) operant conditioning.
    D) <u>culture shock.</u>

Culture shock is the feeling of discomfort or unpleasantness one has upon encountering cultural norms that are different from one's own. In this case, the student encountered a very different cultural norm about bathroom behavior and felt an instance of culture shock.

A: We're told that the student felt a sense of disgust about a particular behavior, not that he felt his entire culture was superior to Chinese culture.
B: Behaviors regarding body modesty aren't inherently a part of the material aspects of culture.
C: While the student may have originally learned toilet training through some form of operant conditioning, that does not explain his current reaction.

Passage 9 Explanation

Having other people present typically leads an individual to experience **physiological arousal**. The impact this arousal has on performance depends on the type of task the individual is performing. It has been found that in the presence of groups individuals tend to demonstrate **dominant responses**, or responses which are **well-rehearsed and familiar** to the individual. When the task is **complicated** performance will be **impaired**.

Key terms: physiological arousal, dominant responses
Cause and effect: the presence of other people increases performance on familiar, dominant behaviors, and decreases performance on complicated or novel tasks

Social facilitation is seen when researchers watch individuals performing tasks and then introduce confederates who observe the individuals performing. The **percentage of success** of those individuals is recorded before the **confederates are introduced and after** they are introduced. The participants are classified according to their proficiency in the task as being either high performers or low performers. A study in which researchers observed **basketball players** and recorded their percentage of shots made before and after introducing confederates was conducted with the results presented as follows:

Cause and effect: the effect of observers on basketball performers was observed.

Table 1 Performance in the presence of others

Performance Level	Before Confederates	After Confederates
High performers	68%	74%
Low performers	42%	36%

Table 1 shows us that high performers do better when being watched and low performers do worse.

Groups also impact individual behavior through **deindividuation**. This refers to people feeling that they are **less personally responsible** for their behavior in a group and as a result behaving in ways they normally wouldn't while alone. Deindividuation changes individual behavior through **anonymity** and **diverting** the individual's **attention away from his own values**. An example of the deindividuation that can occur in a group was provided by researchers who observed children Trick-or-Treating for Halloween. The researchers put out candy and instructed children to only take one piece. Conditions that fostered children **only taking one piece** included having the children **asked their name, being alone, and having a mirror** present in front of the candy.

Key terms: deindividuation
Cause and effect: deindividuation creates anonymity and reduces a person's focus on their own values, leading to behavior that's not normal for the person.

Finally, the **opinions** of a group tend to **become more extreme** after group discussion. This effect is known as **polarization**. A reason for this is that the group is likely to **hear more arguments** of the opinion the group is **favoring**. Group members will hear these arguments and become more persuaded and also continue to further the argument in more extreme directions.

Key terms: polarization, norm, social comparison

Cause and effect: Group discussions tend to make the group's opinion more extreme since arguments that favor the group opinion are heard more than contrary opinions.

47. According to the data, what group might be most likely to perform well in front of a group?
    A) Good students performing novel calculations
    B) Poor singers performing a song
    C) Unskilled mechanics changing a tire
    D) **An experienced factory worker performing a duty on an assembly line**

    Answer: D – According to the data individuals who perform best in front of groups are those who are good at their task and for whom the task is routine.

48. Which of the following would NOT be a way to avoid groupthink?
    A) Have group members with a variety of views on the topic
    B) Record individual views before topics are discussed
    C) **Include individuals in positions of authority in the group**
    D) Present all sides on the issue

    Answer: C – If individuals in positions of authority are in the group then the group members may be more inclined to try to curry favor with these individuals, which could lead to groupthink.

49. What could be done to avoid inflammatory rhetoric in online commentary?
    A) Allow individuals to gravitate towards topics they feel passionate about
    B) Allow the online group to rebuke the commentators
    C) **Require users to use their actual names**
    D) Ask difficult questions, requiring non-dominant answers

    Answer: C – According to the passage, individuals often behave in ways they would not normally behave if they feel they are anonymous and have been deindividuated.

50. A group member presenting a more extreme opinion than another group member who he views as high status in order to appear favorable to the group is known as what process?
    A) **Upward social comparison**
    B) Downward social comparison
    C) Lateral social comparison
    D) Inverse social comparison

    Answer: A – In an upward social comparison, individuals compare themselves with group members who are seen as having high status.

51. Each of the following factors would help the low performing group in the study to perform better EXCEPT:
  I. Become more familiar with the task
 II. Perform in front of observers
III. Place observers behind one-way mirrors such that the subjects do not know they are being observed
    A) I only
    B) **<u>II only</u>**
    C) III only
    D) I and III only

Answer: B – Both factors I and III could improve the performance of the low-performing group. Since this is an EXCEPT question, the right answer is choice (B), II only.

Passage 10 Explanation

Alzheimer's Disease (AD) is a form of dementia with a prevalence of 2 to 3% in people over the age of 65, with this rate doubling every 5 years. AD is **irreversible and its effects can be debilitating**, necessitating long-term care at a high cost. The biggest risk factor for AD is **aging**. However, a **hereditary link** has been established, with a two to four-fold increase in the incidence of AD among those with a first-degree relative with AD.

Key terms: Alzheimer's disease
Cause and effect: Genetic factors and aging lead to AD.

Severe cholinergic deficits in the cerebral cortex, specifically in the **basal forebrain** from the **hippocampus to neocortex**, have been found in those with AD. Thus it is hypothesized that a cause of AD is the **reduced ability of the brain to synthesize acetylcholine**. These findings have led to attempts to treat AD with cholinergic agonists, a strategy that has proven to be quite effective in treating some forms of dementia. However, **attempts to increase acetylcholine** in those with AD has been **less effective**, perhaps due to permanent changes in brain structure of those with AD. These changes can be seen in post-mortem examinations of the brain, in which **amyloid plaques and neurofibrillary tangles** can be seen, both considered the hallmark signs of AD.

Key terms: cholinergic deficits, basal forebrain, hippocampus, neocortex, amyloid plaques, neuro-fibrillary tangles
Contrast: increase acetylcholine is effective with some dementia but not AD

Frequently concordant with the development of AD are other behavioral and emotional issues, such as **depression, anxiety, aggression, and paranoia**, among other issues. Disorders such as these may be the **primary presenting issue** for many families of individuals with AD. Thus, **treatment of these issues is indicated**. These issues may be treated as they are typically treated in individuals without AD. However, **preventative strategies** for avoiding the development of these issues **is indicated** in those who have developed AD. Preventative strategies include encouraging and maintaining wellness behaviors, such as exercise and active behavior, support groups, and other psychoeducation, among other efforts.

Opinion: patients with AD should engage in both prevention and treatment of the emotional issues that come with AD.

The following is a small case study of a **75 year-old individual** who presented at a medical center for **complaints about forgetting** things, such as where he places things at his home, sometimes **getting lost** on the way home from the store, and **feeling sad** often. However, he is still able to remember incidents from his past and the names of his family members. Tests were conducted to assess his intelligence, memory, and difficulties with daily living skills, with the test given and the results in terms of age-normed percentile given:

Table 1 Patient Assessment results

Intelligence Test	Memory Test	Daily Living Skills Functioning Test
30%	32%	39%

Table 1 indicates that the patient is performing well below average on measures of memory, intelligence, and daily living skills.

52. What type of memory appears intact in the man?
    A) Anterograde, but not retrograde
    B) **Retrograde, but not anterograde**
    C) Both retrograde and anterograde
    D) Neither retrograde nor anterograde

    Answer: B – The man has difficulty remembering new things, which involves anterograde memory, but is still able to remember things from the past, using retrograde memory.

53. The relative ineffectiveness of cholinergic agonists in treatment of AD suggests what type of neural process is NOT possible in AD?
    A) Neural pruning
    B) Neural conditioning
    C) **Neuroplasticity**
    D) Neural networking

    Answer: C – As stated in the paragraph drugs which increase acetylcholine are not very effective in treatment of AD because of permanent changes in the brain, implying new neural connections are not able to be made, a process called neuroplasticity.

54. What is the expected prevalence of AD for a man as old as the man in the case study?
    A) 2-3%
    B) 4-6%
    C) **8-12%**
    D) 16-24%

    Answer: C – According to the passage, the prevalence rate for AD among those over age 65 is 2-3%, with the prevalence rate doubling every 5 years after age 65, which would be 8-12%.

55. Which of the following topics would NOT be helpful to know more about when attempting to diagnose the man with AD?
    A) His IQ when he was younger
    B) If someone in his family has AD
    C) His mental health status now
    D) **If amyloid plaques are present in his brain**

    Answer: D – The presence of amyloid plaques are only observable through a post-mortem brain examination.

These questions are **NOT** related to a passage.

56. What best describes the relationship between symbols and language?
- A) Symbols can result in group socialization; language allows for both group socialization and individual socialization.
- B) Symbols help sustain continuity of a culture; language can be interpreted and reinterpreted over time.
- C) **Symbols carry shared meaning in a culture; language constitutes a subcategory of symbols which is a set of representations that conveys meaning about the world.**
- D) Symbols are a subcategory of language which, unlike language, are only understood by certain members of a culture.

The correct choice is (C). Symbols are defined as representations with shared meaning among the individuals within a culture or subculture. Language is a subcategory of symbols, and is defined as a set of symbolic representations that conveys meaning about the world.

A: Socialization is the adoption of group norms by individuals. Both symbols and language allow for, and can result in, socialization.
B: Both symbols and language can help sustain continuity of a culture, and both can be interpreted and reinterpreted over time.
D: Incorrect because language is a subcategory of symbols. Also incorrect because symbols are shared by members of a culture or subculture, which is the opposite of being understood only by certain individuals within that culture or subculture.

57. Which of the following are examples of demographic transitions in Thompson's demographic transitions model?
I. Immigrants from a poorer country enter a richer country in large numbers.
II. **Lower birthrates and lower mortality in a country over time result in the percentage of elderly citizens increasing, and the percentage of young citizens decreasing.**
III. Members of a minority ethnic group flee their homeland on a large scale to avoid persecution by the ethnic majority.
- A) I only
- B) **II only**
- C) I and II
- D) I, II and III.

Demographic transitions in Thompson's model refer to a society with high birthrates and high death rates transitioning to a society with low birthrates and low death rates. It often results in an aging population. Choice (II) describes these, and is correct. Choices (I) and (III) describe shifts that are not within the definition of Thompson's demographic transition model. As such, (B) is the correct response.

58. A person with a very visible bruise on his hand worries that it will lead to worse blood circulation, and possibly loss of hand function. After some time passes and the bruise remains, he finds that he is unable to move his hand more than a little, even though tests show his blood circulation in his hand and arm is normal and no other medical causes are detected explaining the person's loss of hand function. What best characterizes this person's condition?
- A) Body dysmorphic disorder
- B) Generalized anxiety disorder
- C) **Conversion disorder**
- D) Hypochondriasis

Conversion disorder occurs when excessive anxiety causes loss of functioning in all or part of a patient. Here, the person's loss of hand function is attributable only to excessive anxiety and not to medical causes; this defines conversion disorder, and makes (C) the correct answer.

A: Body dysmorphic disorder occurs when a subject perceives a defect in the appearance of part of his or her body, and becomes excessively preoccupied with this defect; here, the anxiety relates not to appearance but to loss of function.

B: Generalized anxiety disorder affects a wide spectrum of life areas and everyday functions; the prompt, by contrast, describes anxiety with a much more narrow effect.

D: Hypochondriasis is characterized by a person who is excessively preoccupied with the idea that he or she has a serious illness. Although this is the case in the prompt, hypochondria is not associated with actual loss of body function. This makes conversion disorder the better response.

59. A patient experiencing memory loss symptoms consults with two medical professionals in an attempt to find the cause of his condition. The first person he sees focuses on possible past head injuries, and runs several medical tests on the patient. The second person he sees asks about the patient's environment, his social life, and his stress levels; he also conducts a personality evaluation of the patient. What best characterizes the differing approaches of the two medical professionals?

    A) **<u>The first is using a biomedical approach, while the second is using a biopsychosocial approach.</u>**
    B) The first is using a biopsychosocial approach, while the second is using a biomedical approach.
    C) The first is using a biological approach, while the second is using a psychological approach.
    D) The first is using a biological approach, while the second is using a sociological approach.

Here, (A) is correct. A biomedical approach involves a search for underlying pathologies or injuries which may be causing psychological problems; a biopsychosocial approach combines such biomedical inquires with a search for factors related to the patient's mental processes and social environment.

B: This is the reverse of the correct answer.
C: The biopsychosocial approach includes a psychological component, but also includes other elements.
D: The biopsychosocial approach includes a sociological component, but also includes other elements.

APPENDIX A: SCORE CONVERSION CHART

Table 1 Raw Score to Scaled Score Conversion for Science Sections

These scores are rough estimates. The AAMC has not yet released extensive data on the conversion of raw scores to scaled scores. These estimates are based on the most recent data from official AAMC practice tests.

Raw Score (Number of Questions Correct)	Scaled Score	Percentile*
58-59	132	99.9
56-57	131	99
54-55	130	98
51-53	129	96
47-50	128	88
43-46	127	77
39-42	126	61
36-38	125	50
33-35	124	39
30-32	123	25
27-29	122	14
23-26	121	6
19-22	120	2
16-18	119	1
0-15	118	0.1

* Percentile rank is given in this table as an example of how percentile correlates with scaled score, taken from recent actual MCAT exams. This is for illustration purposes only and does not represent performance of test-takers from the material in this exam.

APPENDIX B: SELF-STUDY OUTLINE

PSYCHOLOGY

I. Sensation

1. Thresholds CL: _____

_____
_____
_____
_____
_____

2. Weber's Law CL: _____

_____
_____
_____
_____
_____

3. Signal Detection theory CL: _____

_____
_____
_____
_____
_____

4. Sensory adaptation CL: _____

_____
_____
_____
_____

Particular Senses

1. Vision CL: _____

_____
_____
_____
_____
_____

a) Parallel Processing CL: _____

_____
_____
_____
_____
_____

b) Feature detection CL: _____

_____
_____
_____
_____
_____

2. Hearing and Auditory Processing CL: _____

_____
_____
_____
_____
_____

3. Auditory processing CL: _____

_____
_____
_____
_____
_____

4. Somatosensation and Pain CL: _____

_____
_____
_____
_____
_____

5. Kinesthetic sense CL: _____

_____
_____
_____
_____
_____

Perception

1. Bottom-up / Top-down processing CL: _____

_____
_____
_____
_____
_____

2. Perceptual organization – depth, form, motion, constancy CL: _____

_____
_____
_____
_____
_____

3. Gestalt principles CL: _____

_____
_____
_____
_____
_____

II. Consciousness and Thinking

Consciousness

1. States of consciousness CL: _____

_____
_____
_____
_____

    a) Alertness CL: _____

_____
_____
_____
_____

b) Sleep CL: _____

_____
_____
_____
_____
_____

    i. Stages and cycles of sleep CL: _____

_____
_____
_____
_____
_____

    ii. Dreaming CL: _____

_____
_____
_____
_____
_____

    iii. Sleep disorders CL: _____

_____
_____
_____
_____
_____

c) Hypnosis CL: _____

_____
_____
_____
_____
_____

d) Meditation CL: _____

_____
_____
_____
_____
_____

2. Drugs that change conscious perception CL: _____

_____
_____
_____
_____
_____

   a) Types of drugs CL: _____

_____
_____
_____
_____
_____

   b) Drug addiction CL: _____

_____
_____
_____
_____
_____

Memory and Attention

1. Selective Attention CL: _____

_____
_____
_____
_____

2. Divided Attention CL: _____

_____
_____
_____
_____

3. Memory encoding – process and how to increase it CL: _____

_____
_____
_____
_____

4. Memory storage CL: _____

_____
_____
_____
_____
_____

   a) Types CL: _____

_____
_____
_____
_____
_____

   b) Semantic networks CL: _____

_____
_____
_____
_____
_____

   c) Spreading activation CL: _____

_____
_____
_____
_____
_____

5. Memory retrieval, effect of emotion CL: _____

_____
_____
_____
_____
_____

   a) Recall CL: _____

_____
_____
_____
_____
_____

b) Recognition CL: _____

_____
_____
_____
_____
_____

c) Relearning CL: _____

_____
_____
_____
_____
_____

d) Retrieval cues CL: _____

_____
_____
_____
_____
_____

6. Memory loss CL: _____

_____
_____
_____
_____
_____

a) Aging CL: _____

_____
_____
_____
_____
_____

b) Alzheimer's disease CL: _____

_____
_____
_____
_____
_____

c) Korsakoff's syndrome CL: _____

_____
_____
_____
_____
_____

d) Decay CL: _____

_____
_____
_____
_____
_____

e) Interference CL: _____

_____
_____
_____
_____
_____

f) Memory construction and source monitoring CL: _____

_____
_____
_____
_____
_____

Cognition and Language

1. Cognitive development CL: _____

_____
_____
_____
_____
_____

a) Piaget CL: _____

_____
_____
_____
_____
_____

b) Later adulthood CL: _____

_____
_____
_____
_____
_____

c) Effect of language CL: _____

_____
_____
_____
_____
_____

d) Role of culture, heredity, environmental CL: _____

_____
_____
_____
_____
_____

2. Problem solving CL: _____

_____
_____
_____
_____
_____

a) Approaches CL: _____

_____
_____
_____
_____
_____

b) Barriers CL: _____

_____

_____

_____

_____

_____

c) Hueristics CL: _____

_____

_____

_____

_____

_____

   i. Biases CL: _____

_____

_____

_____

_____

_____

   ii. Intuition CL: _____

_____

_____

_____

_____

_____

   iii. Emotion CL: _____

_____

_____

_____

_____

_____

   iv. Overconfidence CL: _____

_____

_____

_____

_____

_____

v. Belief perseverance CL: _____

_____

_____

_____

_____

_____

3. Intelligence CL: _____

_____

_____

_____

_____

_____

    a) Various definitions and levels of ability CL: _____

_____

_____

_____

_____

_____

    b) Effect of heredity, environment CL: _____

_____

_____

_____

_____

_____

4. Theories of language development CL: _____

_____

_____

_____

_____

_____

    a) Learning CL: _____

_____

_____

_____

_____

_____

    b) Nativist CL: ____

_____
_____
_____
_____
_____

    c) Interactionist CL: ____

_____
_____
_____
_____
_____

III. Emotion and Stress

Emotion

1. Cognitive component CL: ____

_____
_____
_____
_____
_____

2. Physiological component CL: ____

_____
_____
_____
_____
_____

3. Behavioral component CL: ____

_____
_____
_____
_____
_____

4. Universal emotions CL: _____

_____
_____
_____
_____
_____

5. James-Lange theory CL: _____

_____
_____
_____
_____
_____

6. Cannon-Bard theory CL: _____

_____
_____
_____
_____
_____

7. Schachter-Singer theory CL: _____

_____
_____
_____
_____
_____

Stress

1. Stress appraisal CL: _____

_____
_____
_____
_____
_____

2. Stressors CL: _____

_____

_____

_____

_____

_____

3. Responses to stress: physiological, emotional, behavioral CL: _____

_____

_____

_____

_____

_____

4. Stress management CL: _____

_____

_____

_____

_____

_____

IV. Behavior and Personality

Biology influences behavior

1. Neurotransmitters CL: _____

_____

_____

_____

_____

_____

2. Endocrine effects CL: _____

_____

_____

_____

_____

_____

3. Genetic factors CL: _____

_____

_____

_____

_____

_____

    a) Temperament CL: _____

_____

_____

_____

_____

_____

    b) Interaction between heredity and environment CL: _____

_____

_____

_____

_____

_____

4. Environment and experience effect behavior CL: _____

_____

_____

_____

_____

_____

Attitudes and Motivation

1. Influences on motivation CL: _____

_____

_____

_____

_____

_____

    a) Instinct CL: ____

---

    b) Arousal CL: ____

---

    c) Drive CL: ____

---

    d) Needs CL: ____

---

2. Link between motivation and behavior CL: ____

---

    a) Drive Reduction Theory CL: ____

---

b) Incentive Theory CL: _____

_____
_____
_____
_____
_____

c) Cognitive Theories CL: _____

_____
_____
_____
_____
_____

d) Need-based Theories CL: _____

_____
_____
_____
_____
_____

3. Specific behaviors explained by theories CL: _____

_____
_____
_____
_____
_____

a) Eating CL: _____

_____
_____
_____
_____
_____

b) Sex CL: _____

_____
_____
_____
_____
_____

   c) Drug use CL: _____

_____
_____
_____
_____
_____

   d) Others CL: _____

_____
_____
_____
_____
_____

4. Regulation of motivation: biological factors, cultural factors CL: _____

_____
_____
_____
_____
_____

5. Components of attitudes CL: _____

_____
_____
_____
_____
_____

   a) Cognitive CL: _____

_____
_____
_____
_____
_____

   b) Affective CL: _____

_____
_____
_____
_____
_____

c) Behavioral CL: _____

_____
_____
_____
_____
_____

6. Cognitive dissonance CL: _____

_____
_____
_____
_____
_____

7. Behavior and attitude affect each other CL: _____

_____
_____
_____
_____
_____

Personality

1. Perspectives on Personality CL: _____

_____
_____
_____
_____
_____

a) Psychoanalytic CL: _____

_____
_____
_____
_____
_____

b) Humanistic CL: _____

_____
_____
_____
_____
_____

c) Trait CL: _____

_____
_____
_____
_____
_____

d) Social cognitive CL: _____

_____
_____
_____
_____
_____

e) Biological CL: _____

_____
_____
_____
_____
_____

f) Behaviorist CL: _____

_____
_____
_____
_____
_____

2. Explaining behavior situationally CL: _____

_____
_____
_____
_____
_____

The Presence of Other People

1. Social facilitation CL: _____

_____
_____
_____
_____
_____

2. Deindividuation CL: _____

_____
_____
_____
_____
_____

3. Bystander effect CL: _____

_____
_____
_____
_____
_____

4. Social loafing CL: _____

_____
_____
_____
_____
_____

5. Peer pressure CL: _____

_____
_____
_____
_____
_____

Behavior Change and Learning

1. Habituation CL: _____

_____
_____
_____
_____
_____

2. Classical Conditioning CL: _____

_____
_____
_____
_____
_____

   a) Stimuli CL: _____

_____
_____
_____
_____
_____

      i. Neutral CL: _____

_____
_____
_____
_____
_____

      ii. Conditioned CL: _____

_____
_____
_____
_____
_____

iii. Unconditioned CL: _____

_____
_____
_____
_____
_____

b) Responses CL: _____

_____
_____
_____
_____
_____

i. Conditioned CL: _____

_____
_____
_____
_____
_____

ii. Unconditioned CL: _____

_____
_____
_____
_____

c) Acquisition CL: _____

_____
_____
_____
_____

d) Extinction CL: _____

_____
_____
_____
_____

e) Spontaneous recovery CL: _____

_____

_____

_____

_____

_____

f) Generalization CL: _____

_____

_____

_____

_____

_____

g) Discrimination CL: _____

_____

_____

_____

_____

_____

3. Operant Conditioning CL: _____

_____

_____

_____

_____

_____

a) Shaping CL: _____

_____

_____

_____

_____

_____

b) Extinction CL: _____

_____

_____

_____

_____

_____

c) Reinforcement CL: _____

_____
_____
_____
_____
_____

    i. Positive CL: _____

_____
_____
_____
_____
_____

    ii. Negative CL: _____

_____
_____
_____
_____
_____

    iii. Primary CL: _____

_____
_____
_____
_____
_____

    iv. Conditional CL: _____

_____
_____
_____
_____
_____

d) Reinforcement Schedules CL: _____

_____
_____
_____
_____
_____

i. Fixed ratio CL: _____

_____
_____
_____
_____
_____

ii. Variable ratio CL: _____

_____
_____
_____
_____
_____

iii. Fixed interval CL: _____

_____
_____
_____
_____
_____

iv. Variable interval CL: _____

_____
_____
_____
_____
_____

e) Punishment CL: _____

_____
_____
_____
_____
_____

f) Escape CL: _____

_____
_____
_____
_____
_____

g) Avoidance CL: _____

_____
_____
_____
_____
_____

4. Observational learning CL: _____

_____
_____
_____
_____
_____

    a) Modeling CL: _____

_____
_____
_____
_____
_____

    b) Mirror Neurons CL: _____

_____
_____
_____
_____
_____

    c) Vicarious Emotions CL: _____

_____
_____
_____
_____
_____

5. Attitude change CL: _____

_____
_____
_____
_____
_____

a) Elaboration Likelihood Model CL: _____

_____
_____
_____
_____
_____

   i. Central and Peripheral route processing CL: _____

_____
_____
_____
_____
_____

b) Social Cognitive theory CL: _____

_____
_____
_____
_____
_____

c) Factors that affect attitude change CL: _____

_____
_____
_____
_____
_____

   i. Changing behavior CL: _____

_____
_____
_____
_____
_____

   ii. Characteristics of the message and target CL: _____

_____
_____
_____
_____
_____

iii. Social factors CL: _____

_____
_____
_____
_____
_____

V. Identity and Interaction

Identity

1. Self-concept CL: _____

_____
_____
_____
_____
_____

2. Identity CL: _____

_____
_____
_____
_____
_____

3. Social Identity CL: _____

_____
_____
_____
_____
_____

4. Self-esteem CL: _____

_____
_____
_____
_____
_____

5. Self-efficacy CL: _____

_____

_____

_____

_____

6. Locus of control in self-identity CL: _____

_____

_____

_____

_____

7. Stages of identity development CL: _____

_____

_____

_____

_____

_____

a) Erikson CL: _____

_____

_____

_____

_____

_____

b) Vygotsky CL: _____

_____

_____

_____

_____

c) Kohlberg CL: _____

_____

_____

_____

_____

d) Freud CL: _____

_____
_____
_____
_____
_____

8. Social factors on identity development CL: _____

_____
_____
_____
_____
_____

    a) Imitation CL: _____

_____
_____
_____
_____
_____

    b) Role-taking CL: _____

_____
_____
_____
_____
_____

    c) Reference group CL: _____

_____
_____
_____
_____
_____

Interaction

1. Attribution theory CL: _____

_____
_____
_____
_____

   a) Fundamental attribution error CL: _____

_____
_____
_____
_____
_____

   b) Cultural impact on attribution CL: _____

_____
_____
_____
_____
_____

  2. Self-perception shapes perception of others CL: _____

_____
_____
_____
_____
_____

  3. Perception of environment affects perception of others CL: _____

_____
_____
_____
_____
_____

  4. Prejudice CL: _____

_____
_____
_____
_____
_____

   a) Power CL: _____

_____
_____
_____
_____
_____

b) Prestige CL: _____

_____
_____
_____
_____
_____

c) Class CL: _____

_____
_____
_____
_____
_____

d) Emotion CL: _____

_____
_____
_____
_____
_____

e) Cognition CL: _____

_____
_____
_____
_____
_____

f) Discrimination CL: _____

_____
_____
_____
_____
_____

   i. How power, prestige, class affect discrimination CL: _____

_____
_____
_____
_____
_____

5. Stereotypes CL: _____

_____

_____

_____

_____

_____

   a) Self-fulfilling prophecy CL: _____

_____

_____

_____

_____

_____

   b) Stereotype threat CL: _____

_____

_____

_____

_____

_____

6. Interaction between animals CL: _____

_____

_____

_____

_____

_____

   a) Signals used by animals CL: _____

_____

_____

_____

_____

_____

7. Social behaviors CL: _____

_____

_____

_____

_____

_____

a) Attraction CL: _____

_____
_____
_____
_____
_____

b) Aggression CL: _____

_____
_____
_____
_____
_____

c) Attachment CL: _____

_____
_____
_____
_____
_____

d) Social support CL: _____

_____
_____
_____
_____
_____

VI. Psychological Disorders

1. Psychological disorders CL: _____

_____
_____
_____
_____
_____

a) Biomedical approach CL: _____

_____
_____
_____
_____
_____

b) Biopsychosocial approach CL: _____

_____
_____
_____
_____
_____

c) Classification schemes and types CL: _____

_____
_____
_____
_____
_____

   i. Anxiety CL: _____

_____
_____
_____
_____
_____

   ii. Somatoform CL: _____

_____
_____
_____
_____
_____

   iii. Mood CL: _____

_____
_____
_____
_____
_____

    iv. Schizophrenia CL: _____

_____

_____

_____

_____

_____

    v. Dissociative CL: _____

_____

_____

_____

_____

_____

    vi. Personality CL: _____

_____

_____

_____

_____

_____

    d) Incidence and prevalence CL: _____

_____

_____

_____

_____

_____

2. Psychological disorders as nervous system disorders CL: _____

_____

_____

_____

_____

_____

    a) Schizophrenia CL: _____

_____

_____

_____

_____

_____

b) Depression CL: _____

_____

_____

_____

_____

_____

c) Alzheimer's CL: _____

_____

_____

_____

_____

_____

d) Parkinson's CL: _____

_____

_____

_____

_____

_____

SOCIOLOGY

I. Social Influences on Behavior

1. Peer pressure CL: _____

_____
_____
_____
_____
_____

2. Group polarization CL: _____

_____
_____
_____
_____
_____

3. Groupthink CL: _____

_____
_____
_____
_____
_____

4. Culture CL: _____

_____
_____
_____
_____
_____

   a) Assimilation CL: _____

_____
_____
_____
_____
_____

    b) Multiculturalism CL: _____

_____
_____
_____
_____
_____

    c) Subculture CL: _____

_____
_____
_____
_____
_____

5. Socialization CL: _____

_____
_____
_____
_____
_____

    a) Norms CL: _____

_____
_____
_____
_____
_____

    b) Socializing Agents CL: _____

_____
_____
_____
_____
_____

      i. Family CL: _____

_____
_____
_____
_____
_____

    ii. Peers CL: _____

_____
_____
_____
_____
_____

    iii. Media CL: _____

_____
_____
_____
_____
_____

    iv. Workplace CL: _____

_____
_____
_____
_____
_____

6. Deviance CL: _____

_____
_____
_____
_____
_____

    a) Stigma CL: _____

_____
_____
_____
_____
_____

7. Obedience CL: _____

_____
_____
_____
_____
_____

a) Conformity CL: _____

_____

_____

_____

_____

_____

II. Social Interactions

1. Types of Group CL: _____

_____

_____

_____

_____

_____

   a) Status CL: _____

_____

_____

_____

_____

_____

   b) Roles CL: _____

_____

_____

_____

_____

_____

   c) Groups CL: _____

_____

_____

_____

_____

_____

d) Networks CL: _____

_____
_____
_____
_____
_____

e) Organizations CL: _____

_____
_____
_____
_____
_____

2. Influences on interaction CL: _____

_____
_____
_____
_____
_____

a) Responses to emotional displays CL: _____

_____
_____
_____
_____
_____

  i. Gender CL: _____

_____
_____
_____
_____
_____

  ii. Culture CL: _____

_____
_____
_____
_____
_____

3. Manipulating perception by others CL: _____

_____
_____
_____
_____
_____

a) Front stage vs. Back stage CL: _____

_____
_____
_____
_____
_____

b) Dramaturgy CL: _____

_____
_____
_____
_____
_____

4. Discrimination CL: _____

_____
_____
_____
_____
_____

a) Individual discrimination CL: _____

_____
_____
_____
_____
_____

b) Institutional discrimination CL: _____

_____
_____
_____
_____
_____

5. Ethnocentrism CL: _____

_____

_____

_____

_____

_____

    a) In-group vs. Out-group CL: _____

_____

_____

_____

_____

_____

    b) Cultural relativism CL: _____

_____

_____

_____

_____

_____

III. Structure of Society

Analyzing social structures

1. Functionalism CL: _____

_____

_____

_____

_____

2. Conflict theory CL: _____

_____

_____

_____

_____

3. Symbolic interaction CL: _____

_____
_____
_____
_____
_____

4. Social constructionism CL: _____

_____
_____
_____
_____
_____

5. Institutions that shape society CL: _____

_____
_____
_____
_____
_____

    a) Education CL: _____

_____
_____
_____
_____
_____

    b) Family CL: _____

_____
_____
_____
_____
_____

    c) Religion CL: _____

_____
_____
_____
_____
_____

d) Government CL: _____

_____
_____
_____
_____
_____

e) Economy CL: _____

_____
_____
_____
_____
_____

f) Health care CL: _____

_____
_____
_____
_____
_____

6. Culture CL: _____

_____
_____
_____
_____
_____

a) Material culture CL: _____

_____
_____
_____
_____

b) Symbolic culture CL: _____

_____
_____
_____
_____

c) Language CL: _____

_____

_____

_____

_____

_____

d) Values CL: _____

_____

_____

_____

_____

_____

e) Beliefs CL: _____

_____

_____

_____

_____

_____

   i. Norms CL: _____

_____

_____

_____

_____

_____

f) Rituals CL: _____

_____

_____

_____

_____

_____

7. Social groups placement within the culture CL: _____

_____

_____

_____

_____

_____

8. Evolution CL: _____

_____
_____
_____
_____
_____

Demographics

1. Age CL: _____

_____
_____
_____
_____
_____

2. Gender CL: _____

_____
_____
_____
_____
_____

3. Race CL: _____

_____
_____
_____
_____
_____

4. Ethnicity CL: _____

_____
_____
_____
_____
_____

5. Immigration CL: _____

_____
_____
_____
_____
_____

6. Sexual orientation CL: _____

_____
_____
_____
_____
_____

7. Demographic shifts CL: _____

_____
_____
_____
_____
_____

    a) Fertility CL: _____

_____
_____
_____
_____
_____

    b) Migration CL: _____

_____
_____
_____
_____
_____

    c) Mortality CL: _____

_____
_____
_____
_____
_____

d) Social movements CL: _____

_____
_____
_____
_____
_____

8. Globalization CL: _____

_____
_____
_____
_____
_____

9. Urbanization CL: _____

_____
_____
_____
_____
_____

IV. Social Inequality

1. Spatial Inequality CL: _____

_____
_____
_____
_____
_____

a) Segregation CL: _____

_____
_____
_____
_____
_____

b) Environmental inequality CL: ____

_____
_____
_____
_____
_____

c) Globalization CL: ____

_____
_____
_____
_____
_____

2. Social Class CL: ____

_____
_____
_____
_____
_____

a) Stratification into classes CL: ____

_____
_____
_____
_____
_____

i. Status CL: ____

_____
_____
_____
_____
_____

ii. Power CL: ____

_____
_____
_____
_____
_____

b) Cultural capital CL: _____

_____
_____
_____
_____
_____

c) Social capital CL: _____

_____
_____
_____
_____
_____

d) Social reproduction CL: _____

_____
_____
_____
_____
_____

e) Privilege CL: _____

_____
_____
_____
_____
_____

f) Prestige CL: _____

_____
_____
_____
_____
_____

3. Class and race, gender, age CL: _____

_____
_____
_____
_____

4. Social mobility CL: _____

_____

_____

_____

_____

_____

   a) Intergenerational CL: _____

_____

_____

_____

_____

_____

   b) Intragenerational CL: _____

_____

_____

_____

_____

_____

   c) Downward CL: _____

_____

_____

_____

_____

_____

   d) Upward CL: _____

_____

_____

_____

_____

_____

   e) Meritocracy CL: _____

_____

_____

_____

_____

_____

5. Poverty CL: _____

_____

_____

_____

_____

a) Relative CL: _____

_____

_____

_____

_____

b) Absolute CL: _____

_____

_____

_____

_____

c) Segregation CL: _____

_____

_____

_____

_____

d) Isolation CL: _____

_____

_____

_____

_____

6. Healthcare Disparities CL: _____

_____

_____

_____

_____

a) Inequality in health status CL: _____

_____

_____

_____

_____

_____

    i. Race CL: _____

_____

_____

_____

_____

_____

    ii. Gender CL: _____

_____

_____

_____

_____

_____

    iii. Class CL: _____

_____

_____

_____

_____

_____

b) Unequal access to healthcare CL: _____

_____

_____

_____

_____

_____

    i. Race CL: _____

_____

_____

_____

_____

_____

ii. Gender CL: _____

_____
_____
_____
_____
_____

iii. Class CL: _____

_____
_____
_____
_____
_____

BIOLOGY

I. The Nervous and Endocrine Systems

Nervous system

1. Neurons CL: _____

_____
_____
_____
_____
_____

   a) Reflex Arc CL: _____

_____
_____
_____
_____
_____

   b) Neurotransmitters CL: _____

_____
_____
_____
_____
_____

2. Peripheral nervous system CL: _____

_____
_____
_____
_____
_____

3. Central nervous system CL: _____

_____
_____
_____
_____
_____

a) Brainstem CL: _____

_____
_____
_____
_____
_____

b) Cerebellum CL: _____

_____
_____
_____
_____
_____

c) Diencephalon CL: _____

_____
_____
_____
_____
_____

d) Cerebrum CL: _____

_____
_____
_____
_____
_____

e) Cerebral cortex CL: _____

_____
_____
_____
_____
_____

  i. Voluntary movement CL: _____

_____
_____
_____
_____
_____

        ii. Information processing CL: _____

_____

_____

_____

_____

_____

        iii. Lateralization CL: _____

_____

_____

_____

_____

_____

    4. Lab techniques for studying the brain CL: _____

_____

_____

_____

_____

_____

Endocrine system

    1. Components CL: _____

_____

_____

_____

_____

_____

    2. Effects on behavior CL: _____

_____

_____

_____

_____

_____

3. Negative feedback CL: _____

_____

_____

_____

_____

_____

II. Sense Perception

1. Sensation CL: _____

_____

_____

_____

_____

_____

   a) Thresholds CL: _____

_____

_____

_____

_____

_____

   b) Sensory adaptation CL: _____

_____

_____

_____

_____

_____

   c) Sensory receptors CL: _____

_____

_____

_____

_____

_____

      i. Pathways CL: _____

_____
_____
_____
_____
_____

      ii. Types CL: _____

_____
_____
_____
_____
_____

  2. Vision CL: _____

_____
_____
_____
_____
_____

    a) Structure of the eye CL: _____

_____
_____
_____
_____
_____

    b) Function of the eye CL: _____

_____
_____
_____
_____
_____

    c) Visual processing CL: _____

_____
_____
_____
_____
_____

　　　i. Brain pathways CL: _____

_____

_____

_____

_____

_____

3. Hearing CL: _____

_____

_____

_____

_____

_____

　　a) Structure and function of the ear CL: _____

_____

_____

_____

_____

_____

　　b) Hair cells CL: _____

_____

_____

_____

_____

_____

　　c) Auditory processing CL: _____

_____

_____

_____

_____

_____

　　　i. Brain pathways CL: _____

_____

_____

_____

_____

_____

4. Taste CL: _____

_____
_____
_____
_____
_____

   a) Chemoreceptors CL: _____

_____
_____
_____
_____
_____

5. Smell CL: _____

_____
_____
_____
_____
_____

   a) Olfactory cells CL: _____

_____
_____
_____
_____
_____

   b) Pheromones CL: _____

_____
_____
_____
_____
_____

   c) Olfactory processing CL: _____

_____
_____
_____
_____
_____

i. Brain pathways CL: _____

_____
_____
_____
_____
_____

6. Pain perception CL: _____

_____
_____
_____
_____
_____

7. Kinesthetic sense CL: _____

_____
_____
_____
_____
_____

8. Vestibular sense CL: _____

_____
_____
_____
_____
_____

APPENDIX C: SELF-STUDY GLOSSARY

Absolute poverty
Deprivation of basic human needs including access to food, water, shelter, safety. Was set as $1.25/day in 2005 by the World Bank.

Acquisition
The phase of conditioning in which the conditioned stimulus is paired with the unconditioned stimulus and the animal is learning to give a conditioned response.

Adrenal medulla
Gland just above the kidneys that releases: epinephrine, norepinephrine, dopamine, enkephalin

Aggression
Acts carried out either with an intention to cause harm or to increase relative social dominance.

Altruism
Acting for the good of others at one's own expense and with no expectation of benefit.

Alzheimer's disease
Most common form of dementia. No cure, develops with age and worsens as it progresses, eventually fatal. Starts with simple absent-mindedness, then deepening confusion and eventual debilitating cognitive deficits.

Anterior pituitary
Gland that releases: growth hormone, thyroid stimulating hormone, adrenocoricotropic hormone, beta-endorphin, follicle stimulating hormone, luteinizing hormone, prolactin

Anxiety disorders
Excessive anxiety or fear. Includes Generalized anxiety disorder, Phobias, Panic, OCD, PTSD

Assimilation
Process of one culture or language beginning to resemble that of another group.

Attachment theory
Study of long-term relationships, especially between infants and their primary caregiver. Includes several attachment patterns: secure, anxious, avoidant, ambivalent, disorganized

Attitudes, components
A positive or negative feeling towards something or someone. Consists of Emotion (I like wine); Behavior (I will drink wine if offered); Cognition (I know red wine is good for my heart)

Attraction
A process between two people which draws them together and leads to friendship and romance.

Attribution theory
A process of explaining what happens by attributing causes to the environment, or attributing certain thoughts or feelings to other people.

Auditory pathway

Outer ear, auditory canal, tympanic membrane, middle ear (malleus, incus, stapes), inner ear (cochlea), Organ of Corti, Vestibulocochlear nerve, thalamus, temporal lobe

Avoidance learning

A behavior prevents a negative stimulus (e.g. pressing a lever before the noise starts keeps it silent)

Behaviorist perspective of personality

Personality is a learning process of operant conditioning controlled by the environment. People have response tendencies which create behavior patterns. Childhood not the crucial period as the environment-based learning continues through life.

Biases

Cognitive or motivational forces that result in repeated, systematic deviations from rational judgment. (e.g. availability heuristic, congruence bias, outcome bias)

Biological perspective of personality

Personality reflects the functioning of physiological processes in the brain. Influenced by hormone levels, neurotransmitter levels, size and development of various brain structures. Associated with Eysenck's Three Factor Model

Body dysmorphic disorder

Somatoform disorder in which the patient has excessive concern with a perceived defect or deficiency in their body.

Brain study methods

Electrophysiology (EEG), Neuroimaging (PET, fMRI), Effects of brain damage (strokes)

Brainstem

Part of the CNS that connects the spinal cord to the brain. Medulla oblongata, pons, and midbrain (mesencephalon). Regulates the CNS, controls sleep cycle, heart rate, breathing, eating, etc.

Bystander effect

The more individuals are present, the less likely someone will offer help.

Cannon-Bard theory

Emotional expression is hypothalamic, emotional feeling is dorsal thalamus. Physiology and subjective feeling are independent. Physiological arousal does not have to precede subjective feeling of emotion.

Central route processing

A method of shaping attitudes that asks the audience to think more, to analyze the content of the message. Depends on the cognitive ability and motivation of the audience.

Cerebellum

Coordination, precision, timing of movement (gait, posture, complex tasks like typing or playing the piano)

Cerebrum

Uppermost part of the brain including the cerebral cortex (front lobe, parietal lobe, temporal lobe, occipital lobe) and subcortical structures (hippocampus, basal ganglia, olfactory bulb)

Circadian rhythm	A built-in rhythm of an organism that is roughly 24hrs long but can adjust to external stimuli. Present in plants, animals, fungi, bacteria.
Classical conditioning	A form of learning that pairs neutral stimuli with natural stimuli in which the learner is able to pair this neutral stimuli with the response normally given to the natural stimuli (ring a bell and a dog salivates)
Cognitive dissonance	Mental discomfort when someone holds two contradictory beliefs at once.
Cognitive theories of motivation	Motivation is based on cognitive process. For example, to reduce cognitive dissonance, or in goal-setting theory to reach a particular end state.
Concrete operational stage	Piaget Stage 3: 7-11 yrs. Child can solve problems in a logical fashion. Can begin to understand induction, but still have trouble with deduction.
Conditional reinforcement	A stimulus that an organism learns to desire due to its pairing with another reinforcer (e.g. money or a clicker noise in dog training)
Conditioned response	A response to a conditioned stimulus which usually mimics an unconditioned response. (e.g. salivating in response to food is an unconditioned response; salivating in response to a bell is a conditioned response.)
Conditioned stimuli	A neutral stimulus that is paired with an unconditioned stimulus and comes to elicit the response. (e.g. the bell before the food)
Conflict theory	A variety of approaches to sociology that focus on inequality between social groups and the power differentials that exist between them. Most strongly associated with Karl Marx.
Conformity	Matching behavior to social norms as a result of direct or unconscious pressure. Conforming behavior occurs both in groups and while alone.
Consciousness altering drugs	Drugs that cross the blood-brain barrier to have an effect on the central nervous system. Common categories: anxiolytics, euphoriants, stimulants, depressants, hallucinogens
Conversion disorder	Somatoform disorder in which a patient suffers numbness, blindness or paralysis with no identifiable medical cause.
Cultural capital	Non-economic assets that provide value to an individual and that can promote social mobility (e.g. education, dress, attractiveness, humor)
Cultural relativism	An attempt to study societies while minimizing ethnocentric bias.
Deindividuation	When an individual loses a sense of self-awareness when in a group.

Demographic shift

The increase in the median age of a country due to rising life expectancy and/or reduced birth rate. Has happened in nearly every country in the world as it becomes more economically developed.

Depression

A low mood that leaves subject feeling sad, hopeless, worried. Characterized by disruptions to sleep and eating and loss of pleasure.

Deviance

Actions that violate social norms, either explicit rules (e.g. committing a crime) or informal mores (e.g. being atheist in a religious society).

Diencephalon

Region of embryonic neural tube that leads to the thalamus, subthalamus, hypothalamus, epithalamus.

Discrimination

When an animal learns to responsed to one conditioned stimulus but gives either a different response or no response at all to a slightly different stimulus.

Dissociative disorders

Mental disorders involving breakdown in memory, awareness and identity. Includes dissociative identity disorder (formerly multiple personality disorder), dissociative amnesia, and depersonalization disorder

Divided attention

The ability of the brain to perform multiple tasks at once (such as driving a car and talking on the phone). The brain has limited attention resources and as multiple tasks are added, especially in the same modality (listening to the radio and listening to a conversation), performance drops.

Dramaturgical approach

A perspective on sociology that focuses on the context of human behavior rather than the causes, viewing everyday social interactions as a form of performance in which people are playing roles.

Drive reduction theory

Motivation results from an organism's desire to reduce a drive (hunger, thirst, sex)

Elaboration likelihood model

A process of persuasion in which attitudes are influenced both by high elaboration factors (e.g. evaluating and processing information) and low elaboration ones (e.g. the attractiveness of the person making the appeal).

Emotion components

Cognition: evaluation of events, Physiology: bodily responses, Motivation: motor responses an emotion generates, Expression: facial and vocal signals of the feeling, Feelings: subjective experience of the emotion.

Endocrine organs

Hypothalamus, Pineal Gland, Pituitary, Thyroid, Adrenal Medulla, Testes, Ovaries

Environmental justice

The effort to fairly distribute environmental benefits (clean water, parkland) and environmental burdens (industrial facilities, pollution) across all of society.

MCAT PSYCHOLOGY AND SOCIOLOGY: STRATEGY AND PRACTICE

Erikson stages of psychosocial identity development	0-2 yrs, Hopes, Trust vs. Mistrust 2-4 yrs, Will, Autonomy vs. Shame 4-5 yrs, Purpose, Initiative vs. Guilt 5-12 yrs, Competence, Industry vs. Inferiority 13-19 yrs, Fidelity, Identity vs. Role Confusion 20-39, Love, Intimacy vs. Isolation 40-64 yrs, Care, Generativity vs. Stagnation 65-death, Wisdom, Ego Integrity vs. Despair
Escape learning	A behavior stops a negative stimulus (e.g. silencing an obnoxious noise to encourage a lever press)
Ethnocentrism	The process of judging another culture by the values and standards of your own culture.
Extinction	When the conditioned stimulus stops generating a conditioned response.
Eysenck's three factor model	Model of personality based on activity of reticular formation and limbic system. Personality made up of 1. Extraversion 2. Neuroticism 3. Psychoticism.
Feature detection	Specialized nerve cells in the brain respond to particular features such as edges, angles, or movement. These feature detection neurons fire in response to images that have specific characteristics.
Fertility	The average number of expected children born to a woman assuming that the woman will survive from birth to the end of her reproductive life.
Fixed interval	Reinforcement after the first response, after a fixed time has elapsed (e.g. after a food pellet is given, no food pellets will be dispensed for 5 minutes. After 5 minutes, the first lever press will get a food pellet)
Fixed ratio	Reinforcement after a fixed number of responses (e.g. a food pellet after every 5 lever presses)
Foot in the door phenomenon	Getting someone to agree to a small request increases the likelihood they will then agree to a much larger one.
Formal operational stage	Piaget Stage 4: Age 11 onwards. Can do hypothetical and deductive reasoning and think about abstract concepts.
Freud stages of psychosexual identity development	Oral: 0-1yr, oral fixation is a passive immature personality Anal: 1-3yr, anal fixation is obsessively neat/organized personality Phallic: 3-6yr, fixation can be oedipus complex Latency: 6-12yr, fixation leads to sexual unfulfillment Genital: puberty-death, fixation leads to frigidity, impotence

Front stage vs. back stage	Front stage: how a person behaves when an audience is present, adhering to certain conventions for the audience; Back stage: how a person behaves when no audience is present
Functionalism	A large-scale sociological approach that analyzes particular social structures and functions that influence society as a whole.
Fundamental attribution error	Overvaluing a personality-based explanation rather than environmental explanations. For example, explaining that members of an ethnic group must be poor because they are all lazy, rather than environmental impediments to their ability to get out of poverty.
Generalization	When a new stimulus that is similar to a conditioned stimulus comes to generate the same or similar response.
Gestalt principles	Laws of perceptual organization that guide the brain in making a whole out of sensory parts.
Globalization	Interconnection and interdependence across national boundaries, involving the exchange of culture, ideas, goods, etc.
Group polarization	Groups tend to make decisions that are more extreme than the initial attitudes of the individual members.
Groupthink	A breakdown in decision making in which groups value coherence and loyalty to the in group over critical analysis of the decisions.
Hair cells	Sensory receptors in the organ of Corti on the basilar membrane. Located in the cochlea of the inner ear. The hairs detect sound as vibrations in the tectorial membrane.
Heuristics in problem solving	A quick way to solve a problem using experience when a full exhaustive search would be impossible. Generates results that may not be the best. (e.g. rule of thumb, educated guess, intuition, common sense, stereotypes)
Humanistic perspective on personality	Personality develops as a person grows psychologically. Emphasizes free will and self-actualization. Associated with Maslow's hierarchy of needs.
Hypnosis	A mental state in which the subject is focused intensely on particular thought or memory while being more open to suggestion.
Hypothalamus	Portion of the brain connected to the endocrine system. Produces: Dopamine, Growth Hormone Releasing Hormone, Thyrotropin-releasing hormone, Somatostatin, Gonadotropin-releasing hormone, Corticotropin-releasing hormone, Oxytocin, Vasopressin
Identity	A person's sense of and expression of their group affiliations and individuality.

Incentive theory	Motivation is based on external incentives rather than internal drives. People's varying behaviors result from the different incentives in their environment and the differing values they place on those incentives.
Incidence rate	Total number of newly appearing cases of a disease per unit time, usually given as a proportion (e.g. 5 per 1,000, or 0.045%, or 1 in 100,000)
Inclusive fitness	The ability of an organism to increase its fitness by behaving altruistically to support group members that share its genes. (e.g. a worker honey bee surrenders any possibility of reproducing itself but supporting the hive increases inclusive fitness and the reproduction of its genes through the queen)
Individual discrimination	Treatment of one individual by another in a way that is worse than a normal social interaction owing to some group affiliation. (e.g. charging a higher rate for a cleaning service for a customer in an ethnic minority because "they're messier people")
Ingroup	Any group that a person psychologically identifies as their own.
Innate behaviors	Instinctive behavior that occurs in the absence of any learning or experience. Can be simple or fairly complex behaviors.
Institutional discrimination	Unjust discriminatory treatment of a group by formal organizations such as governments, public institutions, and corporations. Typically codified into set rules. (e.g. racial segregation laws)
Intelligence	Many different definitions (one general ability vs. many different "types" of intelligence) that generally relate to problem-solving ability, abstract thinking, and ability to learn from experience.
Interactionist theory of language development	Language is acquired through social interaction with adults. Emphasizes the role of feedback and reinforcement. Requires modeling of adults.
Intuition in problem solving	The ability to have knowledge or solve a problem without rational inference or reasoning. Subjects typically don't know the process by which they have the intuitive judgment. Associated with the right brain.
James-Lange theory	Emotions start as physiological states in the body and emotions are reactions to those bodily responses.
Kinesthetic sense	Sense of the position of body parts relative to one another.

Kohlberg stages	Stages that represent an individual's ability to reason through ethical and moral questions. Relate not to the outcome (decision made), but the process by which an individual thinks about ethical questions.
	        Pre-conventional: obedience and punishment, self-interest
	        Conventional: conformity, authority obedience
	        Post-conventional: universal ethical principles

Korsakoff's syndrome	Neurological disorder due to lack of thiamine (vitamin B1) associated with chronic alcoholism. Involves memory loss, invented memories, lack of insight, and apathy.
Language, brain areas	Wernicke's area: temporal lobe, ability to comprehend speech; Broca's area: frontal lobe, speech production
Learning theory of language development	Language is learned from the environment (not based on inherent biological systems) in some manner similar to operant conditioning. Various theories about what that manner is.
Limbic system	Collection of brain structures involved with emotion, behavior, motivation, long-term memory, smell. Includes hippocampus, amygdala, fornix, mammillary body, etc.
Locus of control	The extent to which individuals believe that they can control events that affect them.
Marginalization	The social exclusion in which individuals or groups are systematically barred from normal opportunities in a society (work, housing, health care, legal services)
Meditation	One of a number of practices meant to induce a mode of consciousness in which the person focuses on an aspect of awareness, emotion, or sense of well-being
Memory encoding	Process of turning sense information into information in the brain (memory) that can later be recalled (e.g. remember what something looks like)
Memory types	Topographic memory, flashbulb memory, declarative memory (explicit memory), procedural memory (implicit memory)
Meritocracy	Political philosophy that holds that power should accrue to individuals demonstrating merit as measured by achievement or intellectual talent.
Mirror neurons	Neurons that fire when an animal exhibits a behavior and when it observes another carrying out that same behavior, as if the observer were the one acting. Present in both motor and sensory cortical areas.

Modelling	A process of learning through imitation of others. "Modelling" can refer to the actions of the person demonstrating the behavior, or the behavior of the learner.
Mood disorders	Depression and bipolar disorder. Disturbance in a person's underlying mood is the main feature of the disorder.
Morbidity	Number of people in ill health per unit time, usually given per 1000 people per year.
Mortality	Number of deaths per unit time, usually given per 1000 people per year.
Multiculturalism	Communities with multiple distinct cultures. Also the ideology that promotes diversity as opposed to assimilation (e.g. publishing official gov't communications in multiple languages)
Nativist theory of language development	Language acquisition must be biologically dependent on the native capacity of the human brain (theories linked most commonly to Chomsky)
Need based theories of motivation	Most common: Maslow's hierarchy of needs: physiology, safety and security, love and friendship, self-esteem and achievement, self actualization.
Negative reinforcement	A stimulus withdrawn to increase a behavior (e.g. silencing an obnoxious noise to encourage pressing a lever)
Neural plasticity	Changes in neural pathways and synapses that occur in response to experience. Can be a change on the level of a single cell or remapping entire chunks of the cortex.
Neurotransmitters	Chemicals used to send signals across a synapse between a neuron and the target cell. Include amino acids, monoamines, peptides, and others (adenosine, acetylcholine, nitric oxide, etc)
Neutral stimuli	A stimulus which initially produces no specific response other than focusing attention (e.g. a noise made by a clicker in dog training)
Nociception	Sensation of pain triggered by mechanical, thermal, or chemical stimuli above a threshold.
Norms	Socially held beliefs about appropriate behavior.
Olfactory pathway	Nose, Olfactory Epithelium, Olfactory Receptor, Olfactory nerve (part of the CNS), Olfactory Bulb, Brain (Piriform Cortex, Amygdala)

Operant conditioning

Conditioning in which behaviors are shaped by their consequences (rather than their antecedents as in classical conditioning). It uses reinforcement and punishment to change behavior, whereas classical conditioning shapes reflexive behavior.

Ovaries

Sex organ of the female that releases: progesterone, estrogens (mainly estradiol), inhibin

Parallel processing

The ability of the brain to process multiple things at once, such as in vision where color, motion, shape, and depth are all processed simultaneously to help the brain identify visual stimulus.

Parkinson's disease

Degenerative disease. Motor difficulties due to death of dopamine-generating cells in the substantia nigra of the midbrain.

Peer pressure

A pressure to change attitudes, values, or behaviors to conform to group norms.

Peripheral route processing

A process of shaping attitudes that depend on the environmental characteristics of the message (attractiveness of the speaker, catchy slogan, seeming expertise). Useful when the idea is essentially weak or the audience unable or unwilling to work to evaluate the merits of the idea.

Personality disorders

Mental disorder involving an enduring set of behaviors or cognitions that cause distress or disability. Includes paranoid, antisocial, borderline, narcissistic, avoidant, obsessive-compulsive.

Pheromones

Chemical secreted or excreted by an animal to trigger a social response from others. Includes alarm, food, and sex pheromones.

Piaget's stages

Sensorimotor, Preoperational, Concrete Operational, Formal Operational

Pineal gland

Portion of the brain that secretes melatonin

Peripheral nervous system

Nerves and ganglia outside the brain/spinal cord. Divided into somatic and autonomic systems.

Positive Reinforcement

A stimulus delivered to increase a behavior (e.g. a food pellet to encourage pressing a lever)

Prejudice

Having a positive or negative view of a person or thing prior to experience with that person or thing. Typically towards people based on some group affiliation. Often unreasonable and difficult to change.

Preoperational stage

Piaget Stage 2: 2 – 7 yrs. Child can speak, imagine symbolically, but not carry out mental operations.

Prestige

A positive esteem of a person or group

Prevalence rate	Total number of people with a given disease at a given point in time, usually given as a proportion (5 per 1,000, or 0.045%, or 1 in 100,000)
Primary reinforcement	A stimulus that an organism desires with no learning (e.g. food, water)
Privilege	A set of unearned advantages accruing to someone owing to membership in a group. (e.g. male privilege in China under the one-child policy resulted in infanticide of female offspring)
Psychological disorders, categories	Anxiety, Somatoform, Mood, Schizophrenia, Dissociative, Personality
Psychoanalytic perspective on personality	Personality is developed by early childhood experiences and influenced by the unconscious part of the mind. Freud said personality develops through psychosexual stages.
Punishment	A consequence that causes a behavior to occur less frequently.
Reference group	A group against which an individual (or other group) is compared. It provides benchmarks against which the traits of an individual can compare herself, either by comparison or by contrast.
Reflex arc	Neural pathway in which afferent nerve synapses with efferent nerve in the spinal cord, generating a response while the signal is still being sent up to the brain.
Relative poverty	Income below some proportion of the median income. Thus poverty is relative to the society one is in.
Residential segregation	The physical separation of different groups into neighborhoods, typically along race, ethnic, or income criteria.
Role taking	3-6 yrs: Egocentric role taking, can't distinguish own perspective from others 6-8 yrs: Subjective role taking, child can tell that others will have different views based on different information 8-10 yrs: Self-reflective role taking, child understands that others have different values 10-12 yrs: Mutual role taking, child simultaneously considers his own view and differing views of others 12+ yrs: Societal role taking, child now considers social and cultural effects on views
Schachter-Singer theory	Emotions depend on physiological arousal and cognitive label. People use their environment or experience to label why they feel the physiological stimulation they do.

Schizophrenia	Mental disorder involving delusions, hallucinations, disorganized thinking, lack of emotion and lack of motivation.
Selective attention	The ability of the brain to focus on a single input and "tune out" other stimuli. "Cocktail Party Effect".
Self-concept	The set of beliefs one has about who one is (gender roles, sexuality, racial identity, personal characteristics, etc.)
Self-efficacy	A belief in one's own ability to achieve goals.
Self-esteem	The cognitive and emotional evaluation a person has of their own worth.
Self-fulfilling prophecy in stereotypes	A person's behavior can change to fit a stereotype if the person believes it themselves. For example, a stereotype that Asians are good at math can lead an Asian student to work exceptionally hard to excel in a math class.
Sensitivity index	A measure of how easily a signal can be detected. Estimated as d' = Hit Rate − False Alarm Rate
Sensorimotor stage	Piaget's Stage 1: infants, toddlers. Knowledge through senses and manipulating objects.
Sensory adaptation	A form of neural adaptation in which the sensory system stops responding to a constant stimulus.
Shaping	Rewarding a series of small behaviors that are a part of the overall behavior desired in order to create larger behavior which would likely never occur on its own.
Signal detection theory	A mathematical theory for measuring how sensitive people are in spotting stimuli correctly and rejecting false signals correctly.
Sleep disorders	Medical disorder of sleep patterns. (e.g. insomnia, narcolepsy, night terrors, sleep apnea, sleepwalking, enuresis)
Social capital	The value of a social network. Collective or economic benefits that result from cooperation between people and groups.
Social cognitive perspective on personality	Personality is developed through observational learning, situational influences, cognitive processes. Focuses on self-efficacy.
Social cognitive theory	Some portion of people's learning occurs not through direct behavior, but by observing the consequences of the behavior of others.
Social constructionism	A theory that people construct their sense of reality and meaning through interaction with others, most powerfully through language.

Social facilitation

The presence of other people will increase performance on familiar tasks but reduce performance on unfamiliar ones.

Social identity

The part of a person's identity that comes from their sense of membership in some social group.

Social loafing

Phenomenon of individuals putting in less effort when working in groups.

Social reproduction

The process of transmitting social inequality to the next generation. Based on differences in financial capital, cultural capital, human capital, and social capital.

Social stratification

A hierarchy of classes of people based on differences in power or privilege. It carries from generation to generation, is present in all societies, and includes beliefs.

Socialization

The process of acquiring and transmitting cultural norms and customs, developing the social skills for a person to participate in society.

Somatoform disorders

Mental disorder that creates physical symptoms that cannot be explained by an actual medical condition. Includes Conversion, Somatization, Hypochondriasis, Body Dysmorphic Disorder, Pain Disorder

Somatosensation

Sensory system throughout the skin, muscles, bones, joints, etc. Processes proprioception, touch, thermoception, nociception.

Spontaneous recovery

After a behavior has extinguished, a conditioned stimulus may once again elicit a conditioned response after a rest period.

Stages of sleep

Stage 1: Drowsy sleep, transition from alpha to theta waves
Stage 2: Conscious awareness gone, theta waves
Stage 3: Slow-wave sleep / Deep sleep, delta waves
REM: dreaming, muscle paralysis

Stereotype threat

Anxiety that one will fulfill a negative stereotype causing decreased performance.

Stereotypes

An idea about a particular group of people which may or may not accurately reflect reality. Cognitive in nature. (as opposed to prejudice which is emotional and discrimination which is behavioral)

Stigma

Social disapproval. Usually based on overt external deformities, personality deviations, or membership in an unfavored group (e.g. antisemitism).

Stress

The body's response to an environmental stressor or challenge. Triggers the sympathetic nervous system.

Subcultures	A group of people within a culture that differentiate themselves from the larger culture.
Symbolic interactionism	A microsociological approach that analyzes behavior – people behave towards the environment based on the meaning they ascribe to things, and that sense of meaning is based on social interaction and individual interpretation.
Testes	Sex organ of the male that releases: androgens (mainly testosterone) from Leydig cells, estradiol and inhibin from Sertoli cells
Thyroid	Gland in the neck which releases: calcitonin, thyroxine, triiodothyronine
Trait perspective of personality	Personality is made up of a number of traits that are heavily influenced by biology. Various theories. "Big Five" theory: 1. extraversion 2. neuroticism 3. openness to experience 4. conscientiousness 5. agreeableness.
Unconditioned response	A natural response that happens with no learning at all. (e.g. salivation in response to food)
Unconditioned stimuli	A natural stimulus that provokes a response with no learning at all. (e.g. food is an unconditioned stimulus for salivation)
Universal emotions	Anger, Disgust, Fear, Happiness, Sadness, Surprise
Urbanization	The process of shifting a population from rural to urban settings, most common in developing countries. By 2010, more than half of the world's population had shifted to urban environments.
Variable interval	Reinforcement after the first response, after a variable time has elapsed (e.g. after a food pellet is dispensed, there is some changing period of time during which no food pellets will be dispensed. After that time is up, the first lever press will get a food pellet.)
Variable ratio	Reinforcement after some changing number of responses (e.g. a food pellet after a changing number of lever presses)
Vestibular sense	The labyrinth of the inner ear provides a sense of spatial orientation, sense of balance, and sense of movement.
Vicarious emotions	When an observer feels the same emotion that someone being observed would feel (e.g. feeling embarrassment when someone else commits a social faux pas)
Visual pathway	Eye, Optic Nerve, Optic Chiasm, Optic Tract, Thalamus, Visual Cortex (occipital lobe)
Voluntary movement control	Posterior part of the front lobe of the cerebral cortex.

Vygotsky and development

Theorized that play is essential in a child's development. Children learn symbolic play (using a stick to pretend it's a horse) and learn social rules through play (e.g. playing house to simulate acceptable social interactions)

Weber's law

States that the ability to distinguish between two physical stimuli depends on a proportional increase in that stimulus (heavier of two masses, louder of two sounds, etc.). For example, a person can tell one mass is heavier than another if there is a 10% difference between them.

We hope you were able to use these practice passages to help raise your MCAT score. If you're still struggling or just need help polishing your score for top schools, consider our one-on-one tutoring program.

Next Step Test Preparation is a national leader in providing one-on-one MCAT tutoring. We believe strongly that one-on-one attention is the best way for students to improve their scores. Our students around the country work individually with top scorers and expert instructors to create customized strategies and study plans. Next Step students improve their scores significantly – even on retakes or after months of self-study.

To learn more, please visit our website http://www.nextsteptestprep.com/ or call us directly at 888-530-NEXT.

Made in the USA
Lexington, KY
05 June 2015